CLEP-31   COLLEGE-LEVEL EXAMINATION
PROGRAM SERIES

*This is your
PASSBOOK for...*

Freshman English

*Test Preparation Study Guide
Questions & Answers*

COPYRIGHT NOTICE

This book is SOLELY intended for, is sold ONLY to, and its use is RESTRICTED to individual, bona fide applicants or candidates who qualify by virtue of having seriously filed applications for appropriate license, certificate, professional and/or promotional advancement, higher school matriculation, scholarship, or other legitimate requirements of education and/or governmental authorities.

This book is NOT intended for use, class instruction, tutoring, training, duplication, copying, reprinting, excerption, or adaptation, etc., by:

1) Other publishers
2) Proprietors and/or Instructors of "Coaching" and/or Preparatory Courses
3) Personnel and/or Training Divisions of commercial, industrial, and governmental organizations
4) Schools, colleges, or universities and/or their departments and staffs, including teachers and other personnel
5) Testing Agencies or Bureaus
6) Study groups which seek by the purchase of a single volume to copy and/or duplicate and/or adapt this material for use by the group as a whole without having purchased individual volumes for each of the members of the group
7) Et al.

Such persons would be in violation of appropriate Federal and State statutes.

PROVISION OF LICENSING AGREEMENTS – Recognized educational, commercial, industrial, and governmental institutions and organizations, and others legitimately engaged in educational pursuits, including training, testing, and measurement activities, may address request for a licensing agreement to the copyright owners, who will determine whether, and under what conditions, including fees and charges, the materials in this book may be used them. In other words, a licensing facility exists for the legitimate use of the material in this book on other than an individual basis. However, it is asseverated and affirmed here that the material in this book CANNOT be used without the receipt of the express permission of such a licensing agreement from the Publishers. Inquiries re licensing should be addressed to the company, attention rights and permissions department.

All rights reserved, including the right of reproduction in whole or in part, in any form or by any means, electronic or mechanical, including photocopying, recording, or by any information storage and retrieval system, without permission in writing from the Publisher.

Copyright © 2024 by
National Learning Corporation

212 Michael Drive, Syosset, NY 11791
(516) 921-8888 • www.passbooks.com
E-mail: info@passbooks.com

PUBLISHED IN THE UNITED STATES OF AMERICA

PASSBOOK® SERIES

THE *PASSBOOK® SERIES* has been created to prepare applicants and candidates for the ultimate academic battlefield – the examination room.

At some time in our lives, each and every one of us may be required to take an examination – for validation, matriculation, admission, qualification, registration, certification, or licensure.

Based on the assumption that every applicant or candidate has met the basic formal educational standards, has taken the required number of courses, and read the necessary texts, the *PASSBOOK® SERIES* furnishes the one special preparation which may assure passing with confidence, instead of failing with insecurity. Examination questions – together with answers – are furnished as the basic vehicle for study so that the mysteries of the examination and its compounding difficulties may be eliminated or diminished by a sure method.

This book is meant to help you pass your examination provided that you qualify and are serious in your objective.

The entire field is reviewed through the huge store of content information which is succinctly presented through a provocative and challenging approach – the question-and-answer method.

A climate of success is established by furnishing the correct answers at the end of each test.

You soon learn to recognize types of questions, forms of questions, and patterns of questioning. You may even begin to anticipate expected outcomes.

You perceive that many questions are repeated or adapted so that you can gain acute insights, which may enable you to score many sure points.

You learn how to confront new questions, or types of questions, and to attack them confidently and work out the correct answers.

You note objectives and emphases, and recognize pitfalls and dangers, so that you may make positive educational adjustments.

Moreover, you are kept fully informed in relation to new concepts, methods, practices, and directions in the field.

You discover that you are actually taking the examination all the time: you are preparing for the examination by "taking" an examination, not by reading extraneous and/or supererogatory textbooks.

In short, this PASSBOOK®, used directedly, should be an important factor in helping you to pass your test.

NONTRADITIONAL EDUCATION

Students returning to school as adults bring more varied experience to their studies than do the teenagers who begin college shortly after graduating from high school. As a result, there are numerous programs for students with nontraditional learning curves. Hundreds of colleges and universities grant degrees to people who cannot attend classes at a regular campus or have already learned what the college is supposed to teach.

You can earn nontraditional education credits in many ways:
- Passing standardized exams
- Demonstrating knowledge gained through experience
- Completing campus-based coursework, and
- Taking courses off campus

Some methods of assessing learning for credit are objective, such as standardized tests. Others are more subjective, such as a review of life experiences.

With some help from four hypothetical characters – Alice, Vin, Lynette, and Jorge – this article describes nontraditional ways of earning educational credit. It begins by describing programs in which you can earn a high school diploma without spending 4 years in a classroom. The college picture is more complicated, so it is presented in two parts: one on gaining credit for what you know through course work or experience, and a second on college degree programs. The final section lists resources for locating more information.

Earning High School Credit

People who were prevented from finishing high school as teenagers have several options if they want to do so as adults. Some major cities have back-to-school programs that allow adults to attend high school classes with current students. But the more practical alternatives for most adults are to take the General Educational Development (GED) tests or to earn a high school diploma by demonstrating their skills or taking correspondence classes.

Of course, these options do not match the experience of staying in high school and graduating with one's friends. But they are viable alternatives for adult learners committed to meeting and, often, continuing their educational goals.

GED Program

Alice quit high school her sophomore year and took a job to help support herself, her younger brother, and their newly widowed mother. Now an adult, she wants to earn her high school diploma – and then go on to college. Because her job as head cook and her family responsibilities keep her busy during the day, she plans to get a high school equivalency diploma. She will study for, and take, the GED tests. Every year, about half a million adults earn their high school credentials this way. A GED diploma is accepted in lieu of a high school one by more than 90 percent of employers, colleges, and universities, so it is a good choice for someone like Alice.

The GED testing program is sponsored by the American Council on Education and State and local education departments. It consists of examinations in five subject areas: Writing, science, mathematics, social studies, and literature and the arts. The tests also measure skills such as analytical ability, problem solving, reading comprehension, and ability to understand and apply information. Most of the questions are multiple choice; the writing test includes an essay section on a topic of general interest.

Eligibility rules for taking the exams vary, but some states require that you must be at least 18. Tests are given in English, Spanish, and French. In addition to standard print, versions in large print, Braille, and audiocassette are also available. Total time allotted for the tests is 7 1/2 hours.

The GED tests are not easy. About one-fourth of those who complete the exams every year do not pass. Passing scores are established by administering the tests to a sample of graduating high school seniors. The minimum standard score is set so that about one-third of graduating seniors would not pass the tests if they took them.

Because of the difficulty of the tests, people need to prepare themselves to take them. Often, they start by taking the Official GED Practice Tests, usually available through a local adult education center. Centers are listed in your phone book's blue pages under "Adult Education," "Continuing Education," or "GED." Adult education centers also have information about GED preparation classes and self-study materials. Classes are generally arranged to accommodate adults' work schedules. National Learning Corporation publishes several study guides that aim to thoroughly prepare test-takers for the GED.

School districts, colleges, adult education centers, and community organizations have information about GED testing schedules and practice tests. For more information, contact them, your nearest GED testing center, or:

GED Testing Service
One Dupont Circle, NW, Suite 250
Washington, DC 20036-1163
1(800) 62-MY GED (626-9433)
(202) 939-9490

Skills Demonstration

Adults who have acquired high school level skills through experience might be eligible for the National External Diploma Program. This alternative to the GED does not involve any direct instruction. Instead, adults seeking a high school diploma must demonstrate mastery of 65 competencies in 8 general areas: Communication; computation; occupational preparedness; and self, social, consumer, scientific, and technological awareness.

Mastery is shown through the completion of the tasks. For example, a participant could prove competency in computation by measuring a room for carpeting, figuring out the amount of carpet needed, and computing the cost.

Before being accepted for the program, adults undergo an evaluation. Tests taken at one of the program's offices measure reading, writing, and mathematics abilities. A take-home segment includes a self-assessment of current skills, an individual skill evaluation, and an occupational interest and aptitude test.

Adults accepted for the program have weekly meetings with an assessor. At the meeting, the assessor reviews the participant's work from the previous week. If the task has not been completed properly, the assessor explains the mistake. Participants continue to correct their errors until they master each competency. A high school diploma is awarded upon proven mastery of all 65 competencies.

Fourteen States and the District of Columbia now offer the External Diploma Program. For more information, contact:

External Diploma Program
One Dupont Circle, NW, Suite 250
Washington, DC 20036-1193
(202) 939-9475

Correspondence and Distance Study

Vin dropped out of high school during his junior year because his family's frequent moves made it difficult for him to continue his studies. He promised himself at the time he dropped out that he would someday finish the courses needed for his diploma. For people like Vin, who prefer to earn a traditional diploma in a nontraditional way, there are about a dozen accredited courses of study for earning a high school diploma by correspondence, or distance study. The programs are either privately run, affiliated with a university, or administered by a State education department.

Distance study diploma programs have no residency requirements, allowing students to continue their studies from almost any location. Depending on the course of study, students need not be enrolled full time and usually have more flexible schedules for finishing their work. Selection of courses ranges from vo-tech to college prep, and some programs place different emphasis on the types of diplomas offered. University affiliated schools, for example, allow qualified students to take college courses along with their high school ones. Students can then apply the college credits toward a degree at that university or transfer them to another institution.

Taking courses by distance study is often more challenging and time consuming than attending classes, especially for adults who have other obligations. Success depends on each student's motivation. Students usually do reading assignments on their own. Written exercises, which they complete and send to an instructor for grading, supplement their reading material.

A list of some accredited high schools that offer diplomas by distance study is available free from the Distance Education and Training Council, formerly known as the National Home Study Council. Request the "DETC Directory of Accredited Institutions" from:

The Distance Education and Training Council
1601 18th Street, NW.
Washington, DC 20009-2529
(202) 234-5100

Some publications profiling nontraditional college programs include addresses and descriptions of several high school correspondence ones. See the Resources section at the end of this article for more information.

Getting College Credit For What You Know

Adults can receive college credit for prior coursework, by passing examinations, and documenting experiential learning. With help from a college advisor, nontraditional students should assess their skills, establish their educational goals, and determine the number of college credits they might be eligible for.

Even before you meet with a college advisor, you should collect all your school and training records. Then, make a list of all knowledge and abilities acquired through experience, no matter how irrelevant they seem to your chosen field. Next, determine your educational goals: What specific field do you wish to study? What kind of a degree do you want? Finally, determine how your past work fits into the field of study. Later on, you will evaluate educational programs to find one that's right for you.

People who have complex educational or experiential learning histories might want to have their learning evaluated by the Regents Credit Bank. The Credit Bank, operated by Regents College of the University of the State of New York, allows people to consolidate credits earned through college, experience, or other methods. Special assessments are available for Regents College enrollees whose knowledge in a specific field cannot be adequately evaluated by standardized exams. For more information, contact the Regents Credit Bank at:

Regents College
7 Columbia Circle
Albany, NY 12203-5159
(518) 464-8500

Credit For Prior College Coursework

When Lynette was in college during the 1970s, she attended several different schools and took a variety of courses. She did well in some classes and poorly in others. Now that she is a successful business owner and has more focus, Lynette thinks she should forget about her previous coursework and start from scratch. Instead, she should start from where she is.

Lynette should have all her transcripts sent to the colleges or universities of her choice and let an admissions officer determine which classes are applicable toward a degree. A few credits here and there may not seem like much, but they add up. Even if the subjects do not seem relevant to any major, they might be counted as elective credits toward a degree. And comparing the cost of transcripts with the cost of college courses, it makes sense to spend a few dollars per transcript for a chance to save hundreds, and perhaps thousands, of dollars in books and tuition.

Rules for transferring credits apply to all prior coursework at accredited colleges and universities, whether done on campus or off. Courses completed off campus, often called extended learning, include those available to students through independent study and correspondence. Many schools have extended learning programs; Brigham Young University, for example, offers more than 300 courses through its Department of Independent Study. One type of extended learning is distance learning, a form of correspondence study by technological means such as television, video and audio, CD-ROM, electronic mail, and computer tutorials. See the Resources section at the end of this article for more information about publications available from the National University Continuing Education Association.

Any previously earned college credits should be considered for transfer, no matter what the subject or the grade received. Many schools do not accept the transfer of courses graded below a C or ones taken more than a designated number of years ago. Some colleges and universities also have limits on the number of credits that can be transferred and applied toward a degree. But not all do. For example, Thomas Edison State College, New Jersey's State college for adults, accepts the transfer of all 120 hours of credit required for a baccalaureate degree – provided all the credits are transferred from regionally accredited schools, no more than 80 are at the junior college level, and the student's grades overall and in the field of study average out to C.

To assign credit for prior coursework, most schools require original transcripts. This means you must complete a form or send a written, signed request to have your transcripts released directly to a college or university. Once you have chosen the schools you want to apply to, contact the schools you attended before. Find out how much each transcript costs, and ask them to send your transcripts to the ones you are applying to. Write a letter that includes your name (and names used during attendance, if different) and dates of attendance, along with the names and addresses of the schools to which your transcripts should be sent. Include payment and mail to the registrar at the schools you have attended. The registrar's office will process your request and send an official transcript of your coursework to the colleges or universities you have designated.

Credit For Noncollege Courses

Colleges and universities are not the only ones that offer classes. Volunteer organizations and employers often provide formal training worth college credit. The American Council on Education has two programs that assess thousands of specific courses and make recommendations on the amount of college credit they are worth. Colleges and universities accept the recommendations or use them as guidelines.

One program evaluates educational courses sponsored by government agencies, business and industry, labor unions, and professional and voluntary organizations. It is the Program on Noncollegiate Sponsored Instruction (PONSI). Some of the training seminars Alice has participated in covered topics such as food preparation, kitchen safety, and nutrition. Although she has not yet earned her GED, Alice can earn college credit because of her completion of these formal job-training seminars. The number of credits each seminar is worth does not hinge on Alice's current eligibility for college enrollment.

The other program evaluates courses offered by the Army, Navy, Air Force, Marines, Coast Guard, and Department of Defense. It is the Military Evaluations Program. Jorge has never attended college, but the engineering technology classes he completed as part of his military training are worth college credit. And as an Army veteran, Jorge is eligible for a service that takes the evaluations one step further. The Army/American Council on Education Registry Transcript System (AARTS) will provide Jorge with an individualized transcript of American Council on Education credit recommendations for all courses he completed, the military occupational specialties (MOS's) he held, and examinations he passed while in the Army. All Army and National Guard enlisted personnel and veterans who enlisted after October 1981 are eligible for the transcript. Similar services are being considered by the Navy and Marine Corps.

To obtain a free transcript, see your Army Education Center for a 5454R transcript request form. Include your name, Social Security number, basic active service date, and complete address where you want the transcript sent. Mail your request to:
AARTS Operations Center
415 McPherson Ave.
Fort Leavenworth, KS 66027-1373

Recommendations for PONSI are published in *The National Guide to Educational Credit for Training Programs;* military program recommendations are in *The Guide to the Evaluation of Educational Experiences in the Armed Forces.* See the Resources section at the end of this article for more information about these publications.

Former military personnel who took a foreign language course through the Defense Language Institute may request course transcripts by sending their name, Social Security number, course title, duration of the course, and graduation date to:

Commandant, Defense Language Institute
Attn: ATFL-DAA-AR
Transcripts
Presidio of Monterey
Monterey, CA 93944-5006

Not all of Jorge's and Alice's courses have been assessed by the American Council on Education. Training courses that have no Council credit recommendation should still be assessed by an advisor at the schools they want to attend. Course descriptions, class notes, test scores, and other documentation may be helpful for comparing training courses to their college equivalents. An oral examination or other demonstration of competency might also be required.

There is no guarantee you will receive all the credits you are seeking – but you certainly won't if you make no attempt.

Credit By Examination

Standardized tests are the best-known method of receiving college credit without taking courses. These exams are often taken by high school students seeking advanced placement for college, but they are also available to adult learners. Testing programs and colleges and universities offer exams in a number of subjects. Two U.S. Government institutes have foreign language exams for employees that also may be worth college credit.

It is important to understand that receiving a passing score on these exams does not mean you get college credit automatically. Each school determines which test results it will accept, minimum scores required, how scores are converted for credit, and the amount of credit, if any, to be assigned. Most colleges and universities accept the American Council on Education credit recommendations, published every other year in the 250-page *Guide to Educational Credit by Examination*. For more information, contact:

The American Council on Education
Credit by Examination Program
One Dupont Circle, Suite 250
Washington, DC 20036-1193
(202) 939-9434

Testing programs:

You might know some of the five national testing programs by their acronyms or initials: CLEP, ACT PEP: RCE, DANTES, AP, and NOCTI. (The meanings of these initialisms are explained below.) There is some overlap among programs; for example, four of them have introductory accounting exams. Since you will not be awarded credit more than once for a specific subject, you should carefully evaluate each program for the subject exams you wish to take. And before taking an exam, make sure you will be awarded credit by the college or university you plan to attend.

CLEP (College-Level Examination Program), administered by the College Board, is the most widely accepted of the national testing programs; more than 2,800 accredited schools award credit for passing exam scores. Each test covers material taught in basic undergraduate courses. There are five general exams – English composition, humanities, college mathematics, natural sciences, and social sciences and history – and many subject exams. Most exams are entirely multiple-choice, but English composition exams may include an essay section. For more information, contact:

    CLEP
    P.O. Box 6600
    Princeton, NJ 08541-6600
    (609) 771-7865

ACT PEP: RCE (American College Testing Proficiency Exam Program: Regents College Examinations) tests are given in 38 subjects within arts and sciences, business, education, and nursing. Each exam is recommended for either lower- or upper-level credit. Exams contain either objective or extended response questions, and are graded according to a standard score, letter grade, or pass/fail. Fees vary, depending on the subject and type of exam. For more information or to request free study guides, contact:

    ACT PEP: Regents College Examinations
    P.O. Box 4014
    Iowa City, IA 52243
    (319) 337-1387
    (New York State residents must contact Regents College directly.)

DANTES (Defense Activity for Nontraditional Education Support) standardized tests are developed by the Educational Testing Service for the Department of Defense. Originally administered only to military personnel, the exams have been available to the public since 1983. About 50 subject tests cover business, mathematics, social science, physical science, humanities, foreign languages, and applied technology. Most of the tests consist entirely of multiple-choice questions. Schools determine their own administering fees and testing schedules. For more information or to request free study sheets, contact:

    DANTES Program Office
    Mail Stop 31-X
    Educational Testing Service
    Princeton, NJ 08541
    1(800) 257-9484

The AP (Advanced Placement) Program is a cooperative effort between secondary schools and colleges and universities. AP exams are developed each year by committees of college and high school faculty appointed by the College Board and assisted by consultants from the Educational Testing Service. Subjects include arts and languages, natural sciences, computer science, social sciences, history, and mathematics. Most tests are 2 or 3 hours long and include both multiple-choice and essay questions. AP courses are available to help students prepare for exams, which are offered in the spring. For more information about the Advanced Placement Program, contact:

    Advanced Placement Services
    P.O. Box 6671
    Princeton, NJ 08541-6671
    (609) 771-7300

NOCTI (National Occupational Competency Testing Institute) assessments are designed for people like Alice, who have vocational-technical skills that cannot be evaluated by other tests. NOCTI assesses competency at two levels: Student/job ready and teacher/experienced worker. Standardized evaluations are available for occupations such as auto-body repair, electronics, mechanical drafting, quantity food preparation, and upholstering. The tests consist of multiple-choice questions and a performance component. Other services include workshops, customized assessments, and pre-testing. For more information, contact:

NOCTI
500 N. Bronson Ave.
Ferris State University
Big Rapids, MI 49307
(616) 796-4699

Colleges and universities:

Many colleges and universities have credit-by-exam programs, through which students earn credit by passing a comprehensive exam for a course offered by the institution. Among the most widely recognized are the programs at Ohio University, the University of North Carolina, Thomas Edison State College, and New York University.

Ohio University offers about 150 examinations for credit. In addition, you may sometimes arrange to take special examinations in non-laboratory courses offered at Ohio University. To take a test for credit, you must enroll in the course. If you plan to transfer the credit earned, you also need written permission from an official at your school. Books and study materials are available, for a cost, through the university. Exams must be taken within 6 months of the enrollment date; most last 3 hours. You may arrange to take the exam off campus if you do not live near the university.

Ohio University is on the quarter-hour system; most courses are worth 4 quarter hours, the equivalent of 3 semester hours. For more information, contact:

Independent Study
Tupper Hall 302
Ohio University
Athens, OH 45701-2979
1(800) 444-2910
(614) 593-2910

The University of North Carolina offers a credit-by-examination option for 140 independent study (correspondence) courses in foreign languages, humanities, social sciences, mathematics, business administration, education, electrical and computer engineering, health administration, and natural sciences. To take an exam, you must request and receive approval from both the course instructor and the independent studies department. Exams must be taken within six months of enrollment, and you may register for no more than two at a time. If you are not near the University's Chapel Hill campus, you may take your exam under supervision at an accredited college, university, community college, or technical institute. For more information, contact:

Independent Studies
CB #1020, The Friday Center
UNC-Chapel Hill
Chapel Hill, NC 27599-1020
1(800) 862-5669 / (919) 962-1134

The Thomas Edison College Examination Program offers more than 50 exams in liberal arts, business, and professional areas. Thomas Edison State College administers tests twice a month in Trenton, New Jersey; however, students may arrange to take their tests with a proctor at any accredited American college or university or U.S. military base. Most of the tests are multiple choice; some also include short answer or essay questions. Time limits range from 90 minutes to 4 hours, depending on the exam. For more information, contact:

Thomas Edison State College
TECEP, Office of Testing and Assessment
101 W. State Street
Trenton, NJ 08608-1176
(609) 633-2844

New York University's Foreign Language Program offers proficiency exams in more than 40 languages, from Albanian to Yiddish. Two exams are available in each language: The 12-point test is equivalent to 4 undergraduate semesters, and the 16-point exam may lead to upper level credit. The tests are given at the university's Foreign Language Department throughout the year.

Proof of foreign language proficiency does not guarantee college credit. Some colleges and universities accept transcripts only for languages commonly taught, such as French and Spanish. Nontraditional programs are more likely than traditional ones to grant credit for proficiency in other languages.

For an informational brochure and registration form for NYU's foreign language proficiency exams, contact:

New York University
Foreign Language Department
48 Cooper Square, Room 107
New York, NY 10003
(212) 998-7030

Government institutes:

The Defense Language Institute and Foreign Service Institute administer foreign language proficiency exams for personnel stationed abroad. Usually, the tests are given at the end of intensive language courses or upon completion of service overseas. But some people – like Jorge, who knows Spanish – speak another language fluently and may be allowed to take a proficiency exam in that language before completing their tour of duty. Contact one of the offices listed below to obtain transcripts of those scores. Proof of proficiency does not guarantee college credit, however, as discussed above.

To request score reports from the Defense Language Institute for Defense Language Proficiency Tests, send your name, Social Security number, language for which you were tested, and, most importantly, when and where you took the exam to:

Commandant, Defense Language Institute
Attn: ATFL-ES-T
DLPT Score Report Request
Presidio of Monterey
Monterey, CA 93944-5006

To request transcripts of scores for Foreign Service Institute exams, send your name, Social Security number, language for which you were tested, and dates or year of exams to:

Foreign Service Institute
Arlington Hall
4020 Arlington Boulevard
Rosslyn, VA 22204-1500
Attn: Testing Office (Send your request to the attention of the testing office of the foreign language in which you were tested)

Credit For Experience

Experiential learning credit may be given for knowledge gained through job responsibilities, personal hobbies, volunteer opportunities, homemaking, and other experiences. Colleges and universities base credit awards on the knowledge you have attained, not for the experience alone. In addition, the knowledge must be college level; not just any learning will do. Throwing horseshoes as a hobby is not likely to be worth college credit. But if you've done research on how and where the sport originated, visited blacksmiths, organized tournaments, and written a column for a trade journal – well, that's a horseshoe of a different color.

Adults attempting to get credit for their experience should be forewarned: Having your experience evaluated for college credit is time-consuming, tedious work – not an easy shortcut for people who want quick-fix college credits. And not all experience, no matter how valuable, is the equivalent of college courses.

Requesting college credit for your experiential learning can be tricky. You should get assistance from a credit evaluations officer at the school you plan to attend, but you should also have a general idea of what your knowledge is worth. A common method for converting knowledge into credit is to use a college catalog. Find course titles and descriptions that match what you have learned through experience, and request the number of credits offered for those courses.

Once you know what credit to ask for, you must usually present your case in writing to officials at the college you plan to attend. The most common form of presenting experiential learning for credit is the portfolio. A portfolio is a written record of your knowledge along with a request for equivalent college credit. It includes an identification and description of the knowledge for which you are requesting credit, an explanatory essay of how the knowledge was gained and how it fits into your educational plans, documentation that you have acquired such knowledge, and a request for college credit. Required elements of a portfolio vary by schools but generally follow those guidelines.

In identifying knowledge you have gained, be specific about exactly what you have learned. For example, it is not enough for Lynette to say she runs a business. She must identify the knowledge she has gained from running it, such as personnel management, tax law, marketing strategy, and inventory review. She must also include brief descriptions about her knowledge of each to support her claims of having those skills.

The essay gives you a chance to relay something about who you are. It should address your educational goals, include relevant autobiographical details, and be well organized, neat, and convey confidence. In his essay, Jorge might first state his goal of becoming an engineer. Then he would explain why he joined the Army, where he got hands-on training and experience in developing and servicing electronic equipment.

This, he would say, led to his hobby of creating remote-controlled model cars, of which he has built 20. His conclusion would highlight his accomplishments and tie them to his desire to become an electronic engineer.

Documentation is evidence that you've learned what you claim to have learned. You can show proof of knowledge in a variety of ways, including audio or video recordings, letters from current or former employers describing your specific duties and job performance, blueprints, photographs or artwork, and transcripts of certifying exams for professional licenses and certification – such as Alice's certification from the American Culinary Federation. Although documentation can take many forms, written proof alone is not always enough. If it is impossible to document your knowledge in writing, find out if your experiential learning can be assessed through supplemental oral exams by a faculty expert.

Earning a College Degree

Nontraditional students often have work, family, and financial obligations that prevent them from quitting their jobs to attend school full time. Can they still meet their educational goals? Yes.

More than 150 accredited colleges and universities have nontraditional bachelor's degree programs that require students to spend little or no time on campus; over 300 others have nontraditional campus-based degree programs. Some of those schools, as well as most junior and community colleges, offer associate's degrees nontraditionally. Each school with a nontraditional course of study determines its own rules for awarding credit for prior coursework, exams, or experience, as discussed previously. Most have charges on top of tuition for providing these special services.

Several publications profile nontraditional degree programs; see the Resources section at the end of this article for more information. To determine which school best fits your academic profile and educational goals, first list your criteria. Then, evaluate nontraditional programs based on their accreditation, features, residency requirements, and expenses. Once you have chosen several schools to explore further, write to them for more information. Detailed explanations of school policies should help you decide which ones you want to apply to.

Get beyond the printed word – especially the glowing words each school writes about itself. Check out the schools you are considering with higher education authorities, alumni, employers, family members, and friends. If possible, visit the campus to talk to students and instructors and sit in on a few classes, even if you will be completing most or all of your work off campus. Ask school officials questions about such things as enrollment numbers, graduation rate, faculty qualifications, and confusing details about the application process or academic policies. After you have thoroughly investigated each prospective college or university, you can make an informed decision about which is right for you.

Accreditation

Accreditation is a process colleges and universities submit to voluntarily for getting their credentials. An accredited school has been investigated and visited by teams of observers and has periodic inspections by a private accrediting agency. The initial review can take two years or more.

Regional agencies accredit entire schools, and professional agencies accredit either specialized schools or departments within schools. Although there are no national accrediting standards, not just any accreditation will do. Countless "accreditation associations" have been invented by schools, many of which have no academic programs and sell phony degrees, to accredit themselves. But 6 regional and about 80 professional accrediting associations in the United States are recognized by the U.S. Department of Education or the Commission on Recognition of Postsecondary Accreditation. When checking accreditation, these are the names to look for. For more information about accreditation and accrediting agencies, contact:

>Institutional Participation Oversight Service Accreditation and State Liaison Division
>U.S. Department of Education
>ROB 3, Room 3915
>600 Independence Ave., SW
>Washington, DC 20202-5244
>(202) 708-7417

Because accreditation is not mandatory, lack of accreditation does not necessarily mean a school or program is bad. Some schools choose not to apply for accreditation, are in the process of applying, or have educational methods too unconventional for an accrediting association's standards. For the nontraditional student, however, earning a degree from a college or university with recognized accreditation is an especially important consideration. Although nontraditional education is becoming more widely accepted, it is not yet mainstream. Employers skeptical of a degree earned in a nontraditional manner are likely to be even less accepting of one from an unaccredited school.

Program Features

Because nontraditional students have diverse educational objectives, nontraditional schools are diverse in what they offer. Some programs are geared toward helping students organize their scattered educational credits to get a degree as quickly as possible. Others cater to those who may have specific credits or experience but need assistance in completing requirements. Whatever your educational profile, you should look for a program that works with you in obtaining your educational goals.

A few nontraditional programs have special admissions policies for adult learners like Alice, who plan to earn their GEDs but want to enroll in college in the meantime. Other features of nontraditional programs include individualized learning agreements, intensive academic counseling, cooperative learning and internship placement, and waiver of some prerequisites or other requirements – as well as college credit for prior coursework, examinations, and experiential learning, all discussed previously.

Lynette, whose primary goal is to finish her degree, wants to earn maximum credits for her business experience. She will look for programs that do not limit the number of credits awarded for equivalency exams and experiential learning. And since well-documented proof of knowledge is essential for earning experiential learning credits, Lynette should make sure the program she chooses provides assistance to students submitting a portfolio.

Jorge, on the other hand, has more credits than he needs in certain areas and is willing to forego some. To become an engineer, he must have a bachelor's degree; but because he is accustomed to hands-on learning, Jorge is interested in getting experience as he gains more technical skills. He will concentrate on finding schools with strong cooperative education, supervised fieldwork, or internship programs.

Residency Requirements

Programs are sometimes deemed nontraditional because of their residency requirements. Many people think of residency for colleges and universities in terms of tuition, with in-state students paying less than out-of-state ones. Residency also may refer to where a student lives, either on or off campus, while attending school.

But in nontraditional education, residency usually refers to how much time students must spend on campus, regardless of whether they attend classes there. In some nontraditional programs, students need not ever step foot on campus. Others require only a very short residency, such as one day or a few weeks. Many schools have standard residency requirements of several semesters but schedule classes for evenings or weekends to accommodate working adults.

Lynette, who previously took courses by independent study, prefers to earn credits by distance study. She will focus on schools that have no residency requirement. Several colleges and universities have nonresident degree completion programs for adults with some college credit. Under the direction of a faculty advisor, students devise a plan for earning their remaining credits. Methods for earning credits include independent study, distance learning, seminars, supervised fieldwork, and group study at arranged sites. Students may have to earn a certain number of credits through the degree-granting institution. But many programs allow students to take courses at accredited schools of their choice for transfer toward their degree.

Alice wants to attend lectures but has an unpredictable schedule. Her best course of action will be to seek out short residency programs that require students to attend seminars once or twice a semester. She can take courses that are televised and videotape them to watch when her schedule permits, with the seminars helping to ensure that she properly completes her coursework. Many colleges and universities with short residency requirements also permit students to earn some credits elsewhere, by whatever means the student chooses.

Some fields of study require classroom instruction. As Jorge will discover, few colleges and universities allow students to earn a bachelor's degree in engineering entirely through independent study. Nontraditional residency programs are designed to accommodate adults' daytime work schedules. Jorge should look for programs offering evening, weekend, summer, and accelerated courses.

Tuition and Other Expenses

The final decisions about which schools Alice, Jorge, and Lynette attend may hinge in large part on a single issue: Cost. And rising tuition is only part of the equation. Beginning with application fees and continuing through graduation fees, college expenses add up.

Traditional and nontraditional students have some expenses in common, such as the cost of books and other materials. Tuition might even be the same for some courses, especially for colleges and universities offering standard ones at unusual times. But for nontraditional programs, students may also pay fees for services such as credit or transcript review, evaluation, advisement, and portfolio assessment.

Students are also responsible for postage and handling or setup expenses for independent study courses, as well as for all examination and transcript fees for transferring credits. Usually, the more nontraditional the program, the more detailed the fees. Some schools charge a yearly enrollment fee rather than tuition for degree completion candidates who want their files to remain active.

Although tuition and fees might seem expensive, most educators tell you not to let money come between you and your educational goals. Talk to someone in the financial aid department of the school you plan to attend or check your library for publications about financial aid sources. The U.S. Department of Education publishes a guide to Federal aid programs such as Pell Grants, student loans, and work-study. To order the free 74-page booklet, *The Student Guide: Financial Aid from the U.S. Department of Education,* contact:

Federal Student Aid Information Center
P.O. Box 84
Washington, DC 20044
1 (800) 4FED-AID (433-3243)

Resources

Information on how to earn a high school diploma or college degree without following the usual routes is available from several organizations and in numerous publications. Information on nontraditional graduate degree programs, available for master's through doctoral level, though not discussed in this article, can usually be obtained from the same resources that detail bachelor's degree programs.

National Learning Corporation publishes study guides for all of these exams, for both general examinations and tests in specific subject areas. To order study guides, or to browse their catalog featuring more than 5,000 titles, visit NLC online at www.passbooks.com, or contact them by phone at (800) 632-8888.

Organizations

Adult learners should always contact their local school system, community college, or university to learn about programs that are readily available. The following national organizations can also supply information:

American Council on Education
One Dupont Circle
Washington, DC 20036-1193
(202) 939-9300

Within the American Council on Education, the Center for Adult Learning and Educational Credentials administers the National External Diploma Program, the GED Program, the Program on Noncollegiate Sponsored Instruction, the Credit by Examination Program, and the Military Evaluations Program.

College-Level Examination Program (CLEP)

1. WHAT IS CLEP?

CLEP stands for the College-Level Examination Program, sponsored by the College Board. It is a national program of credit-by-examination that offers you the opportunity to obtain recognition for college-level achievement. No matter when, where, or how you have learned – by means of formal or informal study – you can take CLEP tests. If the results are acceptable to your college, you can receive credit.

You may not realize it, but you probably know more than your academic record reveals. Each day you, like most people, have an opportunity to learn. In private industry and business, as well as at all levels of government, learning opportunities continually occur. If you read widely or intensively in a particular field, think about what you read, discuss it with your family and friends, you are learning. Or you may be learning on a more formal basis by taking a correspondence course, a television or radio course, a course recorded on tape or cassettes, a course assembled into programmed tests, or a course taught in your community adult school or high school.

No matter how, where, or when you gained your knowledge, you may have the opportunity to receive academic credit for your achievement that can be counted toward an undergraduate degree. The College-Level Examination Program (CLEP) enables colleges to evaluate your achievement and give you credit. A wide range of college-level examinations are offered by CLEP to anyone who wishes to take them. Scores on the tests are reported to you and, if you wish, to a college, employer, or individual.

2. WHAT ARE THE PURPOSES OF THE COLLEGE-LEVEL EXAMINATION PROGRAM?

The basic purpose of the College-Level Examination Program is to enable individuals who have acquired their education in nontraditional ways to demonstrate their academic achievement. It is also intended for use by those in higher education, business, industry, government, and other fields who need a reliable method of assessing a person's educational level.

Recognizing that the real issue is not how a person has acquired his education but what education he has, the College Level Examination Program has been designed to serve a variety of purposes. The basic purpose, as listed above, is to enable those who have reached the college level of education in nontraditional ways to assess the level of their achievement and to use the test results in seeking college credit or placement.

In addition, scores on the tests can be used to validate educational experience obtained at a nonaccredited institution or through noncredit college courses.

Some colleges and universities may use the tests to measure the level of educational achievement of their students, and for various institutional research purposes.

Other colleges and universities may wish to use the tests in the admission, placement, and guidance of students who wish to transfer from one institution to another.

Businesses, industries, governmental agencies, and professional groups now accept the results of these tests as a basis for advancement, eligibility for further training, or professional or semi-professional certification.

Many people are interested in the examination simply to assess their own educational progress and attainment.

The college, university, business, industry, or government agency that adopts the tests in the College-Level Examination Program makes its own decision about how it will use and interpret the test scores. The College Board will provide the tests, score them, and report the results either to the individuals who took the tests or the college or agency that administered them. It does NOT, and cannot, award college credit, certify college equivalency, or make recommendations regarding the standards these institutions should establish for the use of the test results.

Therefore, if you are taking the tests to secure credit from an institution, you should FIRST ascertain whether the college or agency involved will accept the scores. Each institution determines which CLEP tests it will accept for credit and the amount of credit it will award. If you want to take tests for college credit, first call, write, or visit the college you wish to attend to inquire about its policy on CLEP scores, as well as its other admission requirements.

The services of the program are also available to people who have been requested to take the tests by an employer, a professional licensing agency, a certifying agency, or by other groups that recognize college equivalency on the basis of satisfactory CLEP scores. You may, of course, take the tests SOLELY for your own information. If you do, your scores will be reported only to you.

While neither CLEP nor the College Board can evaluate previous credentials or award college credit, you will receive, with your scores, basic information to help you interpret your performance on the tests you have taken.

3. WHAT ARE THE COLLEGE-LEVEL EXAMINATIONS?

In order to meet different kinds of curricular organization and testing needs at colleges and universities, the College-Level Examination Program offers 35 different subject tests falling under five separate general categories: Composition and Literature, Foreign Languages, History and Social Sciences, Science and Mathematics, and Business.

4. WHAT ARE THE SUBJECT EXAMINATIONS?

The 35 CLEP tests offered by the College Board are listed below:

COMPOSITION AND LITERATURE:
- American Literature
- Analyzing and Interpreting Literature
- English Composition
- English Composition with Essay
- English Literature
- Freshman College Composition
- Humanities

FOREIGN LANGUAGES
- French
- German
- Spanish

HISTORY AND SOCIAL SCIENCES
- American Government
- Introduction to Educational Psychology
- History of the United States I: Early Colonization to 1877
- History of the United States II: 1865 to the Present
- Human Growth and Development
- Principles of Macroeconomics
- Principles of Microeconomics
- Introductory Psychology
- Social Sciences and History
- Introductory Sociology
- Western Civilization I: Ancient Near East to 1648
- Western Civilization II: 1648 to the Present

SCIENCE AND MATHEMATICS
- College Algebra
- College Algebra-Trigonometry
- Biology
- Calculus
- Chemistry
- College Mathematics
- Natural Sciences
- Trigonometry
- Precalculus

BUSINESS
- Financial Accounting
- Introductory Business Law
- Information Systems and Computer Applications
- Principles of Management
- Principles of Marketing

CLEP Examinations cover material taught in courses that most students take as requirements in the first two years of college. A college usually grants the same amount of credit to students earning satisfactory scores on the CLEP examination as it grants to students successfully completing the equivalent course.

Many examinations are designed to correspond to one-semester courses; some, however, correspond to full-year or two-year courses.

Each exam is 90 minutes long and, except for English Composition with Essay, is made up primarily of multiple-choice questions. Some tests have several other types of questions besides multiple choice. To see a more detailed description of a particular CLEP exam, visit www.collegeboard.com/clep.

The English Composition with Essay exam is the only exam that includes a required essay. This essay is scored by college English faculty designated by CLEP and does not require an additional fee. However, other Composition and Literature tests offer optional essays, which some college and universities require and some do not. These essays are graded by faculty at the individual institutions that require them and require an additional $10 fee. Contact the particular institution to ask about essay requirements, and check with your test center for further details.

All 35 CLEP examinations are administered on computer. If you are unfamiliar with taking a test on a computer, consult the CLEP Sampler online at www.collegeboard.com/clep. The Sampler contains the same tutorials as the actual exams and helps familiarize you with navigation and how to answer different types of questions.

Points are not deducted for wrong or skipped answers – you receive one point for every correct answer. Therefore it is best that an answer is supplied for each exam question, whether it is a guess or not. The number of correct answers is then converted to a formula score. This formula, or "scaled," score is determined by a statistical process called *equating*, which adjusts for slight differences in difficulty between test forms and ensures that your score does not depend on the specific test form you took or how well others did on the same form. The scaled scores range from 20 to 80 – this is the number that will appear on your score report.

To ensure that you complete all questions in the time allotted, you would probably be wise to skip the more difficult or perplexing questions and return to them later. Although the multiple-choice items in these tests are carefully designed so as not to be tricky, misleading, or ambiguous, on the other hand, they are not all direct questions of factual information. They attempt, in their way, to elicit a response that indicates your knowledge or lack of knowledge of the material in question or your ability or inability to use or interpret a fact or idea. Thus, you should concentrate on answering the questions as they appear to be without attempting to out-guess the testmakers.

5. WHAT ARE THE FEES?

The fee for all CLEP examinations is $55. Optional essays required by some institutions are an additional $10.

6. WHEN ARE THE TESTS GIVEN?

CLEP tests are administered year-round. Consult the CLEP website (www.collegeboard.com/clep) and individual test centers for specific information.

7. WHERE ARE THE TESTS GIVEN?

More than 1,300 test centers are located on college and university campuses throughout the country, and additional centers are being established to meet increased needs. Any accredited collegiate institution with an explicit and publicly available policy of credit by examination can become a CLEP test center. To obtain a list of these centers, visit the CLEP website at www.collegeboard.com/clep.

8. HOW DO I REGISTER FOR THE COLLEGE-LEVEL EXAMINATION PROGRAM?

Contact an individual test center for information regarding registration, scheduling and fees. Registration/admission forms can also be obtained on the CLEP website.

9. MAY I REPEAT THE COLLEGE-LEVEL EXAMINATIONS?

You may repeat any examination providing at least six months have passed since you were last administered this test. If you repeat a test within a period of time less than six months, your scores will be cancelled and your fees forfeited. To repeat a test, check the appropriate space on the registration form.

10. WHEN MAY I EXPECT MY SCORE REPORTS?

With the exception of the English Composition with Essay exam, you should receive your score report instantly once the test is complete.

11. HOW SHOULD I PREPARE FOR THE COLLEGE-LEVEL EXAMINATIONS?

This book has been specifically designed to prepare candidates for these examinations. It will help you to consider, study, and review important content, principles, practices, procedures, problems, and techniques in the form of varied and concrete applications.

12. QUESTIONS AND ANSWERS APPEARING IN THIS PUBLICATION

The College-Level Examinations are offered by the College Board. Since copies of past examinations have not been made available, we have used equivalent materials, including questions and answers, which are highly recommended by us as an appropriate means of preparing for these examinations.

If you need additional information about CLEP Examinations, visit www.collegeboard.com/clep.

THE COLLEGE-LEVEL EXAMINATION PROGRAM

How The Program Works

CLEP examinations are administered at many colleges and universities across the country, and most institutions award college credit to those who do well on them. The examinations provide people who have acquired knowledge outside the usual educational settings the opportunity to show that they have learned college-level material without taking certain college courses.

The CLEP examinations cover material that is taught in introductory-level courses at many colleges and universities. Faculties at individual colleges review the tests to ensure that they cover the important material taught in their courses. Colleges differ in the examinations they accept; some colleges accept only two or three of the examinations while others accept nearly all of them.

Although CLEP is sponsored by the College Board and the examinations are scored by Educational Testing Service (ETS), neither of these organizations can award college credit. Only accredited colleges may grant credit toward a degree. When you take a CLEP examination, you may request that a copy of your score report be sent to the college you are attending or plan to attend. After evaluating your scores, the college will decide whether or not to award you credit for a certain course or courses, or to exempt you from them. If the college gives you credit, it will record the number of credits on your permanent record, thereby indicating that you have completed work equivalent to a course in that subject. If the college decides to grant exemption without giving you credit for a course, you will be permitted to omit a course that would normally be required of you and to take a course of your choice instead.

What the Examinations Are Like

The examinations consist mostly of multiple-choice questions to be answered within a 90-minute time limit. Additional information about each CLEP examination is given in the examination guide and on the CLEP website.

Where To Take the Examinations

CLEP examinations are administered throughout the year at the test centers of approximately 1,300 colleges and universities. On the CLEP website, you will find a list of institutions that award credit for satisfactory scores on CLEP examinations. Some colleges administer CLEP examinations to their own students only. Other institutions administer the tests to anyone who registers to take them. If your college does not administer the tests, contact the test centers in your area for information about its testing schedule.

Once you have been tested, your score report will be available instantly. CLEP scores are kept on file at ETS for 20 years; and during this period, for a small fee, you may have your transcript sent to another college or to anyone else you specify. (Your scores will never be sent to anyone without your approval.)

APPROACHING A COLLEGE ABOUT CLEP

The following sections provide a step-by-step approach to learning about the CLEP policy at a particular college or university. The person or office that can best assist students desiring CLEP credit may have a different title at each institution, but the following guidelines will lead you to information about CLEP at any institution.

Adults returning to college often benefit from special assistance when they approach a college. Opportunities for adults to return to formal learning in the classroom are now widespread, and colleges and universities have worked hard to make this a smooth process for older students. Many colleges have established special service offices that are staffed with trained professionals who understand the kinds of problems facing adults returning to college. If you think you might benefit from such assistance, be sure to find out whether these services are available at your college.

How to Apply for College Credit

STEP 1. Obtain the General Information Catalog and a copy of the CLEP policy from the colleges you are considering. If you have not yet applied for admission, ask for an admissions application form too.

Information about admissions and CLEP policies can be obtained by contacting college admissions offices or finding admissions information on the school websites. Tell the admissions officer that you are a prospective student and that you are interested in applying for admission and CLEP credit. Ask for a copy of the publication in which the college's complete CLEP policy is explained. Also get the name and the telephone number of the person to contact in case you have further questions about CLEP.

At this step, you may wish to obtain information from external degree colleges. Many adults find that such colleges suit their needs exceptionally well.

STEP 2. If you have not already been admitted to the college you are considering, look at its admission requirements for undergraduate students to see if you can qualify.

This is an important step because if you can't get into college, you can't get college credit for CLEP. Nearly all colleges require students to be admitted and to enroll in one or more courses before granting the students CLEP credit.

Virtually all public community colleges and a number of four-year state colleges have open admission policies for in-state students. This usually means that they admit anyone who has graduated from high school or has earned a high school equivalency diploma.

If you think you do not meet the admission requirements, contact the admissions office for an interview with a counselor. Colleges do sometimes make exceptions, particularly for adult applicants. State why you want the interview and ask what documents you should bring with you or send in advance. (These materials may include a high school transcript, transcript of previous college work, completed application for admission, etc.) Make an extra effort to have all the information requested in time for the interview.

During the interview, relax and be yourself. Be prepared to state honestly why you think you are ready and able to do college work. If you have already taken CLEP examinations and scored high enough to earn credit, you have shown that you are able to do college work. Mention this achievement to the admissions counselor because it may increase your chances of being accepted. If you have not taken a CLEP examination, you can still improve your chances of being accepted by describing how your job training or independent study has helped prepare you for college-level work. Tell the counselor what you have learned from your work and personal experiences.

STEP 3. Evaluate the college's CLEP policy.

Typically, a college lists all its academic policies, including CLEP policies, in its general catalog. You will probably find the CLEP policy statement under a heading such as Credit-by-Examination, Advanced Standing, Advanced Placement, or External Degree Program. These sections can usually be found in the front of the catalog.

Many colleges publish their credit-by-examination policies in a separate brochure, which is distributed through the campus testing office, counseling center, admissions office, or registrar's office. If you find a very general policy statement in the college catalog, seek clarification from one of these offices.

Review the material in the section of this guide entitled Questions to Ask About a College's CLEP Policy. Use these guidelines to evaluate the college's CLEP policy. If you have not yet taken a CLEP examination, this evaluation will help you decide which examinations to take and whether or not to take the free-response or essay portion. Because individual colleges have different CLEP policies, a review of several policies may help you decide which college to attend.

STEP 4. If you have not yet applied for admission, do so early.

Most colleges expect you to apply for admission several months before you enroll, and it is essential that you meet the published application deadlines. It takes time to process your application for admission; and if you have yet to take a CLEP examination, it will be some time before the college receives and reviews your score report. You will probably want to take some, if not all, of the CLEP examinations you are interested in before you enroll so you know which courses you need not register for. In fact, some colleges require that all CLEP scores be submitted before a student registers.

Complete all forms and include all documents requested with your application(s) for admission. Normally, an admissions decision cannot be reached until all documents have been submitted and evaluated. Unless told to do so, do not send your CLEP scores until you have been officially admitted.

STEP 5. Arrange to take CLEP examination(s) or to submit your CLEP score(s).

You may want to wait to take your CLEP examinations until you know definitely which college you will be attending. Then you can make sure you are taking tests your college will accept for credit. You will also be able to request that your scores be sent to the college, free of charge, when you take the tests.

If you have already taken CLEP examinations, but did not have a copy of your score report sent to your college, you may request the College Board to send an official transcript at any time for a small fee. Use the Transcript Request Form that was sent to you with your score report. If you do not have the form, you may find it online at www.collegeboard.com/clep.

Your CLEP scores will be evaluated, probably by someone in the admissions office, and sent to the registrar's office to be posted on your permanent record once you are enrolled. Procedures vary from college to college, but the process usually begins in the admissions office.

STEP 6. Ask to receive a written notice of the credit you receive for your CLEP score(s).

A written notice may save you problems later, when you submit your degree plan or file for graduation. In the event that there is a question about whether or not you earned CLEP credit, you will have an official record of what credit was awarded. You may also need this verification of course credit if you go for academic counseling before the credit is posted on your permanent record.

STEP 7. Before you register for courses, seek academic counseling.

A discussion with your academic advisor can prevent you from taking unnecessary courses and can tell you specifically what your CLEP credit will mean to you. This step may be accomplished at the time you enroll. Most colleges have orientation sessions for new students prior to each enrollment period. During orientation, students are usually assigned an academic advisor who then gives them individual help in developing long-range plans and a course schedule for the next semester. In conjunction with this counseling, you may be asked to take some additional tests so that you can be placed at the proper course level.

External Degree Programs

If you have acquired a considerable amount of college-level knowledge through job experience, reading, or noncredit courses, if you have accumulated college credits at a variety of colleges over a period of years, or if you prefer studying on your own rather than in a classroom setting, you may want to investigate the possibility of enrolling in an external degree program. Many colleges offer external degree programs that allow you to earn a degree by passing examinations (including CLEP), transferring credit from other colleges, and demonstrating in other ways that you have satisfied the educational requirements. No classroom attendance is required, and the programs are open to out-of-state candidates as well as residents. Thomas A. Edison State College in New Jersey and Charter Oaks College in Connecticut are fully accredited independent state colleges; the New York program is part of the state university system and is also fully accredited. If you are interested in exploring an external degree, you can write for more information to:

Charter Oak College
The Exchange, Suite 171
270 Farmington Avenue
Farmington, CT 06032-1909

Regents External Degree Program
Cultural Education Center
Empire State Plaza
Albany, New York 12230

Thomas A. Edison State College
101 West State Street
Trenton, New Jersey 08608

Many other colleges also have external degree or weekend programs. While they often require that a number of courses be taken on campus, the external degree programs tend to be more flexible in transferring credit, granting credit-by-examination, and allowing independent study than other traditional programs. When applying to a college, you may wish to ask whether it has an external degree or weekend program.

Questions to Ask About a College's CLEP Policy

Before taking CLEP examinations for the purpose of earning college credit, try to find the answers to these questions:

1. Which CLEP examinations are accepted by this college?

A college may accept some CLEP examinations for credit and not others - possibly not the one you are considering. The English faculty may decide to grant college English credit based on the CLEP English Composition examination, but not on the Freshman College Composition examination. Or, the mathematics faculty may decide to grant credit based on the College Mathematics to non-mathematics majors only, requiring majors to take an examination in algebra, trigonometry, or calculus to earn credit. For these reasons, it is important that you know the specific CLEP tests for which you can receive credit.

2. Does the college require the optional free-response (essay) section as well as the objective portion of the CLEP examination you are considering?

Knowing the answer to this question ahead of time will permit you to schedule the optional essay examination when you register to take your CLEP examination.

3. Is credit granted for specific courses? If so, which ones?

You are likely to find that credit will be granted for specific courses and the course titles will be designated in the college's CLEP policy. It is not necessary, however, that credit be granted for a specific course in order for you to benefit from your CLEP credit. For instance, at many liberal arts colleges, all students must take certain types of courses; these courses may be labeled the core curriculum, general education requirements, distribution requirements, or liberal arts requirements. The requirements are often expressed in terms of credit hours. For example, all students may be required to take at least six hours of humanities, six hours of English, three hours of mathematics, six hours of natural science, and six hours of social science, with no particular courses in these disciplines specified. In these instances, CLEP credit may be given as 6 hrs. English credit or 3 hrs. Math credit without specifying for which English or mathematics courses credit has been awarded. In order to avoid possible disappointment, you should know before taking a CLEP examination what type of credit you can receive and whether you will only be exempted from a required course but receive no credit.

4. How much credit is granted for each examination you are considering, and does the college place a limit on the total amount of CLEP credit you can earn toward your degree?

Not all colleges that grant CLEP credit award the same amount for individual tests. Furthermore, some colleges place a limit on the total amount of credit you can earn through CLEP or other examinations. Other colleges may grant you exemption but no credit toward your degree. Knowing several colleges' policies concerning these issues may help you decide which college you will attend. If you think you are capable of passing a number of CLEP examinations, you may want to attend a college that will allow you to earn credit for all or most of them. For example, the state external degree programs grant credit for most CLEP examinations (and other tests as well).

5. What is the required score for earning CLEP credit for each test you are considering?

Most colleges publish the required scores or percentile ranks for earning CLEP credit in their general catalog or in a brochure. The required score may vary from test to test, so find out the required score for each test you are considering.

6. What is the college's policy regarding prior course work in the subject in which you are considering taking a CLEP test?

Some colleges will not grant credit for a CLEP test if the student has already attempted a college-level course closely aligned with that test. For example, if you successfully completed English 101 or a comparable course on another campus, you will probably not be permitted to receive CLEP credit in that subject, too. Some colleges will not permit you to earn CLEP credit for a course that you failed.

7. Does the college make additional stipulations before credit will be granted?

It is common practice for colleges to award CLEP credit only to their enrolled students. There are other stipulations, however, that vary from college to college. For example, does the college require you to formally apply for or accept CLEP credit by completing and signing a form? Or does the college require you to validate your CLEP score by successfully completing a more advanced course in the subject? Answers to these and other questions will help to smooth the process of earning college credit through CLEP.

The above questions and the discussions that follow them indicate some of the ways in which colleges' CLEP policies can vary. Find out as much as possible about the CLEP policies at the colleges you are interested in so you can choose a college with a policy that is compatible with your educational goals. Once you have selected the college you will attend, you can find out which CLEP examinations your college recognizes and the requirements for earning CLEP credit.

DECIDING WHICH EXAMINATIONS TO TAKE

If You're Taking the Examinations for College Credit or Career Advancement:

Most people who take CLEP examinations do so in order to earn credit for college courses. Others take the examinations in order to qualify for job promotions or for professional certification or licensing. It is vital to most candidates who are taking the tests for any of these reasons that they be well prepared for the tests they are taking so that they can advance as rapidly as possible toward their educational or career goals.

It is usually advisable that those who have limited knowledge in the subjects covered by the tests they are considering enroll in the college courses in which that material is taught. Those who are uncertain about whether or not they know enough about a subject to do well on a particular CLEP test will find the following guidelines helpful.

There is no way to predict if you will pass a particular CLEP examination, but answers to the questions under the seven headings below should give you an indication of whether or not you are likely to succeed.

1. Test Descriptions

Read the description of the test provided. Are you familiar with most of the topics and terminology in the outline?

2. Textbooks

Examine the suggested textbooks and other resource materials following the test descriptions in this guide. Have you recently read one or more of these books, or have you read similar college-level books on this subject? If you have not, read through one or more of the textbooks listed, or through the textbook used for this course at your college. Are you familiar with most of the topics and terminology in the book?

3. Sample Questions

The sample questions provided are intended to be typical of the content and difficulty of the questions on the test. Although they are not an exact miniature of the test, the proportion of the sample questions you can answer correctly should be a rough estimate of the proportion of questions you will be able to answer correctly on the test.

Answer as many of the sample questions for this test as you can. Check your answers against the correct answers. Did you answer more than half the questions correctly?

Because of variations in course content at different institutions, and because questions on CLEP tests vary from easy to difficult - with most being of moderate difficulty - the average student who passes a course in a subject can usually answer correctly about half the questions on the corresponding CLEP examination. Most colleges set their passing scores near this level, but some set them higher. If your college has set its required score above the level required by most colleges, you may need to answer a larger proportion of questions on the test correctly.

4. Previous Study

Have you taken noncredit courses in this subject offered by an adult school or a private school, through correspondence, or in connection with your job? Did you do exceptionally well in this subject in high school, or did you take an honors course in this subject?

5. Experience

Have you learned or used the knowledge or skills included in this test in your job or life experience? For example, if you lived in a Spanish-speaking country and spoke the language for a year or more, you might consider taking the Spanish examination. Or, if you have worked at a job in which you used accounting and finance skills, Principles of Accounting would be a likely test for you to take. Or, if you have read a considerable amount of literature and attended many art exhibits, concerts, and plays, you might expect to do well on the Humanities exam.

6. Other Examinations

Have you done well on other standardized tests in subjects related to the one you want to take? For example, did you score well above average on a portion of a college entrance examination covering similar skills, or did you obtain an exceptionally high score on a high school equivalency test or a licensing examination in this subject? Although such tests do not cover exactly the same material as the CLEP examinations and may be easier, persons who do well on these tests often do well on CLEP examinations, too.

7. Advice

Has a college counselor, professor, or some other professional person familiar with your ability advised you to take a CLEP examination?

If your answer was yes to questions under several of the above headings, you probably have a good chance of passing the CLEP examination you are considering. It is unlikely that you would have acquired sufficient background from experience alone. Learning gained through reading and study is essential, and you will probably find some additional study helpful before taking a CLEP examination.

If You're Taking the Examinations to Prepare for College

Many people entering college, particularly adults returning to college after several years away from formal education, are uncertain about their ability to compete with other college students. They wonder whether they have sufficient background for college study, and those who have been away from formal study for some time wonder whether they have forgotten how to study, how to take tests, and how to write papers. Such people may wish to improve their test-taking and study skills prior to enrolling in courses.

One way to assess your ability to perform at the college level and to improve your test-taking and study skills at the same time is to prepare for and take one or more CLEP examinations. You need not be enrolled in a college to take a CLEP examination, and you may have your scores sent only to yourself and later request that a transcript be sent to a college if you then decide to apply for credit. By reviewing the test descriptions and sample questions, you may find one or several subject areas in which you think you have substantial knowledge. Select one examination, or more if you like, and carefully read at least one of the textbooks listed in the bibliography for the test. By doing this, you will get a better idea of how much you know of what is usually taught in a college-level course in that subject. Study as much material as you can, until you think you have a good grasp of the subject matter. Then take the test at a college in your area. It will be several weeks before you receive your results, and you may wish to begin reviewing for another test in the meantime.

To find out if you are eligible for credit for your CLEP score, you must compare your score with the score required by the college you plan to attend. If you are not yet sure which college you will attend, or whether you will enroll in college at all, you should begin to follow the steps outlined. It is best that you do this before taking a CLEP test, but if you are taking the test only for the experience and to familiarize yourself with college-level material and requirements, you might take the test before you approach a college. Even if the college you decide to attend does not accept the test you took, the experience of taking such a test will enable you to meet with greater confidence the requirements of courses you will take.

You will find information about how to interpret your scores in WHAT YOUR SCORES MEAN, which you will receive with your score report, and which can also be found online at the CLEP website. Many colleges follow the recommendations of the American Council on Education (ACE) for setting their required scores, so you can use this information as a guide in determining how well you did. The ACE recommendations are included in the booklet.

If you do not do well enough on the test to earn college credit, don't be discouraged. Usually, it is the best college students who are exempted from courses or receive credit-by-examination. The fact that you cannot get credit for your score means that you should probably enroll in a college course to learn the material. However, if your score was close to the required score, or if you feel you could do better on a second try or after some additional study, you may retake the test after six months. Do not take it sooner or your score will not be reported and your fee will be forfeited.

If you do earn the score required to earn credit, you will have demonstrated that you already have some college-level knowledge. You will also have a better idea whether you should take additional CLEP examinations. And, what is most important, you can enroll in college with confidence, knowing that you do have the ability to succeed.

PREPARING TO TAKE CLEP EXAMINATIONS

Having made the decision to take one or more CLEP examinations, most people then want to know if it is worthwhile to prepare for them - how much, how long, when, and how should they go about it? The precise answers to these questions vary greatly from individual to individual. However, most candidates find that some type of test preparation is helpful.

Most people who take CLEP examinations do so to show that they have already learned the important material that is taught in a college course. Many of them need only a quick review to assure themselves that they have not forgotten some of what they once studied, and to fill in some of the gaps in their knowledge of the subject. Others feel that they need a thorough review and spend several weeks studying for a test. A few wish to take a CLEP examination as a kind of final examination for independent study of a subject instead of the college course. This last group requires significantly more study than those who only need to review, and they may need some guidance from professors of the subjects they are studying.

The key to how you prepare for CLEP examinations often lies in locating those skills and areas of prior learning in which you are strong and deciding where to focus your energies. Some people may know a great deal about a certain subject area, but may not test well. These individuals would probably be just as concerned about strengthening their test-taking skills as they are about studying for a specific test. Many mental and physical skills are used in preparing for a test. It is important not only to review or study for the examinations, but to make certain that you are alert, relatively free of anxiety, and aware of how to approach standardized tests. Suggestions on developing test-taking skills and preparing psychologically and physically for a test are given. The following section suggests ways of assessing your knowledge of the content of a test and then reviewing and studying the material.

Using This Study Guide

Begin by carefully reading the test description and outline of knowledge and skills required for the examination, if given. As you read through the topics listed there, ask yourself how much you know about each one. Also note the terms, names, and symbols that are mentioned, and ask yourself whether you are familiar with them. This will give you a quick overview of how much you know about the subject. If you are familiar with nearly all the material, you will probably need a minimum of review; however, if less than half of it is familiar, you will probably require substantial study to do well on the test.

If, after reviewing the test description, you find that you need extensive review, delay answering the sample question until you have done some reading in the subject. If you complete them before reviewing the material, you will probably look for the answers as you study, and then they will not be a good assessment of your ability at a later date.

If you think you are familiar with most of the test material, try to answer the sample questions.

Apply the test-taking strategies given. Keeping within the time limit suggested will give you a rough idea of how quickly you should work in order to complete the actual test.

Check your answers against the answer key. If you answered nearly all the questions correctly, you probably do not need to study the subject extensively. If you got about half the questions correct, you ought o review at least one textbook or other suggested materials on the subject. If you answered less than half the questions correctly, you will probably benefit from more extensive reading in the subject and thorough study of one or more textbooks. The textbooks listed are used at many colleges but they are not the only good texts. You will find helpful almost any standard text available to you., such as the textbook used at your college, or earlier editions of texts listed. For some examinations, topic outlines and textbooks may not be available. Take the sample tests in this book and check your answers at the end of each test. Check wrong answers.

Suggestions for Studying

The following suggestions have been gathered from people who have prepared for CLEP examinations or other college-level tests.

1. Define your goals and locate study materials

First, determine your study goals. Set aside a block of time to review the material provided in this book, and then decide which test(s) you will take. Using the suggestions, locate suitable resource materials. If a preparation course is offered by an adult school or college in your area, you might find it helpful to enroll.

2. Find a good place to study

To determine what kind of place you need for studying, ask yourself questions such as: Do I need a quiet place? Does the telephone distract me? Do objects I see in this place remind me of things I should do? Is it too warm? Is it well lit? Am I too comfortable here? Do I have space to spread out my materials? You may find the library more conducive to studying than your home. If you decide to study at home, you might prevent interruptions by other household members by putting a sign on the door of your study room to indicate when you will be available.

3. Schedule time to study

To help you determine where studying best fits into your schedule, try this exercise: Make a list of your daily activities (for example, sleeping, working, and eating) and estimate how many hours per day you spend on each activity. Now, rate all the activities on your list in order of their importance and evaluate your use of time. Often people are astonished at how an average day appears from this perspective. They may discover that they were unaware how large portions of time are spent, or they learn their time can be scheduled in alternative ways. For example, they can remove the least important activities from their day and devote that time to studying or another important activity.

4. Establish a study routine and a set of goals

In order to study effectively, you should establish specific goals and a schedule for accomplishing them. Some people find it helpful to write out a weekly schedule and cross out each study period when it is completed. Others maintain their concentration better by writing down the time when they expect to complete a study task. Most people find short periods of intense study more productive than long stretches of time. For example, they may follow a regular schedule of several 20- or 30-minute study periods with short breaks between them. Some people like to allow themselves rewards as they complete each study goal. It is not essential that you accomplish every goal exactly within your schedule; the point is to be committed to your task.

5. Learn how to take an active role in studying.

If you have not done much studying for some time, you may find it difficult to concentrate at first. Try a method of studying, such as the one outlined below, that will help you concentrate on and remember what you read.

    a. First, read the chapter summary and the introduction. Then you will know what to look for in your reading.

    b. Next, convert the section or paragraph headlines into questions. For example, if you are reading a section entitled, The Causes of the American Revolution, ask yourself: *What were the causes of the American Revolution?* Compose the answer as you read the paragraph. Reading and answering questions aloud will help you understand and remember the material.

c. Take notes on key ideas or concepts as you read. Writing will also help you fix concepts more firmly in your mind. Underlining key ideas or writing notes in your book can be helpful and will be useful for review. Underline only important points. If you underline more than a third of each paragraph, you are probably underlining too much.

d. If there are questions or problems at the end of a chapter, answer or solve them on paper as if you were asked to do them for homework. Mathematics textbooks (and some other books) sometimes include answers to some or all of the exercises. If you have such a book, write your answers before looking at the ones given. When problem-solving is involved, work enough problems to master the required methods and concepts. If you have difficulty with problems, review any sample problems or explanations in the chapter.

e. To retain knowledge, most people have to review the material periodically. If you are preparing for a test over an extended period of time, review key concepts and notes each week or so. Do not wait for weeks to review the material or you will need to relearn much of it.

Psychological and Physical Preparation

Most people feel at least some nervousness before taking a test. Adults who are returning to college may not have taken a test in many years or they may have had little experience with standardized tests. Some younger students, as well, are uncomfortable with testing situations. People who received their education in countries outside the United States may find that many tests given in this country are quite different from the ones they are accustomed to taking.

Not only might candidates find the types of tests and the kinds of questions on them unfamiliar, but other aspects of the testing environment may be strange as well. The physical and mental stress that results from meeting this new experience can hinder a candidate's ability to demonstrate his or her true degree of knowledge in the subject area being tested. For this reason, it is important to go to the test center well prepared, both mentally and physically, for taking the test. You may find the following suggestions helpful.

1. Familiarize yourself, as much as possible, with the test and the test situation before the day of the examination. It will be helpful for you to know ahead of time:

a. How much time will be allowed for the test and whether there are timed subsections.

b. What types of questions and directions appear on the examination.

c. How your test score will be computed.

d. How to properly answer the questions on the computer (See the CLEP Sample on the CLEP website)

e. In which building and room the examination will be administered. If you don't know where the building is, locate it or get directions ahead of time.

f. The time of the test administration. You might wish to confirm this information a day or two before the examination and find out what time the building and room will be open so that you can plan to arrive early.

g. Where to park your car or, if you wish to take public transportation, which bus or train to take and the location of the nearest stop.

h. Whether smoking will be permitted during the test.

i. Whether there will be a break between examinations (if you will be taking more than one on the same day), and whether there is a place nearby where you can get something to eat or drink.

2. Go to the test situation relaxed and alert. In order to prepare for the test:

a. Get a good night's sleep. Last minute cramming, particularly late the night before, is usually counterproductive.

b. Eat normally. It is usually not wise to skip breakfast or lunch on the day of the test or to eat a big meal just before the test.

c. Avoid tranquilizers and stimulants. If you follow the other directions in this book, you won't need artificial aids. It's better to be a little tense than to be drowsy, but stimulants such as coffee and cola can make you nervous and interfere with your concentration.

d. Don't drink a lot of liquids before the test. Having to leave the room during the test will disturb your concentration and take valuable time away from the test.

e. If you are inclined to be nervous or tense, learn some relaxation exercises and use them before and perhaps during the test.

3. Arrive for the test early and prepared. Be sure to:

a. Arrive early enough so that you can find a parking place, locate the test center, and get settled comfortably before testing begins. Allow some extra time in case you are delayed unexpectedly.

b. Take the following with you:

- Your completed Registration/Admission Form
- Two forms of identification – one being a government-issued photo ID with signature, such as a driver's license or passport
- Non-mechanical pencil
- A watch so that you can time your progress (digital watches are prohibited)
- Your glasses if you need them for reading or seeing the chalkboard or wall clock

c. Leave all books, papers, and notes outside the test center. You will not be permitted to use your own scratch paper; it will be provided. Also prohibited are calculators, cell phones, beepers, pagers, photo/copy devices, radios, headphones, food, beverages, and several other items.

d. Be prepared for any temperature in the testing room. Wear layers of clothing that can be removed if the room is too hot but will keep you warm if it is too cold.

4. When you enter the test room:

a. Sit in a seat that provides a maximum of comfort and freedom from distraction.

b. Read directions carefully, and listen to all instructions given by the test administrator. If you don't understand the directions, ask for help before test timing begins. If you must ask a question after the test has begun, raise your hand and a proctor will assist you. The proctor can answer certain kinds of questions but cannot help you with the test.

c. Know your rights as a test taker. You can expect to be given the full working time allowed for the test(s) and a reasonably quiet and comfortable place in which to work. If a poor test situation is preventing you from doing your best, ask if the situation can be remedied. If bad test conditions cannot be remedied, ask the person in charge to report the problem in the Irregularity Report that will be sent to ETS with the answer sheets. You may also wish to contact CLEP. Describe the exact circumstances as completely as you can. Be sure to include the test date and name(s) of the test(s) you took. ETS will investigate the problem to make sure it does not happen again, and, if the problem is serious enough, may arrange for you to retake the test without charge.

TAKING THE EXAMINATIONS

A person may know a great deal about the subject being tested, but not do as well as he or she is capable of on the test. Knowing how to approach a test is an important part of the testing process. While a command of test-taking skills cannot substitute for knowledge of the subject matter, it can be a significant factor in successful testing.

Test-taking skills enable a person to use all available information to earn a score that truly reflects his or her ability. There are different strategies for approaching different kinds of test questions. For example, free-response questions require a very different tack than do multiple-choice questions. Other factors, such as how the test will be graded, may also influence your approach to the test and your use of test time. Thus, your preparation for a test should include finding out all you can about the test so that you can use the most effective test-taking strategies.

Before taking a test, you should know approximately how many questions are on the test, how much time you will be allowed, how the test will be scored or graded, what types of questions and directions are on the test, and how you will be required to record your answers.

Taking Multiple-Choice Tests

1. Listen carefully to the instructions given by the test administrator and read carefully all directions before you begin to answer the questions.

2. Note the time that the test administrator starts timing the test. As you proceed, make sure that you are not working too slowly. You should have answered at least half the questions in a section when half the time for that section has passed. If you have not reached that point in the section, speed up your pace on the remaining questions.

3. Before answering a question, read the entire question, including all the answer choices. Don't think that because the first or second answer choice looks good to you, it isn't necessary to read the remaining options. Instructions usually tell you to select the best answer. Sometimes one answer choice is partially correct, but another option is better; therefore, it is usually a good idea to read all the answers before you choose one.

4. Read and consider every question. Questions that look complicated at first glance may not actually be so difficult once you have read them carefully.

5. Do not puzzle too long over any one question. If you don't know the answer after you've considered it briefly, go on to the next question. Make sure you return to the question later.

6. Make sure you record your response properly.

7. In trying to determine the correct answer, you may find it helpful to cross out those options that you know are incorrect, and to make marks next to those you think might be correct. If you decide to skip the question and come back to it later, you will save yourself the time of reconsidering all the options.

8. Watch for the following key words in test questions:

all	generally	never	perhaps
always	however	none	rarely
but	may	not	seldom
except	must	often	sometimes
every	necessary	only	usually

When a question or answer option contains words such as always, every, only, never, and none, there can be no exceptions to the answer you choose. Use of words such as often, rarely, sometimes, and generally indicates that there may be some exceptions to the answer.

9. Do not waste your time looking for clues to right answers based on flaws in question wording or patterns in correct answers. Professionals at the College Board and ETS put

a great deal of effort into developing valid, reliable, fair tests. CLEP test development committees are composed of college faculty who are experts in the subject covered by the test and are appointed by the College Board to write test questions and to scrutinize each question that is included on a CLEP test. Committee members make every effort to ensure that the questions are not ambiguous, that they have only one correct answer, and that they cover college-level topics. These committees do not intentionally include trick questions. If you think a question is flawed, ask the test administrator to report it, or contact CLEP immediately.

Taking Free-Response or Essay Tests

If your college requires the optional free-response or essay portion of a CLEP Composition and Literature exams, you should do some additional preparation for your CLEP test. Taking an essay test is very different from taking a multiple-choice test, so you will need to use some other strategies.

The essay written as part of the English Composition and Essay exam is graded by English professors from a variety of colleges and universities. A process called holistic scoring is used to rate your writing ability.

The optional free-response essays, on the other hand, are graded by the faculty of the college you designate as a score recipient. Guidelines and criteria for grading essays are not specified by the College Board or ETS. You may find it helpful, therefore, to talk with someone at your college to find out what criteria will be used to determine whether you will get credit. If the test requires essay responses, ask how much emphasis will be placed on your writing ability and your ability to organize your thoughts as opposed to your knowledge of subject matter. Find out how much weight will be given to your multiple-choice test score in comparison with your free-response grade in determining whether you will get credit. This will give you an idea where you should expend the greatest effort in preparing for and taking the test.

Here are some strategies you will find useful in taking any essay test:

1. Before you begin to write, read all questions carefully and take a few minutes to jot down some ideas you might include in each answer.

2. If you are given a choice of questions to answer, choose the questions you think you can answer most clearly and knowledgeably.

3. Determine in what order you will answer the questions. Answer those you find the easiest first so that any extra time can be spent on the more difficult questions.

4. When you know which questions you will answer and in what order, determine how much testing time remains and estimate how many minutes you will devote to each question. Unless suggested times are given for the questions or one question appears to require more or less time than the others, allot an equal amount of time to each question.

5. Before answering each question, indicate the number of the question as it is given in the test book. You need not copy the entire question from the question sheet, but it will be helpful to you and to the person grading your test if you indicate briefly the topic you are addressing – particularly if you are not answering the questions in the order in which they appear on the test.

6. Before answering each question, read it again carefully to make sure you are interpreting it correctly. Underline key words, such as those listed below, that often appear in free-response questions. Be sure you know the exact meaning of these words before taking the test.

analyze	demonstrate	enumerate	list
apply	derive	explain	outline
assess	describe	generalize	prove
compare	determine	illustrate	rank
contrast	discuss	interpret	show
define	distinguish	justify	summarize

If a question asks you to outline, define, or summarize, do not write a detailed explanation; if a question asks you to analyze, explain, illustrate, interpret, or show, you must do more than briefly describe the topic.

For a current listing of CLEP Colleges

where you can get credit and be tested, write:

CLEP, P.O. Box 6600, Princeton, NJ 08541-6600

Or e-mail: clep@ets.org, or call: (609) 771-7865

HOW TO TAKE A TEST

You have studied long, hard and conscientiously.

With your official admission card in hand, and your heart pounding, you have been admitted to the examination room.

You note that there are several hundred other applicants in the examination room waiting to take the same test.

They all appear to be equally well prepared.

You know that nothing but your best effort will suffice. The "moment of truth" is at hand: you now have to demonstrate objectively, in writing, your knowledge of content and your understanding of subject matter.

You are fighting the most important battle of your life—to pass and/or score high on an examination which will determine your career and provide the economic basis for your livelihood.

What extra, special things should you know and should you do in taking the examination?

I. YOU MUST PASS AN EXAMINATION

A. WHAT EVERY CANDIDATE SHOULD KNOW
   Examination applicants often ask us for help in preparing for the written test. What can I study in advance? What kinds of questions will be asked? How will the test be given? How will the papers be graded?

B. HOW ARE EXAMS DEVELOPED?
   Examinations are carefully written by trained technicians who are specialists in the field known as "psychological measurement," in consultation with recognized authorities in the field of work that the test will cover. These experts recommend the subject matter areas or skills to be tested; only those knowledges or skills important to your success on the job are included. The most reliable books and source materials available are used as references. Together, the experts and technicians judge the difficulty level of the questions.
   Test technicians know how to phrase questions so that the problem is clearly stated. Their ethics do not permit "trick" or "catch" questions. Questions may have been tried out on sample groups, or subjected to statistical analysis, to determine their usefulness.
   Written tests are often used in combination with performance tests, ratings of training and experience, and oral interviews. All of these measures combine to form the best-known means of finding the right person for the right job.

II. HOW TO PASS THE WRITTEN TEST

A. BASIC STEPS

1) Study the announcement

How, then, can you know what subjects to study? Our best answer is: "Learn as much as possible about the class of positions for which you've applied." The exam will test the knowledge, skills and abilities needed to do the work.

Your most valuable source of information about the position you want is the official exam announcement. This announcement lists the training and experience qualifications. Check these standards and apply only if you come reasonably close to meeting them. Many jurisdictions preview the written test in the exam announcement by including a section called "Knowledge and Abilities Required," "Scope of the Examination," or some similar heading. Here you will find out specifically what fields will be tested.

2) Choose appropriate study materials

If the position for which you are applying is technical or advanced, you will read more advanced, specialized material. If you are already familiar with the basic principles of your field, elementary textbooks would waste your time. Concentrate on advanced textbooks and technical periodicals. Think through the concepts and review difficult problems in your field.

These are all general sources. You can get more ideas on your own initiative, following these leads. For example, training manuals and publications of the government agency which employs workers in your field can be useful, particularly for technical and professional positions. A letter or visit to the government department involved may result in more specific study suggestions, and certainly will provide you with a more definite idea of the exact nature of the position you are seeking.

3) Study this book!

III. KINDS OF TESTS

Tests are used for purposes other than measuring knowledge and ability to perform specified duties. For some positions, it is equally important to test ability to make adjustments to new situations or to profit from training. In others, basic mental abilities not dependent on information are essential. Questions which test these things may not appear as pertinent to the duties of the position as those which test for knowledge and information. Yet they are often highly important parts of a fair examination. For very general questions, it is almost impossible to help you direct your study efforts. What we can do is to point out some of the more common of these general abilities needed in public service positions and describe some typical questions.

1) General information

Broad, general information has been found useful for predicting job success in some kinds of work. This is tested in a variety of ways, from vocabulary lists to questions about current events. Basic background in some field of work, such as sociology or economics, may be sampled in a group of questions. Often these are principles which have become familiar to most persons through exposure rather than through formal training. It is difficult to advise you how to study for these questions; being alert to the world around you is our best suggestion.

2) Verbal ability
An example of an ability needed in many positions is verbal or language ability. Verbal ability is, in brief, the ability to use and understand words. Vocabulary and grammar tests are typical measures of this ability. Reading comprehension or paragraph interpretation questions are common in many kinds of civil service tests. You are given a paragraph of written material and asked to find its central meaning.

IV. KINDS OF QUESTIONS

1. Multiple-choice Questions
Most popular of the short-answer questions is the "multiple choice" or "best answer" question. It can be used, for example, to test for factual knowledge, ability to solve problems or judgment in meeting situations found at work.
A multiple-choice question is normally one of three types:
- It can begin with an incomplete statement followed by several possible endings. You are to find the one ending which best completes the statement, although some of the others may not be entirely wrong.
- It can also be a complete statement in the form of a question which is answered by choosing one of the statements listed.
- It can be in the form of a problem – again you select the best answer.

Here is an example of a multiple-choice question with a discussion which should give you some clues as to the method for choosing the right answer:

When an employee has a complaint about his assignment, the action which will best help him overcome his difficulty is to
   A. discuss his difficulty with his coworkers
   B. take the problem to the head of the organization
   C. take the problem to the person who gave him the assignment
   D. say nothing to anyone about his complaint

In answering this question, you should study each of the choices to find which is best. Consider choice "A" – Certainly an employee may discuss his complaint with fellow employees, but no change or improvement can result, and the complaint remains unresolved. Choice "B" is a poor choice since the head of the organization probably does not know what assignment you have been given, and taking your problem to him is known as "going over the head" of the supervisor. The supervisor, or person who made the assignment, is the person who can clarify it or correct any injustice. Choice "C" is, therefore, correct. To say nothing, as in choice "D," is unwise. Supervisors have and interest in knowing the problems employees are facing, and the employee is seeking a solution to his problem.

2. True/False

3. Matching Questions
Matching an answer from a column of choices within another column.

V. RECORDING YOUR ANSWERS

Computer terminals are used more and more today for many different kinds of exams.

For an examination with very few applicants, you may be told to record your answers in the test booklet itself. Separate answer sheets are much more common. If this separate answer sheet is to be scored by machine – and this is often the case – it is highly important that you mark your answers correctly in order to get credit.

VI. BEFORE THE TEST

YOUR PHYSICAL CONDITION IS IMPORTANT

If you are not well, you can't do your best work on tests. If you are half asleep, you can't do your best either. Here are some tips:

1) Get about the same amount of sleep you usually get. Don't stay up all night before the test, either partying or worrying—DON'T DO IT!
2) If you wear glasses, be sure to wear them when you go to take the test. This goes for hearing aids, too.
3) If you have any physical problems that may keep you from doing your best, be sure to tell the person giving the test. If you are sick or in poor health, you relay cannot do your best on any test. You can always come back and take the test some other time.

Common sense will help you find procedures to follow to get ready for an examination. Too many of us, however, overlook these sensible measures. Indeed, nervousness and fatigue have been found to be the most serious reasons why applicants fail to do their best on civil service tests. Here is a list of reminders:

- Begin your preparation early – Don't wait until the last minute to go scurrying around for books and materials or to find out what the position is all about.
- Prepare continuously – An hour a night for a week is better than an all-night cram session. This has been definitely established. What is more, a night a week for a month will return better dividends than crowding your study into a shorter period of time.
- Locate the place of the exam – You have been sent a notice telling you when and where to report for the examination. If the location is in a different town or otherwise unfamiliar to you, it would be well to inquire the best route and learn something about the building.
- Relax the night before the test – Allow your mind to rest. Do not study at all that night. Plan some mild recreation or diversion; then go to bed early and get a good night's sleep.
- Get up early enough to make a leisurely trip to the place for the test – This way unforeseen events, traffic snarls, unfamiliar buildings, etc. will not upset you.
- Dress comfortably – A written test is not a fashion show. You will be known by number and not by name, so wear something comfortable.
- Leave excess paraphernalia at home – Shopping bags and odd bundles will get in your way. You need bring only the items mentioned in the official notice you received; usually everything you need is provided. Do not bring reference books to the exam. They will only confuse those last minutes and be taken away from you when in the test room.

- Arrive somewhat ahead of time – If because of transportation schedules you must get there very early, bring a newspaper or magazine to take your mind off yourself while waiting.
- Locate the examination room – When you have found the proper room, you will be directed to the seat or part of the room where you will sit. Sometimes you are given a sheet of instructions to read while you are waiting. Do not fill out any forms until you are told to do so; just read them and be prepared.
- Relax and prepare to listen to the instructions
- If you have any physical problem that may keep you from doing your best, be sure to tell the test administrator. If you are sick or in poor health, you really cannot do your best on the exam. You can come back and take the test some other time.

VII. AT THE TEST

The day of the test is here and you have the test booklet in your hand. The temptation to get going is very strong. Caution! There is more to success than knowing the right answers. You must know how to identify your papers and understand variations in the type of short-answer question used in this particular examination. Follow these suggestions for maximum results from your efforts:

1) Cooperate with the monitor

The test administrator has a duty to create a situation in which you can be as much at ease as possible. He will give instructions, tell you when to begin, check to see that you are marking your answer sheet correctly, and so on. He is not there to guard you, although he will see that your competitors do not take unfair advantage. He wants to help you do your best.

2) Listen to all instructions

Don't jump the gun! Wait until you understand all directions. In most civil service tests you get more time than you need to answer the questions. So don't be in a hurry. Read each word of instructions until you clearly understand the meaning. Study the examples, listen to all announcements and follow directions. Ask questions if you do not understand what to do.

3) Identify your papers

Civil service exams are usually identified by number only. You will be assigned a number; you must not put your name on your test papers. Be sure to copy your number correctly. Since more than one exam may be given, copy your exact examination title.

4) Plan your time

Unless you are told that a test is a "speed" or "rate of work" test, speed itself is usually not important. Time enough to answer all the questions will be provided, but this does not mean that you have all day. An overall time limit has been set. Divide the total time (in minutes) by the number of questions to determine the approximate time you have for each question.

5) Do not linger over difficult questions

If you come across a difficult question, mark it with a paper clip (useful to have along) and come back to it when you have been through the booklet. One caution if you do this – be sure to skip a number on your answer sheet as well. Check often to be sure that you have not lost your place and that you are marking in the row numbered the same as the question you are answering.

6) Read the questions

Be sure you know what the question asks! Many capable people are unsuccessful because they failed to read the questions correctly.

7) Answer all questions

Unless you have been instructed that a penalty will be deducted for incorrect answers, it is better to guess than to omit a question.

8) Speed tests

It is often better NOT to guess on speed tests. It has been found that on timed tests people are tempted to spend the last few seconds before time is called in marking answers at random – without even reading them – in the hope of picking up a few extra points. To discourage this practice, the instructions may warn you that your score will be "corrected" for guessing. That is, a penalty will be applied. The incorrect answers will be deducted from the correct ones, or some other penalty formula will be used.

9) Review your answers

If you finish before time is called, go back to the questions you guessed or omitted to give them further thought. Review other answers if you have time.

10) Return your test materials

If you are ready to leave before others have finished or time is called, take ALL your materials to the monitor and leave quietly. Never take any test material with you. The monitor can discover whose papers are not complete, and taking a test booklet may be grounds for disqualification.

VIII. EXAMINATION TECHNIQUES

1) Read the general instructions carefully. These are usually printed on the first page of the exam booklet. As a rule, these instructions refer to the timing of the examination; the fact that you should not start work until the signal and must stop work at a signal, etc. If there are any special instructions, such as a choice of questions to be answered, make sure that you note this instruction carefully.

2) When you are ready to start work on the examination, that is as soon as the signal has been given, read the instructions to each question booklet, underline any key words or phrases, such as least, best, outline, describe and the like. In this way you will tend to answer as requested rather than discover on reviewing your paper that you listed without describing, that you selected the worst choice rather than the best choice, etc.

3) If the examination is of the objective or multiple-choice type – that is, each question will also give a series of possible answers: A, B, C or D, and you are called upon to select the best answer and write the letter next to that answer on your answer paper – it is advisable to start answering each question in turn. There may be anywhere from 50 to 100 such questions in the three or four hours allotted and you can see how much time would be taken if you read through all the questions before beginning to answer any. Furthermore, if you

come across a question or group of questions which you know would be difficult to answer, it would undoubtedly affect your handling of all the other questions.

4) If the examination is of the essay type and contains but a few questions, it is a moot point as to whether you should read all the questions before starting to answer any one. Of course, if you are given a choice – say five out of seven and the like – then it is essential to read all the questions so you can eliminate the two that are most difficult. If, however, you are asked to answer all the questions, there may be danger in trying to answer the easiest one first because you may find that you will spend too much time on it. The best technique is to answer the first question, then proceed to the second, etc.

5) Time your answers. Before the exam begins, write down the time it started, then add the time allowed for the examination and write down the time it must be completed, then divide the time available somewhat as follows:
   - If 3-1/2 hours are allowed, that would be 210 minutes. If you have 80 objective-type questions, that would be an average of 2-1/2 minutes per question. Allow yourself no more than 2 minutes per question, or a total of 160 minutes, which will permit about 50 minutes to review.
   - If for the time allotment of 210 minutes there are 7 essay questions to answer, that would average about 30 minutes a question. Give yourself only 25 minutes per question so that you have about 35 minutes to review.

6) The most important instruction is to read each question and make sure you know what is wanted. The second most important instruction is to time yourself properly so that you answer every question. The third most important instruction is to answer every question. Guess if you have to but include something for each question. Remember that you will receive no credit for a blank and will probably receive some credit if you write something in answer to an essay question. If you guess a letter – say "B" for a multiple-choice question – you may have guessed right. If you leave a blank as an answer to a multiple-choice question, the examiners may respect your feelings but it will not add a point to your score. Some exams may penalize you for wrong answers, so in such cases only, you may not want to guess unless you have some basis for your answer.

7) Suggestions
   a. Objective-type questions
      1. Examine the question booklet for proper sequence of pages and questions
      2. Read all instructions carefully
      3. Skip any question which seems too difficult; return to it after all other questions have been answered
      4. Apportion your time properly; do not spend too much time on any single question or group of questions
      5. Note and underline key words – all, most, fewest, least, best, worst, same, opposite, etc.
      6. Pay particular attention to negatives
      7. Note unusual option, e.g., unduly long, short, complex, different or similar in content to the body of the question
      8. Observe the use of "hedging" words – probably, may, most likely, etc.

9. Make sure that your answer is put next to the same number as the question
10. Do not second-guess unless you have good reason to believe the second answer is definitely more correct
11. Cross out original answer if you decide another answer is more accurate; do not erase until you are ready to hand your paper in
12. Answer all questions; guess unless instructed otherwise
13. Leave time for review

b. Essay questions
1. Read each question carefully
2. Determine exactly what is wanted. Underline key words or phrases.
3. Decide on outline or paragraph answer
4. Include many different points and elements unless asked to develop any one or two points or elements
5. Show impartiality by giving pros and cons unless directed to select one side only
6. Make and write down any assumptions you find necessary to answer the questions
7. Watch your English, grammar, punctuation and choice of words
8. Time your answers; don't crowd material

8) Answering the essay question

Most essay questions can be answered by framing the specific response around several key words or ideas. Here are a few such key words or ideas:

M's: manpower, materials, methods, money, management
P's: purpose, program, policy, plan, procedure, practice, problems, pitfalls, personnel, public relations

a. Six basic steps in handling problems:
1. Preliminary plan and background development
2. Collect information, data and facts
3. Analyze and interpret information, data and facts
4. Analyze and develop solutions as well as make recommendations
5. Prepare report and sell recommendations
6. Install recommendations and follow up effectiveness

b. Pitfalls to avoid
1. Taking things for granted – A statement of the situation does not necessarily imply that each of the elements is necessarily true; for example, a complaint may be invalid and biased so that all that can be taken for granted is that a complaint has been registered
2. Considering only one side of a situation – Wherever possible, indicate several alternatives and then point out the reasons you selected the best one
3. Failing to indicate follow up – Whenever your answer indicates action on your part, make certain that you will take proper follow-up action to see how successful your recommendations, procedures or actions turn out to be
4. Taking too long in answering any single question – Remember to time your answers properly

EXAMINATION SECTION

EXAMINATION SECTION
TEST 1

DIRECTIONS: Each question or incomplete statement is followed by several suggested answers or completions. Select the one that BEST answers the question or completes the statement. *PRINT THE LETTER OF THE CORRECT ANSWER IN THE SPACE AT THE RIGHT.*

1. *After completing fighter pilot training, women's access to battle has often been denied.*
   The above sentence contains
   A. a dangling modifier
   B. a euphemism
   C. problems with parallel construction
   D. a split infinitive

   1._____

2. *That is a strange type of a bird.*
   The above sentence contains problems with
   A. split infinitives   B. idiom
   C. parallel construction   D. subject-verb agreement

   2._____

3. *Native Americans are often portrayed or stereotyped as lazy, despite overwhelming evidence to the contrary.*
   The above sentence contains
   A. a dangling modifier   B. a split infinitive
   C. redundancy   D. no errors

   3._____

4. *After the initial excitement had worn off, Jessica decided to carefully weigh her options.*
   The above sentence contains
   A. a dangling modifier   B. an inconsistent verb tense
   C. faulty apposition   D. a split infinitive

   4._____

5. Despite our efforts to rid ourselves of them, the fats in our bodies serve a purpose. Fat cells never die, which is why exercising is better than dieting. Few people understand that almost three-quarters of our calories are burned while we rest.
   Based on the above information, which of the following represents a correct logical inference?
   A. Fat is increasingly harmful to our bodies as we age.
   B. Understanding the way our bodies function is central to good health.
   C. The more a person rests, the more weight he or she will lose.
   D. Dieting is useless.

   5._____

6. **How to Get Out of a Locked Trunk, Philip Weiss:** *Every culture comes up with tests of a person's ability to get out of a _____ situation.*
   Which of the following words provides the appropriate connotation to complete the above sentence?
   A. death-defying   B. sticky   C. flavorful   D. hopeful

7. *Carol has a habit of jumping out of the frying pan and into deep water.*
   The above sentence contains problems with
   A. split infinitives
   B. mixed metaphors
   C. idiom
   D. jargon

8. *When I go skiing I like to purchase a lift ticket. Otherwise you spend all your time walking uphill.*
   The above passage contains
   A. a dangling modifier
   B. problems with parallel construction
   C. a shifting point of view
   D. a split infinitive

9. *Her hopes rise as they draw near to the animal store, and then fell when her parents drove past it.*
   The above sentence contains
   A. a dangling modifier
   B. an inconsistent verb tense
   C. a shifting point of view
   D. problems with subject-verb agreement

10. *The doctor, a very lucrative profession, requires a great deal of education and training.*
    The above sentence contains
    A. a dangling modifier
    B. a shifting point of view
    C. faulty apposition
    D. an inconsistent verb tense

11. *Tony and Kim were devastated to learn that their dog, Sentinel, would have to be put to sleep.*
    The above sentence contains
    A. jargon   B. slang   C. a metaphor   D. a euphemism

12. Which of the following is the CLEAREST description of a particular scene?
    A. A Canadian bridge building official on a windy day in 1886 on a bridge high above the St. Lawrence river saw a group of Caughnawaga Mohawk Indians playing.
    B. On a bridge high above the St. Lawrence river a Canadian bridge-building official saw a group of Caughnawaga Indians playing on a windy day in 1886.
    C. On a windy day in 1886, a Canadian bridge-building official saw a group of Caughnawaga Mohawk Indians playing on a bridge high above the St. Lawrence river.
    D. A group of Caughnawaga Mohawk Indians playing on a windy day in 1886 were seen by a Canadian bridge-building official high above the St. Lawrence river.

13. Which of the following provides the MOST objective point of view on the part of the writer?
    A. A student protest group blocked the entry to the graduate library for 2 hours today.
    B. A group of left-wing radicals blocked our way into the study carrels this afternoon.
    C. Students blocked the entrance to the graduate library that sits like an eyesore on the campus.
    D. These student groups rarely seem to understand what it is they're protesting.

14. *When I saw Gabriel Samuels in the county courthouse, I knew he must have been arrested.*
    The above statement is an example of
    A. a faulty use of cause and effect
    B. an ad hominem attack
    C. circular reasoning
    D. a hasty generalization

15. *The wise politician promises the possible and accepts the inevitable.*
    The above statement contains
    A. elliptical phrases
    B. parallel construction
    C. a shift in point of view
    D. euphemisms

16. *The actor Brad Pitt is so handsome that I know he must be smart.*
    The above statement is an example of
    A. a faulty use of cause and effect
    B. a non sequitur
    C. circular reasoning
    D. a hasty generalization

Questions 17-18.

DIRECTIONS: Questions 17 and 18 are to be answered on the basis of the following passage.

Kill 'Em! Crush 'Em! Eat 'Em Raw!, John McCurty:

    The family resemblance between football and war is, indeed striking. Their languages are similar: "field general," "long bomb," "blitz," "take a shot," "front line," "pursuit," "good hit," "the draft," and so on. Their principles and practices are alike: mass hysteria, the art of intimidation, absolute command and total obedience, territorial aggression, censorship, inflated insignia and propaganda, blackboard maneuvers and strategies, drills, uniforms, formations, marching bands and training camps.

17. The diction in the above passage is BEST characterized as
    A. formal, with slang terms
    B. colloquial with slang terms
    C. formal
    D. colloquial

18. The above passage depends MOST upon
    A. imagery
    B. metaphor
    C. comparison
    D. contrast

Questions 19-25.

DIRECTIONS: Questions 19 through 25 are to be answered on the basis of the following passage.

The Awakening, Kate Chopin

A certain light was beginning to dawn dimly within her—the light which, showing the way, forbids it.(1)
At that early period it served but to bewilder her.(2) It moved her to dreams, to thoughtfulness, to the shadowy anguish which had overcome her the midnight when she had abandoned herself to tears.(3)
In short, Mrs. Pontellier was beginning to realize her position in the universe as a human being, and to recognize her relations as an individual to the world within and about her.(4) This may seem like a ponderous weight of wisdom to descend upon the soul of a young woman of twenty-eight—perhaps more wisdom than the Holy Ghost is usually pleased to vouchsafe to any woman.(5)
But the beginning of things, of a world especially, is necessarily vague, tangled, chaotic, and exceedingly disturbing.(6) How few of us ever emerge from such beginning!(7) How many souls perish in its tumult!(8)
The voice of the sea is seductive; never ceasing, whispering, clamoring, murmuring, inviting the soul to wander for a spell in abysses of solitude; to lose itself in mazes of inward contemplation.(9)
The voice of the sea speaks to the soul.(10) The touch of the sea is sensuous, enfolding the boy in its soft, close embrace.(11)

19. This passage is BEST characterized as a(n)
    A. concrete description of the sea and its dangers
    B. descriptive narrative about Mrs. Pontellier's depression
    C. descriptive narrative about Mrs. Pontellier's soul
    D. account of Mrs. Pontellier's fear of swimming

20. In this passage, the sea is BEST characterized as a(n)
    A. element of nature that encourages deep reflection
    B. dangerous and unpredictable body of water that threatens human life
    C. mysterious force that entices people to abandon their loved ones
    D. element of nature that causes people to reflect upon their childhoods

21. In line 5, the word *ponderous* is used to mean
    A. surprising   B. unexpected   C. thoughtful   D. heavy

22. Lines 6-8 provide a(n)
    A. description of the dangers of the sea
    B. explanation of the causes of Mrs. Pontellier's depression
    C. description of the transformation of Mrs. Pontellier's soul
    D. argument for greater understanding of those suffering from depression

23. Mrs. Pontellier is BEST characterized as a   23.____
    A. middle-aged woman overcome with sadness
    B. young woman just beginning to discover herself
    C. middle-aged women who has discovered a new sense of power
    D. young woman in love with the sea

24. Which of the following words BEST describes Mrs. Pontellier's reaction to this experience?   24.____
    A. Confusion   B. Sorrow   C. Ecstasy   D. Happiness

25. The MAIN implication of this passage is that   25.____
    A. Mrs. Pontellier is a very religious woman
    B. Mrs. Pontellier needs help for her debilitating depression
    C. the sea is a mesmerizing, overwhelming element of nature
    D. the discovery of self is a bewildering and sometimes dangerous process

KEY (CORRECT ANSWERS)

1.	A		11.	D
2.	B		12.	C
3.	C		13.	A
4.	D		14.	A
5.	B		15.	B
6.	B		16.	B
7.	B		17.	A
8.	C		18.	C
9.	B		19.	C
10.	C		20.	A

21. D
22. C
23. B
24. A
25. D

TEST 2

DIRECTIONS: Each question or incomplete statement is followed by several suggested answers or completions. Select the one that BEST answers the question or completes the statement. *PRINT THE LETTER OF THE CORRECT ANSWER IN THE SPACE AT THE RIGHT.*

1. *For a successful stockbroker, Adam is remarkably ingenuous.*
   Which of the following BEST captures the meaning of the word *ingenuous* as used in the above sentence?
   A. Ignorant
   B. Terse
   C. Straightforward, frank
   D. Duplicitous

   1.____

2. *I had every intention of complying to the rules.*
   The above sentence contains problems with
   A. split infinitives
   B. mixed metaphors
   C. idiom
   D. jargon

   2.____

3. The Ring of Time, E.B. White:
   The enchantment grew not out of anything that happened or was performed but out of something that seemed to go round and around and around with the girl, attending her, a steady gleam in the shape of a circle—a ring of ambition, of happiness, of youth.
   The above passage depends MOST heavily on
   A. irony
   B. parallel construction
   C. correlative conjunctions
   D. elliptical phrases

   3.____

4. Which of the following titles utilizes a slang tone?
   A. Just How Do You Suppose That Alice Knows?
   B. Leisure Will Kill You
   C. Gotta Dance
   D. When I Heard the Learn'd Astronomer

   4.____

5. Which of the following presents the BEST sequence of the following sentences to make a coherent paragraph?
   I. One of the most important of these nutrients is nitrogen, derived from the decomposing organic matter—material from living things—in the soil.
   II. If these plants did not have a source for nitrogen, they would not be able to produce their own food, and would quickly die.
   III. Nearly all the world's green plants make their own food using sunlight, water, and nutrients that are drawn from the soil through their roots.
   IV. However, some plants live in wet, marshy areas where much of this organic material, including nitrogen, is washed out of the soil.
   The CORRECT answer is:
   A. I, II, IV, III   B. II, III, I, IV   C. III, I, IV, II   D. III, IV, I, II

   5.____

6. *On his new mountain bike, Justin flew over the hills at a full head of steam.*
   The above sentence contains problems with
   A. split infinitives
   B. mixed metaphors
   C. idiom
   D. jargon

7. *Prior than yesterday, we had never seen such a thing.*
   The above sentence contains problems with
   A. split infinitives
   B. mixed metaphors
   C. idiom
   D. jargon

8. *I _____ under this pressure. Unable to compete, yet unwilling to shut down, I simply stumbled onward.*
   Which of the following words provides the appropriate connotation to complete the above passage?
   A. diminished   B. shriveled   C. suffered   D. thrived

9. *In his lecture on twentieth century art, the professor alluded to Andy Warhol.*
   Which of the following BEST captures the meaning of the word *alluded* as it is used in the above sentence?
   A. Indirectly referred
   B. Directly referred
   C. Footnoted
   D. Introduced

10. Which of the following is the CLEAREST description of a particular scene?
    A. During the dance, which is beautiful to watch, these tin cones strike one another to produce a soft, rhythmic sound.
    B. During the dance these tin cones strike one another to produce a soft, rhythmic sound, which is beautiful to watch.
    C. During the dance these tin cones strike one another to produce a sound that is soft, rhythmic and beautiful to watch.
    D. During this beautiful dance, these tin cones strike one another to produce a soft, rhythmic sound.

11. *Throughout her life, Martina Navratilova has used her differences creating a career marked by determination, skill, and discipline to her advantage.*
    The above sentence contains
    A. redundancy
    B. a faulty modifier
    C. improper punctuation
    D. mixed metaphors

12. *Journalists are trained to approach stories with an amoral perspective.*
    Which of the following BEST captures the meaning of the word *amoral* as it is used in the above sentence?
    A. Subjective   B. Emotional   C. Judgmental   D. Non-judgmental

13. On Going Home, Joan Didion:
    I would like to promise her that she will grow up with a sense of her cousins and of rivers and of great-grandmother's teacups, would like to pledge her a picnic on a river with friend chicken and her hair uncombed, would like to give her home for her birthday, but we live differently now and I can promise her nothing like that.

The above passage depends MOST heavily on
A. parallel construction   B. metaphor
C. analogy   D. coordination

14. *A few countries produce most of the world's toxins, but pollution affected many countries.*
The above sentence contains
A. a false analogy   B. faulty parallel construction
C. a shift in point of view   D. a shift in verb tense

15. *I glanced quickly through the pages of the old family album, unable to believe my eyes.*
The above sentence contains
A. improper punctuation   B. faulty subordination
C. redundancy   D. no errors

16. *Called Skywalkers, they have helped them find a modern expression for old Mohawk traditions of bravery, courage, and endurance.*
The above sentence contains
A. an ambiguous pronoun reference   B. faulty subordination
C. a dangling modifier   D. no errors

17. *One can become rich if you practice frugality.*
The above sentence contains
A. a shift in verb tense   B. a shift in point of view
C. faulty parallel construction   D. a dangling modifier

18. *While English is both a written and an oral language, the Navajo language is almost entirely oral.*
The above sentence contains
A. faulty subordination   B. a misplaced modifier
C. faulty parallel structure   D. no errors

19. *She is different than you.*
The above sentence contains problems with
A. split infinitives   B. mixed metaphors
C. idiom   D. jargon

20. *After starting at the bottom of the ladder, Samson had made it to CEO of the company.*
The above sentence contains
A. jargon   B. a cliché   C. an idiom   D. slang

21. *The representative's remarks were vigorously censured by his colleagues.*
Which of the following BEST captures the meaning of the word *censured* as it is used in the above sentence?
A. Severely criticized   B. Edited or suppressed
C. Applauded   D. Silenced

22. *Whenever she had to warn us about life, my mother told fantastic stories with complicated morals. She tested our ability to _____ realities.*
Which of the following words provides the appropriate connotation to complete the above sentence?
   A. figure out   B. establish   C. make up   D. discern

22.____

23. In a dictionary, this label is applied to terms that were once common but are now rare.
   A. Formal   B. Informal   C. Nonstandard   D. Archaic

23.____

24. *Her skills are weak and her performance only average.*
The above sentence contains
   A. ambiguous modifiers   B. subject-verb agreement
   C. parallel construction   D. elliptical phrasing

24.____

25. *The graduate student cited Freud in her dissertation.*
Which of the following BEST captures the meaning of the word *cited* as it is used in the above sentence?
   A. Thanked   B. Quoted as an authority
   C. Acknowledged   B. Located

25.____

KEY (CORRECT ANSWERS)

1.	C		11.	B
2.	C		12.	D
3.	B		13.	A
4.	C		14.	D
5.	C		15.	C
6.	B		16.	A
7.	C		17.	B
8.	B		18.	D
9.	A		19.	C
10.	D		20.	B

21. A
22. B
23. D
24. D
25. B

TEST 3

DIRECTIONS: Each question or incomplete statement is followed by several suggested answers or completions. Select the one that BEST answers the question or completes the statement. *PRINT THE LETTER OF THE CORRECT ANSWER IN THE SPACE AT THE RIGHT.*

Questions 1-3.

DIRECTIONS: Questions 1 through 3 are to be answered on the basis of the following excerpts.

A. As Henry David Thoreau famously declared, *In Wilderness is the preservation of the World*. But is it? The more one knows of its peculiar history, the more one realizes that wilderness is not quite what it seems.
B. For whatever else a prison does, it demands that one confront it. If you are a prisoner, it might take you a dozen years to realize that the life you hope to create requires, above all else, that it be lived within these walls, for these walls do not go away. Here, of all the world's places, there is everything to accept.
C. I've been around and seen the Taj Mahal and the Grand Canyon and Marilyn Monroe's footprints outside Grauman's Chinese Theater, but I've never seen my mother wash her own hair. Upon matrimony, she began weekly treks to the beauty salon where Julie washed and styled her hair. Her appointment on Fridays at two o'clock was never canceled or rescheduled.
D. The ongoing loss will not be replaced by evolution in any period of time that has meaning for humanity. Extinction is now proceeding thousands of times faster than the production of new species.

1. In which excerpt is the tone meant to be humorous?
   A. A   B. B   C. C   D. D

2. Which excerpt relies MOST heavily on imagery?
   A. A   B. B   C. C   D. D

3. In which excerpt is the writing style MOST colloquial?
   A. A   B. B   C. C   D. D

4. *Just try and do it anyway.*
   The above sentence contains problems with
   A. idiom
   B. mixed metaphors
   C. a split infinitive
   D. jargon

5. *At three or four o'clock in the afternoon, my mother's friends would _____ in her kitchen to tell the story of their days, their small triumphs, and struggles.*
   Which of the following words provides the appropriate connotation to complete the above sentence?
   A. gossip   B. circle up   C. gather   D. collect

6. Which of the following presents the BEST sequence of the following sentences to make a coherent paragraph?
   I. The Portuguese navy was then considered by the Western world to be the most formidable on earth.
   II. Unlike the Portuguese, this fleet had already sailed beyond the China Sea and the Indian Ocean, reaching all the way to the tip of the African continent.
   III. However, on the other side of the world, Chinese navigators were in possession of a navy that was unequaled in numbers, skills, and technology.
   IV. In the early fifteenth century, Portugal's naval ships were inching their way down the west coast of Africa, searching for an ocean passage to India and Asia.
   The CORRECT answer is:
   A. IV, I, III, II   B. IV, II, I, III   C. I, IV, III, II   D. I, III, II, IV

7. The world's various industries produce an estimated 400 million tons of waste each year. The majority of this waste comes from the United States. Ironically, many citizens of the United States refuse to allow waste dumps in their communities and even in their country. As a result, much of this waste is diverted to poorer countries who are in no position to refuse it.
   Based on the above information, which of the following is a CORRECT logical inference?
   A. Other countries find it economically beneficial to dispose of the waste from the United States.
   B. Poor countries have found an economic opportunity in the disposal of waste from richer countries.
   C. It is better for the United States to dump its waste in other countries than its own.
   D. Poor countries are forced to act as dumping grounds for the world's richest countries.

8. The Stunt Pilot, Annie Dillard:
   Nothing on earth is more _____ than knowing we must roll up our sleeves and move back the boundaries of the humanly possible once more.
   Which of the following words provides the appropriate connotation to complete the above sentence?
   A. heart-rending   B. gladdening   C. saddening   D. lovely

9. *The climactic moment of the hike came at the top of Long's Peak.*
   Which of the following BEST captures the meaning of the word *climactic* as it is used in the above sentence?
   A. Traumatic   B. Geographical height
   C. Climate of greatest intensity   D. Point of greatest intensity

10. The issue of child care represents an ongoing crisis in this country. Families are forced to make profound decisions with lifelong effects regarding the care of their children. Many families do not believe it is possible to live adequately on only one salary. Not that conservatives care. If they had their way, women would be back in the kitchen, baking cookies for junior.
    The above passage contains
    A. a shifting point of view
    B. an inconsistent tone
    C. ad hominem attacks
    D. false analogies

11. *That ruler belonged to Mr. Abel as though it grew out of his right hand, as wings grow out of an angel, or a tail out of a devil.*
    The above sentence contains
    A. a false analogy
    B. a euphemism
    C. parallel construction
    D. an elliptical phrase

12. *The diplomat returned to the clinic where he underwent lung surgery in 1991 in a limousine provided by his embassy.*
    The above sentence contains
    A. an inconsistent tone
    B. faulty parallel construction
    C. a misplaced modifier
    D. a dangling modifier

13. Maintenance, Naomi Shihab Nye:
    Somewhere close behind me the outline of Thoreau's small cabin plods along ghost set on _____. It even has the same rueful eyes Henry David had in his book.
    Which of the following words provides the appropriate connotation to complete the above sentence?
    A. haunting
    B. terrifying
    C. startling
    D. scolding

14. *The coarse language of the instructor was a shock to everyone.*
    Which of the following BEST captures the meaning of the word *coarse* as it is used in the above sentence?
    A. Related to a unit of study
    B. Crude
    C. Technical
    D. Emotional

15. *Recuperation is like spring.*
    The above sentence is an example of a(n)
    A. allegory
    B. metaphor
    C. euphemism
    D. analogy

Questions 16-22.

DIRECTIONS: Questions 16 through 22 are to be answered on the basis of the following passage.

4 (#3)

Sonny's Blues, James Baldwin

But houses exactly like the houses of our past yet dominated the landscape, boys exactly like the boys we once had been found themselves smothering in these houses, came down into the streets for light and air and found themselves encircled by disaster.(1) Some escaped the trap, most didn't.(2) Those who got out always left something of themselves behind, as some animals amputate a leg and leave it in the trap.(3) It might be said, perhaps, that I had escaped. after all, I was a school teacher; or that Sonny had, he hadn't lived in Harlem for years.(4) Yet, as the cab moved uptown through streets which seemed, with a rush, to darken with dark people, and as I covertly studied Sonny's face, it came to me that what we both were seeking was that part of ourselves which had been left behind.(5) It's always at the hour of trouble and confrontation that the missing member aches.(6)

16. What is the point of view of this passage?
    A. First person singular
    B. Second person
    C. Third person singular
    D. Third person plural

17. This passage is BEST characterized as a
    A. concrete description of Harlem
    B. descriptive narrative about a traumatic event in the narrator's childhood
    C. concrete explanation of how the narrator escaped from Harlem
    D. descriptive narrative about the narrator's troubled childhood

18. The narrator relies MOST heavily on which of the following to dramatize the emotional experience of leaving and then returning to Harlem?
    A. Metaphor   B. Analogy   C. Imagery   D. Emotional appeal

19. In line 6, the author is speaking of his need to
    A. ease his own suffering over the loss of Sonny
    B. find Sonny
    C. discover his roots
    D. recover that part of himself left behind in Harlem

20. This passage is a description of a
    A. cab ride the author and his brother took to Harlem when they were young boys
    B. cab ride the author took to Harlem when he was a young boy
    C. cab ride to Harlem
    D. train ride to Harlem

21. The descriptive details given in line 1 provide a(n)
    A. precise visual of Harlem
    B. emotional image linking past to present
    C. precise visual image of the narrator's house and neighborhood
    D. distorted emotional image from the narrator's childhood

22. In line 5, the word *covertly* is used to mean
    A. secretly   B. openly   C. fearfully   D. knowingly

23. *Rebecca hurriedly glanced through the contract before signing it.*
    The above sentence contains
    A. redundancy
    B. faulty parallel construction
    C. faulty subordination
    D. no errors

24. *There are many pictures of celebrities who have dined at Sal's Diner on the walls.*
    The above sentence contains
    A. faulty parallel construction
    B. a misplaced modifier
    C. a dangling modifier
    D. no errors

25. *Susanna took great care to ensure her dinner guest complemented one another in education and background.*
    Which of the following BEST captures the meaning of the word *complemented* as it is used in the above sentence?
    A. Balanced
    B. Flattered
    C. Contrasted with
    D. Competed against

KEY (CORRECT ANSWERS)

1.	C		11.	D
2.	B		12.	C
3.	C		13.	A
4.	A		14.	B
5.	C		15.	D
6.	A		16.	A
7.	D		17.	D
8.	B		18.	A
9.	D		19.	D
10.	B		20.	C

21.	B
22.	A
23.	A
24.	B
25.	A

TEST 4

DIRECTIONS: Each question or incomplete statement is followed by several suggested answers or completions. Select the one that BEST answers the question or completes the statement. *PRINT THE LETTER OF THE CORRECT ANSWER IN THE SPACE AT THE RIGHT.*

1. *After seeing the empty coffin, Edward turned white as a sheet.*
   The above sentence contains a(n)
   A. metaphor B. idiom C. cliché D. euphemism

   1.____

2. Which of the following presents the BEST sequence of the following sentences to make a coherent paragraph?
   I. At that time, the American South was an agricultural region that relied on African-American slaves to work plantations where cotton, tobacco, sugar, and other crops were grown.
   II. Most of them promptly tried to secede, or withdraw, from the United States to form their own country, the Confederate States of America.
   III. The United States elections of 1860 brought to power a president, Abraham Lincoln, and a congressional majority who were against the practice of slavery.
   IV. Lincoln's election made it possible that slavery would eventually be outlawed in the United States, and Southern states saw this as a threat to their way of life.
   The CORRECT answer is:
   A. IV, III, I, II B. I, III, IV, II C. III, II, IV, I D. III, I, IV, II

   2.____

3. *The informant was unable to elicit any useful information for his contact.*
   Which of the following BEST captures the meaning of the word *elicit* as it is used in the above sentence?
   A. Reject B. Discuss C. Draw out D. Illegal

   3.____

4. *Though Mildred still drove, she admitted to being blind as a bat.*
   The above sentence contains a(n)
   A. metaphor B. idiom C. cliché D. euphemism

   4.____

5. *Only a single parent can understand the plight of single parents.*
   The above statement is an example of
   A. a faulty use of cause and effect B. an ad hominem attack
   C. circular reasoning D. a hasty generalization

   5.____

Questions 6-9.

DIRECTIONS: Questions 6 through 9 are to be answered on the basis of the following passage.

What We Talk About When We Talk About Love, Raymond Carver

Outside in the backyard, one of the dogs began to bark.(1) The leaves of the aspen that leaned past the window ticked against the glass.(2) The afternoon sun was like a presence in this room, the spacious light of ease and generosity.(3) We could have been anywhere, somewhere enchanted. (4) We raised our glasses again and grinned at each other like children who had agreed on something forbidden.(5)

6. In line 3, the phrase *spacious light of ease and generosity* mainly implies
   A. charitable feeling
   B. joy
   C. contentment
   D. enlightenment

7. What is the point of view of this passage?
   A. First person singular
   B. First person plural
   C. Second person
   D. Third person plural

8. The descriptive details in this passage provide a
   A. view of the room from a child's perspective
   B. sentimental tone
   C. concrete image of the room
   D. visual image and an emotional tone

9. The tone of this passage is BEST characterized as
   A. sentimental   B. nostalgic   C. humorous   D. solemn

10. Which of the following titles is MOST colloquial?
    A. Casa: A Partial Remembrance of A Puerto Rican Childhood
    B. Borges and Myself
    C. Anarchy in the Tenth Grade
    D. How It Feels to Be Colored Me

11. *In 1941, Edward emigrated to avoid persecution.*
    Which of the following BEST captures the meaning of the word *emigrated* as it is used in the above sentence?
    A. Entered   B. Left   C. Returned   D. Challenged

12. Which of the following presents the BEST sequence of the following sentences to make a coherent paragraph?
    I. Cornbread is a food that originated during the settlement of the American Midwest, and is still popular in both urban and rural sections of the country's interior.
    II. Ashcake was mixed from cornmeal and water, made into thick cakes, and baked directly on the cinders and ashes of prairie camp fires.
    III. For many years this method of baking cornbread remained unchanged by people who settled the frontier.

IV. Unlike most American foods, which were variations of dishes that pioneers brought from their home countries, cornbread originated on this continent, in the Kansas Territory, as a direct descendant of the "ashcake" of the Kansas Indians.
The CORRECT answer is:
A. IV, I, II, III   B. I, IV, II, III   C. IV, I, III, II   D. I, IV, III, II

13. When you significantly shorten a passage, restating the MOST important points in your own words, you have _____ the passage.   13.____
    A. plagiarized   B. paraphrased   C. summarized   D. quoted

14. *The driver awaited his eminent passenger.*   14.____
    Which of the following BEST captures the meaning of the word *eminent* as it is used in the above sentence?
    A. Impending   B. Inevitable   C. Anonymous   D. Distinguished

15. *The culprit was described as a 5 foot, tall female with a mole weighing approximately 120 pounds.*   15.____
    The above sentence contains which of the following mistakes?
    A. Faulty parallel construction   B. Faulty coordination
    C. Misplaced modifier   D. Dangling modifier

16. *Harry says he is failing Economics 101 because his teaching assistant doesn't speak English well.*   16.____
    The above statement is an example of
    A. a faulty use of cause and effect   B. an ad hominem attack
    C. circular reasoning   D. a hasty generalization

17. *Opening the lens to take the picture, the camera fell.*   17.____
    The above sentence contains which of the following mistakes?
    A. Faulty parallel construction   B. Faulty coordination
    C. Misplaced modifier   D. Dangling modifier

18. A car driving on the highway has an auto-rental sticker on its bumper.   18.____
    Based on the above information, which of the following is a CORRECT logical inference?
    A. The car is probably a rental car.
    B. The driver is returning the rental car.
    C. The driver doesn't know the area freeways very well.
    D. A tourist is driving the car.

19. A book's glossary contains   19.____
    A. the page numbers where key terms and ideas are discussed
    B. an author's acknowledgments
    C. definitions of unfamiliar words used in the book
    D. a list of the texts the author referred to in the book

Questions 20-24.

DIRECTIONS: Questions 20 through 24 are to be answered on the basis of the following excerpts.

A. It was the book that moved me to the sort of angelic devotion to the female, which is finally a form of exclusion, a tyrannical boundary (albeit usually unwitting) between the real world of men and the dream world of women, a world which was of course dreamed by men, not by the women who were held in deleterious yet tender captivity there.
B. Long before studying geometry, I learned there is a mystical virtue in right angles. There is an unspoken morality in seeking the level and the plumb. A house will stand, a table will bear weight, the sides of a box will hold together, only if the joints are square and the members upright. (The Inheritance of Tools – Best American Essays)
C. So much for endings. Beginnings are always more fun. True connoisseurs, however, are known to favor the stretch in between, since it's the hardest to do anything with. That's about all that can be said for plots, which anyway are just one thing after another, a what and a what and a what. Now try How, and Why.
D. Since humankind is transcendent in intelligence and spirit, so must our species have been released from the iron laws of ecology that bind all other species. No matter how serious the problem, civilized human beings, by ingenuity, force of will and—who knows—divine dispensation, will find a solution

20. In which excerpt is the tone meant to be humorous?
   A. A   B. B   C. C   D. D

21. In excerpt A, the word *deleterious* MOST NEARLY means
   A. harmful   B. distracting   C. sorrowful   D. beneficial

22. In excerpt D, the word *transcendent* MOST NEARLY means
   A. evolved   B. advanced   C. superior   D. enlightened

23. Which excerpt relies MOST heavily on metaphor?
   A. A   B. B   C. C   D. D

24. In which excerpt is the tone intended to be MOST persuasive?
   A. A   B. B   C. C   D. D

25. Pets feel safest when they are at home. They feel least safe in unfamiliar environments, much like humans. These feelings of insecurity influence a pet's ability to communicate and fight. Many pets do fight with other animals, but rarely will they fight to the death. They have a healthy balance of fear and aggression.
The PRIMARY purpose of the above paragraph is to
   A. tell a story   B. persuade   C. inform   D. offer a solution

KEY (CORRECT ANSWERS)

1. C
2. D
3. C
4. C
5. C

6. C
7. B
8. D
9. B
10. D

11. B
12. B
13. C
14. D
15. C

16. D
17. D
18. A
19. C
20. C

21. A
22. C
23. B
24. D
25. C

EXAMINATION SECTION
TEST 1

DIRECTIONS: Each question or incomplete statement is followed by several suggested answers or completions. Select the one that BEST answers the question or completes the statement. *PRINT THE LETTER OF THE CORRECT ANSWER IN THE SPACE AT THE RIGHT.*

1. *The American people don't want a former pot-smoking draft dodger to be the next President of the United States.*
   The above statement is an example of
   A. faulty use of cause and effect
   B. an ad hominem attack
   C. circular reasoning
   D. a hasty generalization

   1._____

2. *Samuel had received explicit instructions about how to handle the exchange.*
   Which of the following BEST captures the meaning of the word *explicit* as it is used in the above sentence?
   A. Implied
   B. Directly expressed
   C. Terse
   D. Duplicitous

   2._____

3. I soon realized I could not take my studies with Professor Adams any _____.
   Which word BEST completes the above sentence?
   A. further
   B. farther
   C. more
   D. far

   3._____

4. The undercover police officer posed as a person with a chemical dependence when he drove a pre-owned automobile to the economically deprived section of town in order to take out the illegal adult entertainment establishment.
   The above sentence contains too many
   A. analogies
   B. metaphors
   C. euphemisms
   D. aphorisms

   4._____

5. Which of the following represents an appropriate level of diction for the occasion?
   A. I want that job that was in the newspaper.
   B. I would like to apply for the position advertised in the Town Daily.
   C. I want to work as a secretary in that job that was in the paper.
   D. All levels are acceptable.

   5._____

6. Which of the following presents the BEST sequence of the following sentences to make a coherent paragraph?
   I. It was later discovered that nearly all of these people had purchased and eaten hamburgers from the same fast-food franchise.
   II. Two of them, young children, eventually died from their ailments.
   III. The hamburgers had been contaminated by a dangerous strain of the bacteria E. coli and had not been properly cooked.
   IV. In 1993, over 600 people in Washington and Nevada became sick with symptoms that indicated food poisoning.
   The CORRECT answer is:
   A. I, III, II, IV
   B. I, III, IV, II
   C. IV, III, I, II
   D. IV, II, I, III

   6._____

21

7. He _____ the pencil down as soon as he was finished with the test.
   Which word BEST completes the above sentence?
   A. did lay   B. lied   C. laid   D. lay

8. Which of the following presents the BEST sequence of the following sentences to make a coherent paragraph?
   I. Beginning in 1531 with fewer than two hundred men, Pizarro took just two years to subdue the Incas and capture Atahualpa, who attempted to bargain for his life by offering Pizarro a fortune in gold.
   II. His harshness is perhaps best illustrated by his treatment of the Incan emperor, Atahualpa.
   III. Pizarro accepted the gold from Atahualpa, and then killed him anyway.
   IV. Francisco Pizarro was among the most fearsome of the Spanish conquistadors
   The CORRECT answer is:
   A. IV, II, I, III   B. IV, I, II, III   C. II, I, III, IV   D. I, III, IV, II

9. *Neither Sari _____ Joshua could spell the final word in the district spelling bee.*
   Which word BEST completes the above sentence?
   A. nor   B. or   C. either   D. and

10. *They promised when the pageant was over that they would take Sarah out to dinner.*
    The above sentence contains which of the following mistakes?
    A. Faulty parallel construction   B. Faulty coordination
    C. Misplaced modifier   D. Dangling modifier

11. King Lear, Act I, Scene I:
    France: Fairest Cordelia, that art most rich being poor,
              Most choice forsaken, and most loved despised, Thee and thy
              virtues here I seize upon.
    France praises Cordelia because
    A. her sense of morality is more important to him than her material wealth
    B. her dowry has increased, since her father want to get rid of her
    C. of her physical beauty and wealth
    D. she loves him above all others

12. *Michaela's group preceded the lunch break.*
    In the above sentence, the word *preceded* is used to mean which of the following?
    A. Occurred simultaneously   B. Came after
    C. Came before   D. Went forward

Questions 13-17.

DIRECTIONS: Questions 13 through 17 are to be answered on the basis of the following passage.

The Story of An Hour, Kate Chopin:

She could see in the open square before her house the tops of trees that were all aquiver with the new spring life.(1) The delicious breath of rain was in the air.(2) In the street below a peddler was crying his wares.(3) The notes of a distant song which someone was singing reached her faintly, and countless sparrows were twittering in the eaves....(4)
She knew that she would weep again when she saw the kind, tender hands folded in death; the fact that had never looked save with love upon her, fixed and gray and dead.(5) But she saw beyond that bitter moment a long procession of years to come that would belong to her absolutely.(6) And she opened and spread her arms out to them in welcome.(7)

13. Which of the following BEST describes the relationship between the two paragraphs in this passage?
    The second paragraph
    A. provides an answer to the questions raised by the first paragraph
    B. contradicts the mood established in the first paragraph
    C. develops and explains the mood established in the first paragraph
    D. illustrates the first paragraph

14. Which of the following MOST accurately characterizes the reason for the woman's mood?
    A. Her husband is dead and she is free.
    B. Although saddened by her husband's death, the weather is so beautiful that she is freed from her sadness for a time.
    C. Her husband is dead and she is overcome with despair.
    D. Although saddened by her husband's death, she looks forward to a life of independence.

15. The descriptive details in the first paragraph establish a
    A. visual image and an emotional tone
    B. tone of sadness and despair
    C. concrete image of the town
    D. concrete image of the room

16. In line 1, the word *aquiver* is used to mean
    A. shivering   B. fluttering   C. shaking   D. blooming

17. This passage is BEST characterized as which of the following? A
    A. descriptive narrative about a self-centered, remorseless woman
    B. dramatization of a woman's overwhelming despair at the loss of her husband
    C. description of the solace one woman finds in nature
    D. descriptive narrative about a woman's dawning sense of independence

18. Which of the following labels in a dictionary indicates that a particular word is used by people who speak a version of a language that is different from the standard version?
    A. Dialect　　　B. Derivative　　　C. Slang　　　D. Archaic

19. *Bob and Sue were a lawyer and a doctor, respectively.*
    In the above sentence, the word *respectively* is used to mean which of the following?
    A. With respect
    B. In the order given
    C. Well respected
    D. Married

20. *She is different than you.*
    The above sentence contains
    A. a split infinitive
    B. a mixed metaphor
    C. a problem with idiom
    D. no errors

21. Spring, Gretel Erlich:
    By mid-March, the lake ice begins to melt where the spring feeds in, and every year the same pair of mallards come ahead of the others and wait. Though there is very little open water, they seem _____. They glide back and forth through a thin estuary, brushing watercress with their elegant folded wings.
    Which of the following words provides the appropriate connotation to complete the above passage?
    A. content　　　B. overjoyed　　　C. subdued　　　D. excited

22. Which of the following presents the BEST sequence of the following sentences to make a coherent paragraph?
    I. In 1552, a Portuguese historian, João do Barros, wrote that he had heard of a place in Africa where there was a "square fortress of masonry built of stones of marvelous size, and there appears to be no mortar joining them."
    II. The ruins were finally rediscovered by a German geologist, Karl Mauch, in the 1860's.
    III. During the Europeans' first explorations of the African continent, one of the many recurring fables about the mysteries of Africa was a story of some great stone monuments on the southeastern plains.
    IV. Incredibly, tales of this place circulated for more than three hundred years before the first European laid eyes upon their source: the ruins of Great Zimbabwe.
    The CORRECT answer is:
    A. III, IV, II, I　　　B. III, I, IV, II　　　C. I, III, II, IV　　　D. I, IV, II, III

23. *That pumpkin pie was more _____ I could eat.*
    Which word BEST completes the above sentence?
    A. from　　　B. of　　　C. than　　　D. then

24. *Opening the door to let in the heat, the vase was broken.*
    The above sentence contains
    A. faulty parallel construction
    B. faulty coordination
    C. misplaced modifier
    D. dangling modifier

    24.____

25. _____ late with _____ laundry.
    Which pair of words BEST completes the above sentence?
    A. Their; they're
    B. They're; their
    C. Their; there
    D. There; their

    25.____

KEY (CORRECT ANSWERS)

1.	B		11.	A
2.	B		12.	C
3.	A		13.	C
4.	C		14.	D
5.	B		15.	A
6.	D		16.	B
7.	C		17.	D
8.	A		18.	A
9.	A		19.	B
10.	C		20.	C

21. A
22. B
23. C
24. D
25. B

TEST 2

DIRECTIONS: Each question or incomplete statement is followed by several suggested answers or completions. Select the one that BEST answers the question or completes the statement. *PRINT THE LETTER OF THE CORRECT ANSWER IN THE SPACE AT THE RIGHT.*

1. Which of the following provides the MOST objective point of view on the part of the writer?
   A. Terrified passengers waited in blistering heat as amusement park officials worked to rescue them from the dangerous and life-threatening ride.
   B. Rescuers left terrified passengers stranded for hours while they tried to figure out how to rescue them.
   C. Rescuers spent four hours retrieving passengers from a roller coaster car that inexplicably stopped in mid-ride.
   D. Passengers stranded on a roller coaster cried and moaned so much that rescuers had to waste valuable time trying to calm them down.

1.____

Questions 2-6.

DIRECTIONS: Questions 2 through 6 are to be answered on the basis of the following passage.

Girl, Jamaica Kincaid:

Wash the white clothes on Monday and put them on the stone heap; wash the color clothes on Tuesday and put them on the clothesline to dry; don't walk bareheaded in the hot sun; cook pumpkin fritters in very hot sweet oil; soak your little cloths right after you take them off; when buying cotton to make yourself a nice blouse, be sure that it doesn't have gum on it, because that way it won't hold up well after a wash; soak salt fish overnight before you cook it; is it true that you sing benna in Sunday school?; always eat your food in such a way that it won't turn someone else's stomach; don't sing benna in Sunday school.

2. What is the point of view of this passage?
   A. First person singular   B. First person plural
   C. Second person   D. Third person singular

2.____

3. What can we infer about the speaker of this passage? S/he
   A. holds a position of authority in relation to the person being spoken to
   B. believes the person being spoken to is ignorant
   C. believes the person being spoken to doesn't listen
   D. has absolute authority over the person being spoken to

3.____

4. This passage can BEST be characterized as
   A. descriptive   B. instructional   C. narrative   D. nostalgic

4.____

5. The descriptive details provided in this passage mainly
   A. provide concrete instructions on how to live
   B. provide a concrete image of speaker's faith
   C. provide a concrete image of the speaker's home
   D. establish setting and tone

6. What can we infer about the person being spoken to in this passage? She
   A. is suborn
   B. is disobedient
   C. is a child
   D. resents the speaker

7. *We all wondered how a girl _____ walked with such a limp could play soccer.*
   Which word BEST completes the above sentence?
   A. who   B. whom   C. that   D. which

8. In a dictionary, these serve as an aid to finding the page on which a word appears.
   A. Cross-references
   B. Part of speech labels
   C. Superscript numbers
   D. Guide words

9. On Being Black and Middle Class, Shelby Steele:
   Black though I may be, it is impossible for me to sit in my single-family house with two cars in the driveway and a swing set in the backyard and not see the role class has _____ in my life.
   Which of the following words provides the appropriate connotation to complete the above sentence?
   A. asserted   B. played   C. oppressed   D. dominated

10. Which of the following presents the BEST sequence of the following sentences to make a coherent paragraph?
    I. Before the Incas were conquered by the Spaniards in the 16th century, they had built temples and palaces as large and magnificent as any in the world.
    II. The Incas, a native people whose empire once encompassed much of western South America, have long been admired for their accomplishments in architecture and art.
    III. The Incas' network of roads ran the length of their empire, from the north, in what is now Peru, to Chile in the south.
    IV. But fewer people know that the Incas were also responsible for what was then the world's greatest all-weather road system.
    The CORRECT answer is:
    A. I, II, IV, III   B. I, IV, III, II   C. II, I, IV, III   D. II, IV, III, I

11. Which of the following provides the MOST objective point of view on the part of the writer?
    A. Cisco Systems continued its hostile takeover of small business by purchasing Cerent, a start-up company.
    B. Cisco Systems recently purchased the small start-up company, Cerent, for a record-breaking amount of money.

C. Cisco Systems solidified its role as a great benefactor and helpmate to smaller businesses by buying the start-up company, Cerent.
D. The small start-up company, Cerent, is lucky that Cisco Systems wanted to buy it, considering Cerent's load of debt.

12. _____ driving to the airport? _____ car should we take?
Which pair of words BEST completes the above sentences?
    A. Whose; who's
    B. Who's; who's
    C. Whose; whose
    D. Who's; whose

13. *Deciding to join the team, the manager shook Susan's hand.*
The above sentence contains
    A. faulty parallel construction
    B. a dangling modifier
    C. a misplaced modifier
    D. faulty coordination

14. King Lear, Act II, Scene IV:
Regan: I pray you father being weak, seem so.
In this excerpt, Regan tells her father, King Lear, that
    A. he looks physically weak and depleted, and should sit down
    B. he is still very powerful
    C. it is unseemly for such a powerful man as him to act so weak
    D. since he no longer has power, he should not act as if he does

15. They Said You Was High Class, Joseph Epstein:
My fantasy, taken up in early adolescence and not quite dropped to this day, is that I can roam freely from social class, _____ everywhere and everywhere welcome.
Which of the following words provides the appropriate connotation to complete the above sentence?
    A. comfortable
    B. uncomfortable
    C. joyous
    D. acknowledged

16. Heaven and Nature, Edward Hoagland:
People with sunny natures do seem to live longer than people who are nervous wrecks; yet mankind didn't evolve out of the animal kingdom by being _____ sunny-minded.
Which of the following words provides the appropriate connotation to complete the above sentence?
    A. casually
    B. reasonably
    C. unduly
    D. exaggeratedly

17. *Camelia _____ that she knew all about advertising, but her interviewer, _____ that she was inexperienced.*
Which pair of words BEST completes the above sentences?
    A. implied; inferred
    B. implied; implied
    C. inferred; inferred
    D. inferred; implied

18. The most significant danger of television does not lie in what it produces, but in what it prevents. If you are watching television, chances are that you are not engaging in the talking, game playing, family festivities and arguments that help children to learn about themselves and their world. The television set interferes with the process that helps turn children into thinking adults.
The PRIMARY purpose of the above passage is to
A. compare   B. classify   C. analyze   D. entertain

18.____

19. *The book was written by someone who teaches at Stanford, so it must be good.*
The above statement is an example of
A. a faulty use of cause and effect   B. an ad hominem attack
C. circular reasoning   D. a hasty generalization

19.____

Questions 20-22.

DIRECTIONS: Questions 20 through 22 are to be answered on the basis of the following passage.

Hills Like White Elephants, Ernest Hemingway:

The girl stood up and walked to the end of the station. Across, on the other side, were fields of grain and trees along the banks of the Ebro. Far away, beyond the river, were mountains. The shadow of a cloud moved across the field of grain and she saw the river through the trees.

20. This passage is BEST characterized as
A. instructive   B. persuasive   C. narrative   D. descriptive

20.____

21. The descriptive details in this passage MAINLY establish
A. setting   B. tone   C. point of view   D. time period

21.____

22. The point of view of this passage is
A. first person singular   B. first person plural
C. third person singular   D. third person plural

22.____

23. _____ you go on a trip, _____ to Indiana or India, you should always use traveler's checks instead of cash.
Which pair of words BEST completes the above sentence?
A. Whether; off   B. Whether; if   C. If; whether   D. If, if

23.____

24. Which of the following provides the MOST objective point of view on the part of the writer?
A. A radical, left-wing professor has violated her students' constitutional rights by refusing to teach male students.
B. A feminist professor at a major university recently announced that she would no longer teach male students.

24.____

C. An embattled feminist professor at a major university works hard to ensure a safe learning environment by only teaching women students.
D. Recently, at a major university, women banded together to throw men out of the classroom of a feminist professor.

25. *Music today is filled with either violence or sex.* 25.____
The above statement is an example of
  A. a false dilemma
  B. a non sequitur
  C. circular reasoning
  D. a hasty generalization

KEY (CORRECT ANSWERS)

1. C
2. C
3. A
4. B
5. D

6. C
7. A
8. D
9. B
10. C

11. B
12. D
13. B
14. D
15. A

16. C
17. A
18. C
19. D
20. D

21. A
22. C
23. C
24. B
25. A

TEST 3

DIRECTIONS: Each question or incomplete statement is followed by several suggested answers or completions. Select the one that BEST answers the question or completes the statement. *PRINT THE LETTER OF THE CORRECT ANSWER IN THE SPACE AT THE RIGHT.*

1. *Fresh peaches and cream was a last minute addition to the dinner party.* 1.____
   The above sentence contains
   A. a dangling modifier B. faulty parallelism
   C. faulty subject-verb agreement D. no errors

2. *The best mouse trap in the world is, in fact, a snake. The copperhead moves in so quickly on its prey that mice have almost no chance of escape once they have been detected.* 2.____
   The PRIMARY purpose of the above passage is to
   A. persuade B. explain C. entertain D. classify

3. *Willa Ames still hasn't repaid the money she borrowed yet.* 3.____
   The above sentence contains
   A. faulty subject-verb agreement B. redundancy
   C. a dangling modifier D. no errors

4. *The high levels of toxic rain in Canada causes resentment against the U.S. where most of the rain originates.* 4.____
   The above sentence contains
   A. a dangling modifier B. faulty parallelism
   C. faulty subject-verb agreement D. no errors

5. *Beth assured her old friend that their troubled past was water over the dam.* 5.____
   The above sentence contains
   A. jargon B. slang C. an idiom D. a cliche

6. Which of the following presents the BEST sequence of the following sentences to make a coherent paragraph? 6.____
   I. Although the Guinness book of world records ignores fossils and honor the American moose's antlers, the size of the Irish Elk's antlers has never even been approached in the history of life.
   II. The Irish Elk, now extinct, was neither exclusively Irish, nor an elk.
   III. It was the largest deer that ever lived, and its enormous antlers were even more impressive.
   IV. Estimates of their total span range up to twelve feet, which seems all the more impressive when we recognize that the antlers were probably shed and regrown every year, as in all other true deer species.
   The CORRECT answer is:
   A. II, I, III, IV B. II, III, I, IV C. I, IV, II, III D. I, III, II, IV

7. A library's microfilm collection consists MAINLY of
   A. old newspaper and magazine articles
   B. reference books
   C. the historical records of the town or institution where it is located
   D. the titles and authors of all the books in the library

8. *The relationship between risk and free-enterprise is intimate and powerful.*
   The primary purpose of a passage based on the above sentence would MOST likely be to
   A. explain a process
   B. narrate an event
   C. persuade
   D. compare

9. *When watching a favorite film, commercials are especially annoying.*
   The above sentence contains
   A. a dangling modifier
   B. a misplaced modifier
   C. faulty subject-verb agreement
   D. unnecessary punctuation

10. *The Secretary of State, as well as her Press Secretary, was severely criticized by the media.*
    The above sentence contains
    A. a dangling modifier
    B. faulty parallelism
    C. faulty subject-verb agreement
    D. no errors

11. *Sun-loving plants, such as, sunflowers and geraniums, thrive in hot, open places.*
    The above sentence contains
    A. unnecessary punctuation
    B. faulty parallelism
    C. faulty subject-verb agreement
    D. no errors

12. *Car-jackers should be prosecuted because they broke the law.*
    The above statement is an example of
    A. a faulty use of cause and effect
    B. an ad hominem attack
    C. circular reasoning
    D. a hasty generalization

13. *A man carrying a guitar case runs out of a bank and down the street.*
    Based on the above information, which of the following is a CORRECT logical inference?
    The man
    A. has probably robbed the bank
    B. is in a hurry
    C. plays in a symphony and is late to practice
    D. exercises with his guitar case

Questions 14-20.

DIRECTIONS: Questions 14 through 20 are to be answered on the basis of the following passage.

Discovery of a Father, Sherwood Anderson:

    He was a man with big shoulders, a powerful swimmer.(1) In the darkness I could feel the movements of his muscles.(2) We swam to the far edge of the pond and then back to where we had left our clothes.(3) The rain continued and the wind blew.(4) Sometimes my father swam on his back, and when he did he took my hand in his large powerful one and moved it over so that it rested always on his shoulder.(5) Sometimes there would be a flash of lightning and I could see his face quite clearly.(6)
    He had become blood of my blood; he the strong swimmer and I the boy clinging to him in the darkness.(7) We swam in silence, and in silence we dressed in our wet clothes and went home.(8)

14. This passage is BEST characterized as a(n)
    A. concrete description of the dangers of swimming during a storm
    B. instructional narrative about swimming
    C. descriptive narrative about a boy's relationship with his father
    D. account of a boy learning how to swim

15. In this passage, the pond and storm are BEST characterized as
    A. elements of nature that encourage reflection
    B. dangerous and unpredictable elements which threaten human connection
    C. mysterious forces that entice people to do dangerous things
    D. elements of nature that encourage a spiritual connection between father and son

16. In line 7, the clause, *He had become blood of my blood*, MOST NEARLY means that
    A. the boy has discovered a deeper emotional connection to his father because of this experience
    B. the boy has just discovered that this man is his biological father
    C. father and son share the same religious beliefs
    D. father and son are alienated from one another

17. Lines 7 and 8 provide a description of the
    A. father's anger
    B. transformation of the son's relationship to his father
    C. son's anger
    D. alienation which separates the son from the father

18. The narrator in this passage relies MOST heavily on which of the following?
    A. Metaphor   B. Analogy
    C. Imagery   D. Emotional appeal

19. In describing the relationship between the two paragraphs in this passage, the second paragraph   19.____
    A. provides an answer to the questions raised by the first paragraph
    B. contradicts the mood established in the first paragraph
    C. illustrates the first paragraph
    D. develops and explains the mood established in the first paragraph

20. The MAIN implication of this passage is that the narrator   20.____
    A. has discovered that he is afraid of his father
    B. has discovered a powerful and mysterious connection to his father
    C. has discovered that he doesn't understand his relationship to his father
    D. and his father do not know how to communicate with one another

21. Which of the following presents the BEST sequence of the following sentences to make a coherent paragraph?   21.____
    I. Begun around 1200, the ceremony has evolved over time through various stages.
    II. After about a hundred years of this phase, tea-drinking became associated with luxury and was practiced by members of high society who often held "tea tournaments," which were much like present-day wine-tastings.
    III. One of the most important Japanese cultural practices is the tea ceremony.
    IV. At first, tea was drunk for medical reasons, by people who made outrageous claims about tea's ability to cure almost any known illness.
    The CORRECT answer is:
    A. III, I, IV, II   B. I, IV, II, III   C. IV, II, III, I   D. III, IV, II, I

22. King Lear, Act V, Scene III: 22.____
    Lear: Come, let's away to prison:
           We two alone will sing like birds I' th' cage:
           When thou dost ask me blessing, I'll kneel down
           and ask of thee forgiveness: so we'll live,
           and pray, and sing, and tell old tales, and laugh
           at gilded butterflies, and hear poor rogues
           talk of court news; and we'll talk with them too,
           who loses and who wins, who's in, who's out;
           and take upon us the mystery of things,
           as if we were God's spies: and we'll wear out,
           in a walled prison, packs and sects of great oones
           that ebb and flow by the moon.
    In the above scene, King Lear tells Cordelia that, while in prison, the two of them will
    A. act as spies so that they can discover the important news of the royal court and use it for their own benefit
    B. tell false tales about members of the royal court, thereby destroying them from within their prison cells

C. entertain themselves with tales and stories, granting no importance to issues of fashion and royal favor, and so will outlive all the schemers outside of prison
D. ignore everything worldly, only concentrating on prayer and meditation, thereby saving their eternal souls

23. Speech on the Signing of the Treaty of Port Elliott, 1855, Chief Seattle:
Yonder sky that has wept tears of compassion upon my people for centuries untold, and which to us appears changeless and eternal, may change. Today is fair. Tomorrow may be overcast with clouds. My words are like the stars that never change.
The diction in the above passage is BEST characterized as
A. formal
B. colloquial
C. slang
D. formal with slang references

23.____

24. Which of the following presents the BEST sequence of the following sentences to make a coherent paragraph?
I. These natives had not yet invented the wheel, and the land around them had none of the animals—horses, donkeys, or camels—that had been domesticated to serve as pack animals in other parts of the world.
II. During the earliest years of their civilizations, the native people of South America, especially the inhabitants of the mountainous Andes region, had no means for transporting heavy loads.
III. Llamas lived on the high plateau of the Andes and, as early as 4,000 years ago, were being used by South American natives as a transport animal.
IV. However, the mountain highlands of South America were populated by another animal that had adapted well to this harsh environment—the gentle llama.
The CORRECT answer is:
A. II, III, I, IV
B. II, I, IV, III
C. III, I, IV, II
D. III, II, IV, I

24.____

25. *Saritha's suitcase felt light as a feather without her books.*
The above sentence contains
A. slang
B. jargon
C. a cliche
D. an idiom

25.____

KEY (CORRECT ANSWERS)

1.	D		11.	A
2.	B		12.	C
3.	B		13.	B
4.	C		14.	C
5.	D		15.	D
6.	B		16.	A
7.	A		17.	B
8.	D		18.	C
9.	A		19.	D
10.	D		20.	B

21. A
22. C
23. A
24. B
25. C

TEST 4

DIRECTIONS: Each question or incomplete statement is followed by several suggested answers or completions. Select the one that BEST answers the question or completes the statement. *PRINT THE LETTER OF THE CORRECT ANSWER IN THE SPACE AT THE RIGHT.*

1. When you restate the relevant information from a passage in your own words, you have _____ the passage.
   A. paraphrased   B. summarized   C. plagiarized   D. quoted

   1._____

Questions 2-7.

DIRECTIONS: Questions 2 through 7 ae to be answered on the basis of the following passage.

The Inheritance of Tools, Scott Russell Sanders:

   I had botched a great many pieces of wood before I mastered the right angle with a saw, botched even more before I learned to miter a joint.(1) The knowledge of these things resides in my hands and eyes and the webwork of muscles, not in the tools.(2) There are machines for sale—powered miter boxes and radial arms, saws, for instance—that will enable any casual soul to cut proper angles in boards. (3) The skill is invested in the gadget instead of the person who uses it, and this is what distinguishes a machine from a tool.(4)

2. What is the point of view of this passage?
   A. First person singular   B. Second person
   C. Third person singular   D. Third person

   2._____

3. This passage is BEST characterized as a(n)
   A. instructive narrative about the proper use of tools
   B. persuasive narrative about the merits of manual tools
   C. reminiscence about the author's childhood experience with tools
   D. descriptive narrative about the author's relationship to manual tools

   3._____

4. The narrator relies MOST heavily on which of the following in this excerpt?
   A. Metaphor   B. Analogy   C. Contrast   D. Persuasion

   4._____

5. In line 2, the word *resides* MOST NEARLY means
   A. informs   B. exists   C. controls   D. moves

   5._____

6. In this passage, power tools are BEST characterized as
   A. tools which require les training to operate than manual tools
   B. emblems of a dangerous trend away from hard work
   C. tools used only by ignorant people
   D. tools used by amateurs, not expert craftsmen who depend on tools to make their living

   6._____

37

7. The MAIN implication of this passage is that
   A. it takes a lot of time to learn how to use manual tools
   B. manual tools are better to use than modern tools
   C. modern tools are better to use than older tools
   D. modern tools rely more on technology than the skill of the craftsman

8. Which of the following presents the BEST sequence of the following sentences to make a coherent paragraph?
   I. The purpose of this monument would be to honor the memory of the Americans who had served and died in the Vietnam War.
   II. When the name of the winner was revealed, artists and architects all over the world were stunned.
   III. The winner was not a nationally famous artist, but a twenty-one-year-old student at Yale University named Maya Lin, unknown to virtually everyone in the fields of art and architecture.
   IV. In 1980, the Vietnam Veterans Memorial Fund announced a competition, open to all Americans, for the design of a monument that would stand on the Mall in Washington, D.C.
   The CORRECT answer is:
   A. I, II, III, IV   B. I, IV, III, II   C. IV, II, III, I   D. IV, I, II, III

9. A woman in a grocery store has her cart loaded with baby food.
   Based on the above information, which of the following is a CORRECT logical inference? She
   A. feeds baby food to her animals   B. is a store employee
   C. probably has a baby   D. likes to eat baby food

10. *Sheryl had to go off of the medicine.*
    The above sentence contains problems with
    A. split infinitives   B. idiom
    C. mixed metaphors   D. jargon

11. *People who hate their jobs are unhappy because they hate what they're doing.*
    The above statement is an example of
    A. a faulty use of cause and effect   B. an ad hominem attack
    C. circular reasoning   D. a hasty generalization

12. *The quarter horse skipped, pranced, galloping onto the track.*
    The above sentence contains problems with
    A. parallel construction   B. elliptical phrasing
    C. a dangling modifier   D. coordination

13. *Camping in Yosemite was more thrilling for us than, staying in the loveliest most exclusive hotels.*
    The above sentence contains
    A. a dangling modifier   B. unnecessary punctuation
    C. faulty subject-verb agreement   D. no errors

14. *I learned the skills of a master carpenter: however, I never learned the necessary patience.*
    The above sentence contains
    A. faulty use of a colon
    B. faulty use of a semicolon
    C. faulty subject-verb agreement
    D. no errors

14.____

15. *Some of the students looked dazed and confused _____ others looked as if they hadn't yet awakened.*
    Which of the following would BEST complete the above sentence?
    A. Parentheses   B. A dash   C. A semicolon   D. A colon

15.____

16. Anarchy in the Tenth Grade, Greg Graffin:
    People asked me, "Dude! Do you party?" It took me about six months to realize it was a synonym for getting high. I did not know what a bong was, or why someone would call it bitchin'.
    The diction in the above passage is BEST characterized as
    A. slang
    B. colloquial, containing slang references
    C. slang, containing colloquial references
    D. informal, containing colloquial references

16.____

Questions 17-21.

DIRECTIONS: Questions 17 through 21 are to be answered on the basis of the following passage.

Heart of Darkness, Joseph Conrad:

The sea-reach of the Thames stretched before us like the beginning of an interminable waterway.(1) In of the offing the sea and the sky were welded together without a joint, and in the luminous space the tanned sails of the barges drifting up with the tide seemed to stand still in the red clusters of canvas sharply peaked, with gleams of varnished spirits.(2) A haze rested on the low shores that ran out to sea in vanishing flatness.(3) The air was dark above Gravesend , and farther back still seemed condensed into a mournful gloom, brooding motionless over the biggest, and the greatest, town on Earth.(4)

17. In line 1, the word *interminable* MOST NEARLY means
    A. wide   B. ongoing   C. endless   D. vast

17.____

18. This passage is BEST characterized as a(n)
    A. objective description of the modern-day Thames
    B. persuasive narrative about the Thames
    C. descriptive narrative about the Thames from a child's point of view
    D. descriptive narrative about the Thames

18.____

19. The narrator relies MOST heavily on which of the following in this excerpt?
    A. Imagery   B. Metaphor   C. Analogy   D. Contrast

19.____

20. The tone of this excerpt is BEST characterized as
    A. despairing
    B. foreboding
    C. humorous
    D. emotionally objective

21. This excerpt is written in which point of view?
    A. First person
    B. Second person
    C. Third Person
    D. Third person plural

22. Which of the following presents the BEST sequence of the following sentences to make a coherent paragraph?
    I. Almost immediately, he noticed a change in the behavior of his co-workers—in the past they had constantly argued with each other, but now they had become unusually friendly.
    II. Almost thirty years ago, a scientist named David Berliner, who was studying human skin tissues, left some samples in open vials around his laboratory.
    III. When Berliner later removed the vials, the group returned to its grouchy ways.
    IV. Berliner's search to solve this mystery has led him to the discovery of human *pheromones*—behavior-influencing chemical compounds that are transmitted from one member of a species to another—in samples of human skin.
    The CORRECT answer is:
    A. II, I, III, IV
    B. II, III, I, IV
    C. IV, II, I, III
    D. IV, III, I, II

23. *This is a personal day, a terrible day, the day to which his entire sojourn has been tending. It is the day he realizes that there are no untroubled countries in this fearfully troubled world.*
    The diction in the above passage is BEST characterized as
    A. colloquial, with slang references
    B. slang
    C. colloquial
    D. formal

24. *The sheepdog herded the animals quickly, chasing and guarding them, but he didn't bite them.*
    The above sentence contains problems with
    A. subordination
    B. coordination
    C. elliptical phrasing
    D. parallel construction

25. *No pain, no gain.*
    The above sentence contains
    A. nouns in apposition to one another
    B. balanced elliptical phrases
    C. a dangling modifier
    D. euphemism

KEY (CORRECT ANSWERS)

1.	A	11.	C
2.	A	12.	A
3.	D	13.	B
4.	C	14.	A
5.	B	15.	C
6.	A	16.	B
7.	D	17.	C
8.	D	18.	D
9.	C	19.	A
10.	B	20.	B

21. A
22. A
23. D
24. D
25. B

EXAMINATION SECTION
TEST 1

DIRECTIONS: Each question or incomplete statement is followed by several suggested answers or completions. Select the one that BEST answers the question or completes the statement. *PRINT THE LETTER OF THE CORRECT ANSWER IN THE SPACE AT THE RIGHT.*

Questions 1-6.

DIRECTIONS: Questions 1 through 6 are to be answered on the basis of the following passage.

Death in the Woods, Sherwood Anderson

    She was an old woman and lived on a farm near the town in which I lived.(1) All country and small-town people have seen such old women, but no one knows must about them.(2) Such an old woman comes into town driving an old worn-out horse or she comes afoot carrying a basket.(3) She may own a few hens and have eggs to sell.(4) She brings them in a basket and takes them to a grocer.(5) There she trades them in.(6) She gets some salt pork and some beans.(7) Then she gets a pound or two of sugar and some flour.(8)
    Afterwards she goes to the butcher's and asks for some dog-meat.(9) She may spend ten or fifteen cents, but when she does she asks for something.(10) Formerly the butchers gave liver to any one who wanted to carry it away.(11) In our family we were always having it.(12) Once one of my brothers got a whole cow's liver at the slaughterhouse near the fairgrounds in our town.(13) We had it until we were sick of it.(14) It never cost a cent.(15) I have hated the thought of it ever since.(16)

1. This passage is BEST characterized as a(n)   1.____
   A. exact description of the old woman's day
   B. narrative explaining why the narrator hates liver so much
   C. descriptive narrative about the conditions of the old woman's life
   D. descriptive narrative about the conditions of the narrator's life

2. What is the point of view of this passage?   2.____
   A. First person
   B. Second person
   C. Third person singular
   D. Third person plural

3. How does the narrator know so much about the old woman's life?   3.____
   A. The townspeople spent a great deal of time gossiping about the old woman's strange habits.
   B. Because the town in which the narrator grew up was so small, people knew everything about one another.
   C. The narrator was very close to the old woman as a child.
   D. She is like many old women the narrator has observed in small towns such as the one he grew up in.

4. The tone of this excerpt is BEST characterized as
   A. despairing
   B. solemn
   C. scolding
   D. emotionally objective

5. The details in line 3 mainly establish
   A. point of view
   B. tone
   C. time period
   D. place

6. How do the townspeople regard the old woman? They
   A. hardly notice her
   B. love her dearly
   C. treat he with pity
   D. treat her with scorn

7. Which of the following essay titles employs a formal tone?
   A. Of Crumpled Wings and Little Girls
   B. Speech on the Signing of the Treaty of Port Elliott, 1855
   C. Of Cruelty and Clemency, and Whether It is Better to be Loved or Feared
   D. All employ a formal tone

8. *Ms. Davies is such a good judge that it is hard to believe she has such terrible taste in clothes.*
   The above statement is an example of
   A. a faulty use of cause and effect
   B. a non sequitur
   C. circular reasoning
   D. a hasty generalization

9. Which of the following presents the BEST sequence of the following sentences to make a coherent paragraph?
   I. In 1773, Phillis Wheatley, a young slave girl who was owned by a Boston tailor named John Wheatley, published a book of poetry.
   II. At an early age, Phillis began to write about God and her neighboring townspeople, and her first poem was printed when she was only fourteen.
   III. African-American literary history began long before African slaves were granted American citizenship—in fact, it began when the original thirteen states were still British colonies.
   IV. Unlike most slaveowners who punished slaves for learning to read and write, the Wheatley family encouraged Phillis's religious and scholarly education.
   The CORRECT answer is:
   A. III, II, I, IV
   B. III, I, IV, II
   C. I, IV, II, III
   D. I, II, IV, III

10. If the River Was Whiskey, T.C. Boyle:
    His shoulders quaked. He huddled and stamped his feet, but he never took his eyes off the tip of the rod. Twitching it suggestively, he reeled with the jerky, hesitant motion that would drive lunker fish to a frenz. Or so he'd read, anyway.
    The diction in the above passage is BEST characterized as
    A. colloquial
    B. formal
    C. informal
    D. slang

11. *The children ran down the hill, skipped across the lawn and into the pool.* 11.____
    The above sentence contains problems with
    A. subordination	B. coordination
    C. parallel construction	D elliptical phrasing

Questions 12-17.

DIRECTIONS: Questions 12 through 17 are to be answered on the basis of the following passage.

An Occurrence at Owl Creek Bridge, Ambose Bierce:

A man stood upon a railroad bridge in Northern Alabama, looking down into the swift waters twenty feet below.(1) The man's hands were behind his back, the wrists bound with a cord.(2) A rope loosely encircled his neck.(3) It was attached to a stout cross-timber above his head, and the slack feel to the level of his knees.(4) Some loose boards laid upon the sleepers supporting the metals of the railway supplied a footing for him and his executioners two private soldiers of the Federal army, directed by a sergeant, who in civil life may have been a deputy sheriff.(5) At a short remote upon the same temporary platform was an officer in the uniform of his rank, armed.(6) He was a captain.(7)

12. This passage is BEST characterized as a 12.____
    A. concrete description of the preparations for a hanging
    B. descriptive narrative about a man who is about to die
    C. vivid argument against the use of capital punishment
    D. descriptive narrative about a man preparing for a dramatic escape

13. What is the point of view of this passage? 13.____
    A. First person	B. Second person
    C. Third person singular	D. Third person plural

14. The tone of this excerpt is BEST characterized as 14.____
    A. solemn	B. humorous
    C. fantastic	D. emotionally objective

15. The descriptive details in sentence 5 MAINLY establish 15.____
    A. point of view	B. tone	C. setting	D. situation

16. The narrator relies MOST heavily on which of the following in this excerpt? 16.____
    A. Imagery	B. Metaphor	C. Analogy	D. Contrast

17. In sentence 5, the word *civil* MOST NEARLY means 17.____
    A. military	B. civilian	C. polite society	D. peacetime

18. Falling Into Life, Leonard Kriegel: 18.____
    My legs were lifeless, useless, but their loss had created a dancing image in whose shadowy _____ I recognized a strange but potentially interesting new self. I world survive.

Which of the following words provides the appropriate connotation to complete the above sentence?
A. Gyrations   B. Shaking   C. Twitching   D. Silence

19. A parenthetical citation typically lists
    A. an author's last name
    B. an author's last name and the page number where the referenced material can be found
    C. an author's last name and the title of the referenced work
    D. the title of the referenced work, and the date of its first publication

20. Miss U.S.A., Studs Terkel:
    You used to sit around the TV and watch Miss America and it was exciting, we thought glamorous. Fun, we thought. But by the time I was eight or nine, I didn't feel comfortable. Soon I'm hitting my adolescence like fourteen, but I'm not doing any dating and I'm feeling awkward and ugly.
    The diction in the above passage is BEST characterized as
    A. slang, with some colloquial references
    B. formal
    C. colloquial
    D. slang

21. Which of the following presents the BEST sequence of the following sentences to make a coherent paragraph?
    I. Marion Walter Jacobs was born in Louisiana in 1930 and grew up in the Delta, where he acquired the deep blues tradition of the region.
    II. Like many Delta blues musicians, Walter moved north to pursue a career among the larger blues audiences of Chicago.
    III. Walter discovered that a small hand-held microphone could amplify the harmonica's sound to take on an entirely different tone—a sound more like a saxophone's.
    IV. It was in Chicago that he took on the stage name of Little Walter, and made the simple breakthrough that would irreversibly change the sound of blues music.
    The CORRECT answer is:
    A. II, I, IV, III   B. I, IV, II, III   C. I, II, III, IV   D. I, II, IV, III

22. *The duties of the position include babysitting, house-cleaning, and preparation of meals.*
    The above sentence contains problems with
    A. subordination   B. coordination
    C. elliptical phrasing   D. parallel construction

23. *I never have and never will accept a bribe.*
    The above sentence contains problems with
    A. subordination   B. coordination
    C. elliptical phrasing   D. parallel construction

24. *We will abide by the new rules.*
    In the above sentence, the phrase *abide by* is an example of a(n)
    A. idiom
    B. cliche
    C. slang expression
    D. simile

25. Which of the following presents the BEST sequence of the following sentences to make a coherent paragraph?
    I. The ancient Egyptians later discovered a better writing material—the thin bark of the papyrus reed, a plant that grew near the mouth of the Nile River.
    II. Although the tablets were cheap and easy to produce, they had two major disadvantages: they were difficult to store, and once the clay had dried and hardened a person could not write on them.
    III. People wrote on these tablets by pressing a sharpened stick into the wet clay.
    IV. The earliest known writing materials were thin clay tablets, used in Mesopotamia more than 5,000 years ago.
    The CORRECT answer is:
    A. IV, III II, I
    B. I, III, II, IV
    C. IV, I, III, II
    D. II, IV, III, I

KEY (CORRECT ANSWERS)

1. C
2. A
3. D
4. B
5. C

6. A
7. D
8. B
9. B
10. A

11. C
12. A
13. C
14. D
15. C

16. A
17. B
18. A
19. B
20. D

21. D
22. D
23. C
24. A
25. A

TEST 2

DIRECTIONS: Each question or incomplete statement is followed by several suggested answers or completions. Select the one that BEST answers the question or completes the statement. *PRINT THE LETTER OF THE CORRECT ANSWER IN THE SPACE AT THE RIGHT.*

Questions 1-6.

DIRECTIONS: Questions 1 through 6 are to be answered on the basis of the following passage.

A Distant Episode, Paul Bowles:

     The September sunsets were at their reddest the week the Professor decided to visit Ain Tadourit, which is in the warm country.(1) He came down out of the high, flat region in the evening by bus, with two small overnight bags full of maps, sun lotions, and medicines.(2) Ten years ago he had been in the village for three days; long enough, however to establish a fairly firm friendship with a café keeper, who had written him several times during the first year after his visit, if never since.(3) "Hassan Ramani," the Professor said over and over, as the bus bumped downward through ever warmer layers of air.(4) Now facing the flaming sky in the west, and now facing the sharp mountains, the car followed the dusty trail down the canyons into the air which began to smell of other things besides the endless ozone of the heights: orange blossoms, pepper, sun-baked excrement, burning olive oil, rotten fruit.(5) He closed his eyes happily and lived for an instant in a purely olfactory world.(6)

1. This passage is BEST characterized as a
   A. description of a sunset at Ain Tadourit
   B. descriptive narrative about a harrowing bus ride
   C. descriptive narrative about the Professor's trip to visit an old friend
   D. descriptive narrative about a trip the Professor took to visit his friend ten years before

2. The information in sentence 3 mainly establishes
   A. setting   B. point of view   C. tone   D. situation

3. In sentence 4, *Hassan Ramani* MOST likely refer to the
   A. Professor's friend
   B. town to which the Professor is traveling
   C. town which the Professor has just left
   D name of the country in which the Professor is traveling

4. Sentences 5 and 6 provide a
   A. description of Ain Tadourit
   B. vivid contrast between the world the Professor has just left, and the one he is about to enter
   C. physical connection between past and present
   D. description of the Professor's alienation from the town around him

5. In sentence 6, the word *olfactory* MOST NEARLY means
   A. sensual   B. smell   C. imaginary   D. past

6. The author relies MOST heavily on which of the following in this excerpt?
   A. Imagery   B. Metaphor   C. Analogy   D. Contrast

7. A recent study concluded that almost 90 percent of children from upper- and middle class families entered college, whereas fewer than 20 percent of children from lower-working-class families did.
   Based on the above information, which of the following is a CORRECT logical inference?
   A. The children of lower-working-class children are not as smart as children from upper- and middle-class families.
   B. The families of lower-working-class children don't emphasize school.
   C. There is a relationship between college attendance and social class.
   D. Children from upper- and middle-class families enjoy school more than other students.

8. Wounded Chevy at Wounded Knee, Diana Hume George:
   I was fifteen when I started my romance with Indians, and I only knew that I was in love with life outside the constricting white mainstream and with all the energy that _____ on the outer reaches of cultural stability.
   Which of the following words provides the appropriate connotation to complete the above sentence?
   A. exists   B. lies dormant   C. vibrates   D. explodes

Questions 9-14.

DIRECTIONS: Questions 9 through 14 are to be answered on the basis of the following passage.

The Distance of the Moon, Italo Calvino:

   How well I know!—old Qfwfq cried,—the rest of you can't remember, but I can.(1) We had her on top of us all the time, that enormous Moon: when she was full—nights as bright as day, but with a butter-colored light—it looked as if she were going to crush us; when she was new, she rolled around the sky like a black umbrella blown by the wind; and when she was waxing, she came forward with her horns so low she seemed about to stick into the peak of a promontory and get caught there.(2) But the whole business of the Moon's phases worked in a different way then: because the distances from the Sun were different, and the orbits, and the angle of something or other, I forget what; as for eclipses, with Earth and Moon stuck together the way they were, why, we had eclipses every minute: naturally, those two big monsters managed to put each other in the shade constantly, first one, then the other(3).

9. This passage is BEST characterized as a(n)
   A. historical description of the moon's orbit
   B. descriptive narrative about the narrator's childhood
   C. fantastic description of the moon's orbit
   D. descriptive narrative about the narrator's love of astronomy

10. What is the point of view of this passage?
    A. First person
    B. Second person
    C. Third person singular
    D. Third person plural

11. The author relies MOST heavily on which of the following in this excerpt?
    A. Fact   B. Metaphor   C. Analogy   D. Imagery

12. In sentence 2, the word *promontory* MOST NEARLY means
    A. stage   B. mountain   C. building   D. range

13. The tone of this passage is BEST described as
    A. humorous   B. sarcastic   C. fantastic   D. ironic

14. Which writing technique does the author rely on MOST heavily?
    A. Subordination
    B. Parallel structure
    C. Repetition
    D. Fragmentation

15. *Just 3 weeks after raising the speed limit on that stretch of highway, three young people were killed in car accidents.*
    The above statement is an example of
    A. a faulty use of cause and effect
    B. an ad hominem attack
    C. circular reasoning
    D. a hasty generalization

16. Most young people go into the Army with the same mindset. They are young, scared, and advised that joining the Army will free them from probation if they have committed any minor crimes. Young men are told they will come out as men. This, combined with the free rent, free food and adventure, convinces them to join. Then they learn about the real Army.
    Based on the above information, which of the following is a CORRECT logical inference?
    A. Parents shouldn't encourage their children to join the Army.
    B. The Army lies in its advertisements and recruiting efforts.
    C. The experience of being in the Army is different from what most people expect.
    D. One way to become a "man" is to join the Army.

17. Kubota, Garret Hongo:
    He gave his testimony to me and I held it at first _____ in my conscience like it was an heirloom too delicate to expose to strangers and anyone outside of the world Kubota made with his words.

Which of the following words provides the appropriate connotation to complete the above sentence?
A. happily   B. absently   C. gingerly   D. cautiously

18. Which of the following provides the CLEAREST description of a scene?
    A. With a small gathering of people toward a shelter at the edge of a field in northern Indiana, I walked silently in the dusk of a late summer evening.
    B. In the dusk of a late summer evening, I walked silently with a small gathering of people toward a shelter at the edge of a field in northern Indiana.
    C. At the edge of a field in northern Indiana, I walked silently in the dusk of a late summer evening with a small gathering of people toward a shelter.
    D. Toward a shelter at the edge of a field in northern Indiana I walked in the dusk of a late summer evening silently with a small gathering of people.

19. *She finished the project according with schedule.*
    The above sentence contains problems with
    A. split infinitives   B. subject-verb agreement
    C. parallel construction   D. idiom

20. Which of the following provides the MOST objective point of view on the part of the writer?
    A. Central City School Board Members recently voted to eliminate several district positions in order to cut costs.
    B. Central City School Board Members finally voted to eliminate some wasteful jobs from the bloated budget.
    C. Many workers will soon find themselves unemployed thanks to the recent decision by the Central City School Board to fire them.
    D. Lazy workers will soon have to look elsewhere for work thanks to the Central City School Board.

21. Which of the following presents the BEST sequence of the following sentences to make a coherent paragraph?
    A. The Apollo space program, conducted by the National Aeronautics and Space Administration (NASA), had reached its goal, set eight years earlier, of landing a man on the moon.
    B. In the United States, public support for the cost of NASA missions began to fade even before the Apollo 11 landing—the Apollo program ended up costing a total of $25 billion—and as a result the final two Apollo flights were scrapped.
    C. On July 20, 1969, astronauts Neil Armstrong and Edwin "Buzz" Aldrin stepped onto the surface of the moon and accomplished what is still considered to be one of the greatest achievements of human history.
    D. The Apollo 11 landing is so widely celebrated that few people care to know about the controversy created by this and other government-funded space programs.

22. Counters and Cable Cars, Stephen Jay Gould:
We also respect an authenticity of place. Genuine objects out of context and milieu may foster intrigue, but rarely _____. London Bridge dismantled and reassembled in America becomes a mere curiosity.
Which of the following words provides the appropriate connotation to complete the above sentence?
   A. happiness   B. inspiration   C. joy   D. reflection

23. *One day our culinary class assignment was to cook a five course dinner. You were graded on well your part of the meal turned out.*
The above passage contains
   A. a shifting point of view
   B. faulty parallel construction
   C. a split infinitive
   D. faulty apposition

24. *Sarah is late for dinner, but at least she brought good wine.*
The above sentence contains
   A. a shifting point of view
   B. an inconsistent verb tense
   C. a dangling modifier
   D. faulty parallel construction

25. *Patients should try if possible to avoid getting in and out of bed.*
The above sentence contains
   A. a shifting point of view
   B. faulty parallel construction
   C. a split infinitive
   D. a misplaced modifier

KEY (CORRECT ANSWERS)

1.	C		11.	D
2.	D		12.	B
3.	A		13.	C
4.	B		14.	A
5.	B		15.	A
6.	A		16.	C
7.	C		17.	D
8.	C		18.	B
9.	C		19.	D
10.	A		20.	A

21. D
22. B
23. A
24. B
25. C

TEST 3

DIRECTIONS: Each question or incomplete statement is followed by several suggested answers or completions. Select the one that BEST answers the question or completes the statement. *PRINT THE LETTER OF THE CORRECT ANSWER IN THE SPACE AT THE RIGHT.*

1. *Though only 12 years old, Harvard accepted Stuart as a student.*
   The above sentence contains
   A. faulty parallel construction
   B. problems with subject-verb agreement
   C. a misplaced modifier
   D. a dangling modifier

2. *Some of them are friends whom we see at the store or who live in our town.*
   The above sentence contains
   A. elliptical phrasing
   B. parallel construction
   C. appositive nouns
   D. misplaced modifiers

3. *These are the kitchen rules: Coffee to be made only by staff. Coffee service to stop at 3:00 P.M. Doughnuts in cabinet.*
   The above announcement contains
   A. problems with elliptical phrasing
   B. faulty parallel construction
   C. faulty subordination
   D. faulty coordination

4. *Doctors are criticized for doing too much when they're not needed, and too little when you are.*
   The above sentence contains
   A. a split infinitive
   B. a dangling modifier
   C. a shifting point of view
   D. faulty parallel construction

5. Which of the following provides the MOST objective point of view on the part of the writer?
   A. Pilots confirmed our worst fears today, admitting that they often nap during flights.
   B. Terrified passengers discover that their pilots are often napping on the job.
   C. Pilots for a major airline admitted to acting recklessly and endangering the lives of passengers by taking naps during flights.
   D. Pilots for a major airline recently acknowledged that many of them take naps during flights.

Questions 6-11.

DIRECTIONS: Questions 6 through 11 are to be answered on the basis of the following passage.

The Hollow Nut, Colette:

Next year, Bel-Gazou will be past nine years old.(1) She will have ceased to proclaim those inspired truths that confound her pedagogues.(2) Each day carries her farther from that first stage of her life, so full, so wise, so perpetually mistrustful, so loftily disdainful of experience, of good advice, and humdrum wisdom.(3) Next year, she will come back to the sands that glid her, to the salt butter and the foaming cider.(4) She will find again her dilapidated hut, and her citified feet will once more acquire their natural horny soles, slowly roughened on the flints and ridges of the rough ground.(5) But she may well fail to find again her childish subtlety and the keenness of her senses that can taste a scene, feel a color, and see—"thin as a hair, thin as a blade of grass" —the cadence of an imaginary song.(6)

6. This passage is BEST characterized as a
    A. descriptive narrative about the loss of childhood
    B. descriptive narrative about the author's childhood
    C. concrete description of Bel-Gazou's love for her summer home
    D. descriptive narrative about the author's love for Bel-Gazou

7. In sentence 2, the word *pedagogues* MOST NEARLY means
    A. admirers   B. friends   C. teachers   D. critics

8. In sentence 3, which of the following stylistic techniques does the author mainly rely on?
    A. Repetition   B. Coordination
    C. Subordination   D. Parallel structure

9. The details in sentence 3 mainly serve to
    A. detail the negative aspects of childhood which Bel-Gazou will soon outgrow
    B. detail the positive aspects of childhood which will be lost as Bel-Gazou grows up
    C. describe and chastise Bel-Gazou's bad behavior
    D. provide a psychological portrait of childhood

10. In sentence 6, *cadence* MOST NEARLY means
    A. melody   B. rhythm   C. words   D. imagery

11. The MAIN implication of this passage is that
    A. although Bel-Gazou must leave her beloved summer cottage, it will still be waiting when she returns next year
    B. it is time for Bel-Gazou to leave her childish world behind
    C. childhood is a time of carefree joy and curiosity
    D. the sensibilities which characterize childhood are fleeting

12. The Stone Horse, Barry Lopez:
    I waited until I held his eye. I assured him I would not tell anyone else how to get there. He looked at me with _____ despair, like a man who had been robbed twice, whose belief in human beings was offered without conviction.
    Which of the following words provides the appropriate connotation to complete the above passage?
    A. suffering   B. stoical   C. sad   D. intense

13. Which of the following presents the BEST sequence of the following sentences to make a coherent paragraph?
    I. The guide apparently didn't understand the question because he answered by saying "Kangaroo," which is an Aboriginal term meaning, "I don't know."
    II. Perhaps the worst mistake ever made in translation by an explorer is the word "kangaroo."
    III. Upon seeing one of the creatures, Cook turned to one of the native Australians he had brought along as a guide and asked what it was.
    IV. It entered the language in 1770 through the famous English sea captain, James Cook, while he was exploring the coast of Australia.
    The CORRECT answer is:
    A. IV, II, III, I   B. III, I, IV, II   C. II, IV, III, I   D. II, III, I, IV

14. *When I was in the fourth grade, I was called upon to participate in a school-wide spelling bee in an auditorium filled with restless students. Waiting nervously in my seat, I chewed my fingernails and tugged my socks.*
    The PRIMARY purpose of the above passage is to
    A. tell a story   B. offer a solution
    C. describe something   D. define something

15. *The young woman was _____ and fashionable.*
    Which of the following words provides the appropriate connotation to complete the above sentence?
    A. skeletal   B. chubby   C. skinny   D. slender

16. *Upon seeing the washed-out bridge, our bikes screeched to a halt.*
    The above sentence contains
    A. faulty parallel construction   B. faulty coordination
    C. a misplaced modifier   D. a dangling modifier

17. *Harold intended on doing things differently.*
    The above sentence contains problems with
    A. mixed metaphors   B. jargon
    C. idiom   D. split infinitives

18. *Joe is a man who means what he says, and says what he means.*
    The above sentence contains
    A. parallel construction   B. elliptical phrasing
    C. a dangling modifier   D. a false analogy

19. *History became popular, and historians became alarmed.*
    The above sentence contains
    A. parallel construction
    B. elliptical phrasing
    C. a dangling modifier
    D. a false analogy

20. *The candidate will make a good President because he speaks so well in front of the cameras.*
    The above statement is an example of
    A. a faulty use of cause and effect
    B. a non sequitur
    C. circular reasoning
    D. a hasty generalization

Questions 21-25.

DIRECTIONS: Questions 21 through 25 are to be answered on the basis of the following passage.

Walls, Kenneth McClane:

The prisons—at least the prisons I have encountered—are infinitely more hellish than our Hollywood dream makers relate.(1) Inmates in these places are not planning breakouts or prison riots; they are not planning anything.(2) To dream of escape is to believe that one has something worthy of salvaging; to believe, that is, in the proposition of a self-orchestrated future.(3) The prisons I have visited are spirit killers: the inmates—no matter how smart, capable, or engaging—have little sense of their own inextinguishable worth, their own human possibility.(4) And this is not by accident.(5)

21. This passage is BEST characterized as a
    A. persuasive narrative advocating the use of harsh punishment for prison inmates
    B. persuasive narrative against poor treatment of inmates in prisons
    C. descriptive narrative about the psychological effects of prisons on inmates
    D. descriptive narrative about the author's experience as an inmate

22. In sentence 3, the word *proposition* MOST NEARLY means
    A. impossibility   B. offer   C. bargain   D. idea

23. The MAIN purpose of sentence 5 is to
    A. create a transition into the next paragraph
    B. conclude the paragraph
    C. blame prisoners' problems on the prison staff and wardens
    D. answer the question raised in the first sentence of the paragraph

24. The MAIN implication of this passage is that
    A. most prisoners fail to take advantage of the amount of free-time they have in prison to plan for their futures
    B. prisons deliberately work to undermine the prisoners' sense of self and worth

C. most prisoners bide their time in prison by planning for their future outside the prison walls
D. prisons rightfully work to undermine the prisoners' sense of self and worth

25. What can we infer about the author of this passage? 25.____
He
   A. has no opinion on the facts he presents in this paragraph
   B. believes these prisoners have been punished enough and should be freed
   C. is in favor of the kind of punishment he describes in this paragraph
   D. is against the kind of punishment he describes in this paragraph

---

KEY (CORRECT ANSWERS)

1.	D		11.	D
2.	A		12.	B
3.	B		13.	C
4.	C		14.	A
5.	D		15.	D
6.	A		16.	D
7.	C		17.	C
8.	D		18.	B
9.	B		19.	A
10.	B		20.	B

21. C
22. D
23. A
24. B
25. D

TEST 4

DIRECTIONS: Each question or incomplete statement is followed by several suggested answers or completions. Select the one that BEST answers the question or completes the statement. *PRINT THE LETTER OF THE CORRECT ANSWER IN THE SPACE AT THE RIGHT.*

1. *Katrice's new neighbor seemed nutty as a fruitcake.*
   The above sentence contains a(n)
   A. cliche   B. euphemism   C. metaphor   D. idiom

   1.____

2. Which of the following is an example of a reference book?
   A. African-American Biographies
   B. Webster's New American Dictionary
   C. Collier's Encyclopedia
   D. All of the above

   2.____

3. Which of the following provides the CLEAREST description of a scene?
   A. When I was a child, my great-grandfather used to read to me; I remember him pointing to a tree, a cloud a dog, and naming them in the Miami language, giving them back to me in the language of his own childhood.
   B. Reading to me as a child, my great-grandfather used to give them back to me in the language of his own Miami childhood, pointing to a tree, a cloud, a dog.
   C. Pointing to a tree, a cloud, a dog, and naming them in the Miami language, giving them back to me in the language of his own childhood, my great-grandfather used to read to me as a child.
   D. Giving them back to me in the Miami language of his own childhood, my great-grandfather used to pointing to a tree, a cloud, a dog, reading to me as a child.

   3.____

4. A Homemade Education, Malcolm X:
   It was because of my letters that I happened to stumble upon starting to acquire some kind of a homemade education.
   The diction in the above passage is BEST characterized as
   A. colloquial   B. formal
   C. slang   D. colloquial, with slang references

   4.____

5. *She worked the fields all morning, bending for the strawberries, and the _____ she worked up evaporated in the dry air, cooling her hot skin.*
   Which of the following words provides the appropriate connotation to complete the above sentence?
   A. saltwater   B. perspiration   C. stink   D. sweat

   5.____

58

6. Which of the following presents the BEST sequence of the following sentences to make a coherent paragraph?
   I. An amateur should practice this toe-raising technique by sitting well back in a chair with the legs together and straightened, the feet flexed or bent at the ankles.
   II. While keeping your knees straight, your feet should then be arched, slowly, working through the arches to the balls of the feet, and finally onto the points of the toes, which should be squeezed together to increase their ability to support your weight.
   III. Ballet dancers follow a strict code of artistic expectations that usually prohibits them from moving their bodies into positions that do not follow straight, well-balanced lines.
   IV. The dancers' code is so strict that when raising themselves onto their toes, the toes are expected to follow the straight line suggested by the rest of the leg, rather than flexing or "knuckling under."
   The CORRECT answer is:
   A. IV, III, I, II   B. IV, I, II, III   C. III, IV, I, II   D. III, II, I, IV

7. *Patrick enjoyed playing with fire by missing his deadlines.*
   The above sentence contains a(n)
   A. split infinitives   B. subject-verb agreement
   C. parallel construction   D. idiom

8. *She is capable to finish the job.*
   The above sentence contains problems with
   A. split infinitives   B. subject-verb agreement
   C. parallel construction   D. idiom

9. *That we die may be the meaning of life. That we communicate may be the measure of life.*
   The above sentence contains
   A. parallel construction   B. elliptical phrasing
   C. a dangling modifier   D. a false analogy

10. *The shooter celebrated, racing past me. It was obvious that the elephant would never _____ again.*
    Which of the following words provides the appropriate connotation to complete the above sentence?
    A. stand   B. rise   C. walk   D. get up

Questions 11-16.

DIRECTIONS: Questions 11 through 16 are to be answered on the basis of the following passage.

The Stunt Pilot, Annie Dillard:

In 1975, with a newcomer's willingness to try anything once, I attended the Bellingham Air Show.(1) The Bellingham airport was a wide clearing in a forest of tall Douglas firs; its runways suited small planes.(2) It was June.(3) People wearing blue or tan zipped jackets stood loosely on the concrete walkways and runways outside the coffee shop.(4) At that latitude in June, you stayed outside because you could, even most of the night, if you could think up something to do.(5) The sky did not darken until ten o'clock or so, and it never got very dark.(6) Your life parted and opened in the sunlight.(7) You tossed your dark winter routines, thought up mad projects, and improvised everything from hour to hour.(8) Being a stunt pilot seemed the most reasonable thing in the world; you could wave your arms in the air all day and night, and sleep next winter.(9)

11. This passage is BEST characterized as a descriptive narrative about the author's
    A. first experience at an air show
    B. experiences in her new home of Bellingham
    C. new acquaintances
    D. favorite season

12. In sentence 5, the narrative shifts point of view from
    A. first person singular to first person plural
    B. first person to second person
    C. second person to third person
    D. first person to third person

13. The shift in point of view mainly serves to
    A. create a sense of communal experience in which the reader is included
    B. create a sense of communal experience from which the reader is excluded
    C. underscore the author's position within the community
    D. underscore the author's position outside the community

14. The MAIN purpose of sentence 7 is to
    A. describe the author's growing sense of self
    B. describe the quality of light
    C. introduce the author's state of mind
    D. introduce the emotional effects of the season

15. In sentence 8, which of the following stylistic techniques does the author mainly rely on?
    A. Repetition
    B. Coordination
    C. Subordination
    D. Parallel structure

16. The tone of this passage is BEST described as
    A. humorous   B. sarcastic   C. exuberant   D. fantastic

17. *She kept herself busy as a bee all summer long.*
    The above sentence contains a(n)
    A. cliche B. idiom C. metaphor D. euphemism

18. *Actors are often more interesting on the screen than in the flesh.*
    The above sentence contains
    A. parallel construction B. elliptical phrasing
    C. a dangling modifier D. a false analogy

19. Which of the following provides the MOST objective point of view on the part of the writer?
    A. In Othello, Desdemona is another sexist stereotype created by a man.
    B. In Othello, Desdemona acts out of a sense of love, even though that love results in her death.
    C. Desdemona is a boring character who never learns to take control of her own life.
    D. Othello kills his wife, Desdemona, because she is too spineless to stand up for herself.

20. *As I dance, whirling and _____, I feel happier than I have ever felt in my life.*
    Which of the following words provides the appropriate connotation to complete the above sentence?
    A. pleased B. happy C. joyous D. content

21. Which of the following is the CLEAREST explanation?
    A. Developing a code for the U.S. military which would become one of the most successful codes in military history during World War II, a group of Navajo Indians used their unique language.
    B. A group of Navajo Indians during World War II developed a code for the U.S. military which would become one of the most successful codes in military history using their unique language.
    C. One of the most successful codes in military history was developed during World War II from the unique language used by Navajo Indians.
    D. During World War II, a group of Navajo Indians used their unique language to develop a code for the U.S. military which would become one of the most successful codes in military history.

22. *Work with a friend who is in your class or who is good at math.*
    The above sentence contains
    A. elliptical phrases B. parallel construction
    C. euphemisms D. a dangling modifier

23. *I know that the crime rate has increased because the drinking age was lowered.*
    The above statement is an example of
    A. a faulty use of cause and effect B. an ad hominem attack
    C. circular reasoning D. a hasty generalization

24. *To please the children, some presents were opened Christmas Eve.* 24.____
    The above sentence contains
    A. faulty parallel construction
    B. faulty subject-verb agreement
    C. a misplaced modifier
    D. a dangling modifier

25. *It was crystal clear to Maria that Anthony was lying.* 25.____
    The sentence above contains a(n)
    A. metaphor   B. idiom   C. cliché   D. euphemism

KEY (CORRECT ANSWERS)

1.	A	11.	A
2.	D	12.	B
3.	A	13.	A
4.	B	14.	D
5.	D	15.	D
6.	C	16.	C
7.	D	17.	A
8.	B	18.	A
9.	A	19.	B
10.	B	20.	C

21.	D
22.	B
23.	A
24.	D
25.	C

EXAMINATION SECTION
TEST 1

DIRECTIONS: Each question or incomplete statement is followed by several suggested answers or completions. Select the one that BEST answers the question or completes the statement. *PRINT THE LETTER OF THE CORRECT ANSWER IN THE SPACE AT THE RIGHT.*

Questions 1-5.

DIRECTIONS: Questions 1 through 5 are to be answered on the basis of the selection below.

The school term ended. I was selected as valedictorian of my class and assigned to write a paper to be delivered at graduation. One morning the principal summoned me to his office.

"Well, Richard Wright, here's your speech," he said with smooth bluntness and shoved a stack of stapled sheets across his desk.

"What speech?" I asked as I picked up the papers.

"The speech you're to say the night of graduation," he said.

"But, professor, I've written my speech already," I said.

He laughed confidently, indulgently.

"Listen, boy, you're going to speak to both white and colored people that night. What can you alone think of saying to them?
You have no experience..."

I burned.

"I know that I'm not educated, professor," I said. "But the people are coming to hear the students, and I won't make a speech that you've written."

He leaned back in his chair and looked at me in surprise.

"You know, we've never had a boy in this school like you before," he said. "You've had your way around here. Just how you managed to do it, I don't know. But, listen, take this speech and say it. I know what's best for you. You can't afford to just say anything before those white people that night." He paused and added meaningfully: "The superintendent of schools will be there; you're in a position to make a good impression on him. I've been a principal for more years than you are old, boy. I've seen many a boy and girl graduate from this school, and none of them was too proud to recite a speech I wrote for them.

I had to make up my mind quickly; I was faced with a matter of principle. I wanted to graduate, but I did not want to make a public speech that was not my own.

"Professor, I'm going to say my own speech that night," I said.

He grew angry.

"You're just a young, hotheaded fool," he said. He toyed with a pencil and looked up at me. "Suppose you don't graduate?"

"But I passed my examinations," I said.

"Look, mister," he shot at me, "I'm the man who says who passes at this school."

I was so astonished that my body jerked. I had gone to this school for two years and I had never suspected what kind of man the principal was; it simply had never occurred to me to wonder about him.

"Then I don't graduate," I said flatly.

I turned to leave.

"Say, you. Come here," he called.

I turned and faced him; he was smiling at me in a remote superior sort of way.

"You know, I'm glad I talked to you," he said. "I was seriously thinking of placing you in the school system, teaching. But, now, I don't think that you'll fit."

He was tempting me, baiting me; this was the technique that snared black young minds into supporting the southern way of life.

"Look, professor, I may never get a chance to go to school again," I said.

"But I like to do things right. You're just a young, hot fool," he said. "Wake up, boy. Learn the world you're living in. You're smart and I know what you're after. I've kept closer track of you than you think. I know your relatives. Now, if you play safe," he smiled and winked, "I'll help you to go to school, to college."

"I want to learn, professor," I told him. "But there are some things I don't want to know."

Adapted from <u>Black Boy,</u> the
Autobiography of Richard Wright

1. The conflict between Richard and the principal of the school concerns   1.____

    A. whose speech is better—Richard's or the principal's
    B. whether there should be a prepared speech at graduation or informal remark
    C. whether the speech that is given should be written by Richard or the principal
    D. whether the superintendent of schools should be allowed to hear the speech

2. As used in the next to the last paragraph of the selection, the word *track* means a(n)

   A. watching or an observing
   B. athletic competition
   C. footprint
   D. route or course

3. Richard's words and actions in this incident can be BEST explained by Richard's

   A. fear of what the principal could do to him
   B. always wanting to get his own way in everything
   C. realizing that the principal knew what was best for him
   D. belief that, as a matter of principle, he had to be true to what he considered to be right

4. The principal was surprised at Richard's reaction when he handed him the speech because

   A. Richard had always been a cooperative student
   B. no other student had ever acted this way with the principal before
   C. Richard had promised to do whatever the principal told him to do
   D. Richard could barely read and write

5. The frequent use of quotation marks in this passage indicates that

   A. a conversation is going on
   B. the titles of short stories, poems, and other short works being mentioned
   C. the characters do not always mean exactly what their words are saying
   D. that writer does not understand the proper uses of quotation marks

Questions 6-10.

DIRECTIONS: Questions 6 through 10 are to be answered on the basis of the selection below.

We call it Sunrise Dance. But it lasts for four days. It's the biggest ceremony of the White Mountain Apache — when a girl passes from childhood to womanhood. When my time came at 14, I didn't want to have one. I felt embarrassed. All my friends would be watching me. But my parents really wanted it. My mother — she never had one — explained it was important, "Then you will live strong to an old age." So I didn't say no.

My parents prepared for a year. They asked relatives, "Help us so our daughter's dance will be a good one." Older relatives helped choose my sponsors; I call them Godparents. One morning my mother and father took an eagle feather to Godmother Foster and placed it at her foot saying, "Would you prepare a dance for my daughter?" Mrs. Foster picked up the feather. "Yes."

We held the dance at the fairgrounds at Whiteriver. There was room for everyone to camp. One Friday evening Godmother dressed me and pinned an eagle feather on my head. It will help me live until my hair turns gray. The abalone shell pendant on my forehead is the symbol of Changing Woman, mother of all Apache people.

The most important thing Godmother does in the whole ceremony is to massage my body. She is giving me all her knowledge. That night for hours around the fire, I follow a crown dancer who <u>impersonates</u> a protective spirit. We all believe the spirit is present.

Saturday is like an endurance test. Men begin the chants at dawn. They are really praying. Grandmother tells me to dance while kneeling on a buckskin pad facing the sun—the Creator. In that position, Apache women grind corn. When the times comes for running, I go fast around a sacred cave, so nobody evil will ever catch up with me. Rain begins, and my costume, which weighs ten pounds, gets heavier and heavier. But I don't fall. I don't even get tired.

I'm really glad I had a sunrise dance. It made me realize how much my parents care for me and want me to grow up right. They know my small age is past and treat me like a woman. If I have a daughter, I want her to have a sunrise dance, too.

Adapted from the February 1980 issue
of <u>National Geographic Magazine</u>

6. A young Apache girl participates in the ceremony described above when she

   A. is born
   B. is about to enter womanhood
   C. is about to be married
   D. needs godparents

7. The speaker of this selection changed her feelings toward her sunrise dance from

   A. anger to resignation
   B. embarrassment to humiliation
   C. refusal to resignation
   D. embarrassment to pride

8. In paragraph four, the word *impersonates* means

   A. acts the part of   B. dances with
   C. obeys   D. challenges

9. We can conclude that the sunrise dance

   A. is performed each week
   B. brings rain for the crops
   C. will make the speaker live a long time
   D. is a traditional Apache ritual

10. The MOST important part of the ceremony, according to the speaker, is the

    A. eagle feather   B. massage
    C. chanting men   D. sacred cave

Questions 11-15.

DIRECTIONS: Questions 11 through 15 are to be answered on the basis of the following passage.

I really knew I would like New York, but I thought I'd like it immediately, as I had liked the red brick of Venice and London's massive, somber houses. I didn't know that, for a newly arrived European visitor, there was a "New York sickness," like seasickness, air sickness, and mountain sickness.

In Europe, you stop along the streets, meet people, drink, eat, and linger. On Sundays, you get dressed and take a <u>stroll</u> for the sole pleasure of greeting friends. These streets are filled with a community spirit that changes from hour to hour. You do not go for walks in New York; you fly through it. It is a city in motion. Each street looks the same as any other. I feel like anybody, anywhere. I know nobody, nowhere.

In Europe, we become attached to a neighborhood, to a cluster of houses or a street corner, and we are no longer free. But hardly have you entered New York than your life is cut to New York size. You can gaze down in the evening from the top of the Queensborough Bridge, in the morning from New Jersey, at noon from the Empire State Building. Your world is much larger when you live in New York.

I have learned to love New York, especially its sky. In European cities where roofs are low, the sky crawls close to the earth and seems tamed. The New York sky is beautiful because the skyscrapers push it back, very far over our heads. Pure and lovely as a wild beast, it guards and watches over the city. This sky stretches into the distance over all America. It is the whole world's sky.

That thought alone is enough to lend softness to the world's harshest city.

Adapted from "New York"
by Jean-Paul Sartre

11. The author's purpose in writing this passage is to

    A. criticize New York
    B. praise Europe
    C. compare New York with Europe
    D. praise New York

12. The word *stroll* in paragraph two means a

    A. nap   B. walk   C. look   D. ride

13. The author's feelings about New York change from

    A. uneasiness to love   B. love to hatred
    C. fear to shock   D. uneasiness to hatred

14. The word *it* in paragraph four refers to

    A. skyscrapers   B. the beast
    C. New York   D. the sky

15. We can conclude from this passage that the author

    A. dislikes Europe now that he has discovered New York
    B. has travelled widely
    C. left Europe permanently
    D. was seasick on his journey to New York

Questions 16-20.

DIRECTIONS: Read the passages below and select from the words in each question the one that BEST completes the passages. Study the sample below and then proceed on your own.

Sample: Jim Hawkins in TREASURE ISLAND boarded a huge ship and __1__ off that day to go in search of a hidden treasure.

1. A. drove   B. called   C. sailed   D. nodded

The CORRECT answer is C.

The Burgos' house was a poor one with a thatched roof of palm leaves, but there was the warmth of a loving home within. Paula, the mother, kept a small __16__ nearby. She grew vegetables and grain to help feed the family, selling the produce to buy food and clothing. Since she had no one with whom to leave her small daughter, Paula would take Julia on her trips to the market. Down by the river, while the washing was done in the stream, Julia and her sisters played in the grass, smelled the flowers, climbed the trees, and bathed in a pond they called the Deep Well. It was then that the child began to recognize and love __17__.

Life was simple for the Burgos family. Their world was limited to the countryside surrounding their house. But it seemed __18__ and wondrous to Julia. Her eyes would discover the beauty of every wild flower, the living miracle of a bird's nest tucked away in a bush. Years later __19__ about her childhood, she confided, "I would cry disconsolately over the leaves of a MORIVINI because it would not awaken." The MORIVINI is a plant so sensitive that its leaves shrivel and die if someone touches it.

If Julia's childhood was poor in material wealth, it was rich in vital experiences and in emotions. Unfortunately, it also abounded in __20__. One by one she saw six of her brothers die. The first time she saw her mother cry over the loss of one of her sons, Julia was devastated. She would not accept that the dead child had to be buried. "Why don't they place him on a raft and cast him off to sea?" she asked.

16. A. factory   B. garden   C. warehouse   D. dairy   16.___
17. A. families   B. bathing   C. exercise   D. nature   17.___
18. A. enormous   B. poor   C. boring   D. small   18.___
19. A. forgetting B. singing   C. reminiscing D. complaining 19.___
20. A. love   B. sorrow   C. fear   D. anger   20.___

Questions 21-35.

DIRECTIONS: The sentences numbered 21 through 35 make up the paragraph that follows. There is one error either in sentence structure, spelling, punctuation, or incorrect usage in each sentence. Find the error in each sentence and write the CORRECTION in the space at the right.

Sample:
A. On the last day of our vacation, we saw men skiing down a mountain that was the best part of the vacation for me.
B. If we go back next year I plan to take skiing lessons.
C. They shouldnt be expensive.

Answers:
A. mountain. That
B. year,
C. shouldn't or should not

21. You are now at the mid-point in this examination in english. 21._____
22. Have you notice anything about the test so far? 22._____
23. You should of noticed it; it is about beginnings and endings. 23._____
24. In a week, you are probably gonna experience an ending and a beginning of your own. 24._____
25. We are referring to the commencement exercises that represent your graduation from High School. 25._____
26. Commencement ceremonies can be a beginning or an ending it depends on how you look at it. 26._____
27. Some students see there graduation as the completion of their formal education. 27._____
28. Others sees it as the first step to higher education or employment. 28._____
29. Are you looking at it as a beginning or an ending. 29._____
30. Both views are probably true. Because every ending begins something else. 30._____
31. As someone once said Every exit is an entrance somewhere else." 31._____
32. It is also true that each beginning contain's its own ending. 32._____
33. For example the beginning of life also contains the beginning of the end. 33._____
34. The moment we are born we begin both living and dieing. 34._____
35. "That's life," you may be thinking, and your right. 35._____

Questions 36-40.

DIRECTIONS: A dictionary page has been reprinted below. Use the information on this dictionary page to answer Questions 36 through 40.

pan·e·gyr·ist \,pan-ə-'jir-əst\ *n.* A person who formally praises a person or event.

pan·el \'pan-l\ *n.* **1** A section or part of a wall, ceiling, or door, often sunk below the level of the frame; especially, a thin and usually rectangular board set in a frame, as in a door. **2** A thin, flat piece of wood on which a picture is painted. **3** A painting on such a surface. **4** A lengthwise strip or band sewn in a dress; as, an embroidered *panel* on a skirt. **5** A list or group of persons appointed for some service; especially, a group of persons called to serve on a jury. **6** A group of no less than three persons, often experts in various fields, conducting before an audience an unrehearsed discussion on a topic of interest, either to a special audience or to the general public; a similar group, usually of persons well-known to the public, acting as players in a quiz game or guessing game conducted by a master of ceremonies on a radio or television program. — *v.*; **pan·eled** or **pan·elled**; **pan·el·ing** or **pan·el·ling** \-l(-)ing\. To furnish, fit, trim, or decorate with panels; as, to *panel* a wall.

pan·el·ing or **pan·el·ling** \'pan-l(-)ing\ *n.* **1** Wood or other material made into panels. **2** Panels considered collectively.

pan·el·ist \'pan-l-əst\ *n.* A member of a panel for discussion or entertainment.

pang \'pang\ *n.* **1** A sudden sharp attack of pain; a throe. **2** A sudden sharp feeling of any emotion; as, a *pang* of regret.

pan·han·dle \'pan-,hand-l\ *n.* **1** The handle of a pan. **2** An arm or projection of land shaped like the handle of a pan.

pan·han·dle \'pan-,hand-l\ *v.*; **pan·han·dled**; **pan·han·dling** \-l(-)ing\. To approach people on the street and beg for money. — **pan·han·dler** \-lər\ *n.*

pan·ic \'pan-ik\ *n.* **1** A sudden, terrifying fright, especially without reasonable cause. **2** A sudden, widespread fear in financial circles, causing hurried selling of securities and a rapid fall in prices. — *v.*; **pan·icked** \-ikt\; **pan·ick·ing** \-ik-ing\. **1** To affect with panic; to be affected with panic; as, one who *panics* easily. **2** *Slang*. To call forth a show of appreciation on the part of someone. The comedian's performance *panicked* the audience. — **pan·icky** \'pan-ik-ē\ *adj.* — **pan·ic-strick·en** \'pan-ik-,strik-n\ *adj.*

pan·i·cle \'pan-ik-l\ *n.* A flower cluster, loosely branched and often in the shape of a pyramid, in which the branches of the flowerless main stem are elongated clusters in the form of a raceme, blooming from the bottom toward the top and outward, as in the oat.

pan·nier \'pan-yər, 'pan-ē-ər\ *n.* **1** A large basket, especially one of wicker, carried on the back of an animal or the shoulder of a person. **2** A framework worn by women to expand their skirts at the hips. **3** An overskirt puffed out at the sides and back.

pan·o·ply \'pan-ə-plē\ *n.*; *pl.* **pan·o·plies**. **1** A full suit of armor. **2** Anything defending or protecting completely by covering; anything forming a magnificent covering or environment. The automobiles in the parade were covered with *panoplies* of flowers and bunting. — **pan·o·plied** \-plēd\ *adj.*

pan·o·ra·ma \,pan-r-'am-ə, -'äm-, -'am-\ *n.* **1** A picture that is unrolled little by little as a person looks at it. **2** A clear, complete view in every direction. **3** A complete view or treatment of any subject; as, a *panorama* of history. — **pan·o·ram·ic** \-'am-ik\ *adj.*

pan·pipe \'pan-,pīp\ *n.* A wind instrument consisting of a series of hollow reeds or pipes of different lengths, closed at one end and bound together with the mouth pieces in an even row.

panpipe

pan·sy \'pan-zē\ *n.*; *pl.* **pan·sies**. [From medieval English *pensee*, there borrowed from medieval French *pensée*, meaning literally "thought".] A low-growing, commonly annual plant belonging to the violet group and derived from the wild pansy or Johnny-jump-up, with small purple and violet flowers and, in its various garden forms, with showy five-petaled flowers that are usually of cream, violet, or yellow.

pant \'pant\ *v.* **1** To breathe hard or quickly; to gasp; as, to *pant* from running. **2** To want intensely; to long. **3** To breathe or say quickly and with difficulty. — *n.* **1** One of a series of short, quick breaths, as after exercise; a gasp. **2** A puff, as of a steam engine.

pan·ta·lets or **pan·ta·lettes** \,pant-l-'ets\ *n. pl.* Long, loose drawers with ruffles around each ankle, worn by women and girls.

pan·ta·loon \,pant-l-'ün\ *n.* **1** A clown. **2** [in the plural] Trousers.

pan·the·ism \'pan(t)th-ē-,iz-m\ *n.* **1** Any doctrine or belief that the universe taken as a whole is God. **2** The worship of gods of various creeds or religions at one time, as at one period in ancient Rome.

pantalets

pan·ther \'pan(t)th-r\ *n.* **1** The leopard. **2** In America, the cougar.

pant·ies \'pant-ēz\ *n. pl.*; *sing.* **pant·ie** or **panty** \'pant-ē\. A child's or woman's undergarment covering the lower trunk, with a closed crotch and very short legs.

pan·to·mime \'pant-m-,īm\ *n.* **1** A performer skilled in the art of conveying emotions and ideas without the use of words. **2** A play in which the actors use few or no words. **3** Silent movements or facial expressions that show how a person feels about something. — *v.*; **pan·to·mimed**; **pan·to·mim·ing**. To represent by pantomime. — **pan·to·mim·ist** \-,ī-məst, -,im-əst\ *n.*

pan·to·then·ic ac·id \'pant-ə-,then-ik\. A substance in the vitamin-B complex that promotes growth, found especially in liver and yeast.

pan·try \'pan-trē\ *n.*; *pl.* **pan·tries**. A small room where food and dishes are kept.

pants \'pan(t)s\ *n. pl.* **1** Trousers. **2** Drawers; especially, panties.

j joke; ng sing; ō flow; ȯ flaw; ȯi coin; th thin; <u>th</u> this; ü loot; u̇ foot; y yet; yü few; yu̇ furious; zh vision

36. A word that originally comes from French meaning *thought* is
    A. panoply
    B. panicle
    C. pansy
    D. pantheism

37. If I had a *panoramic* view of the countryside, I would see
    A. only those things that are moving
    B. in all directions
    C. part of the scene
    D. only the grass

38. In an illustration on the page, an example of a musical instrument is a
    A. pantalet
    B. pantaloon
    C. pannier
    D. panpipe

39. A word that has at least six different meanings as a noun is
    A. pant
    B. pantomine
    C. panel
    D. panic

40. The play was performed as a _____ , so that the audience had to watch the actors' faces and movements very carefully.
    Select the word that BEST completes the above sentence.
    A. panelist
    B. pantomine
    C. panegyrist
    D. panic

Questions 41-43.

DIRECTIONS: Questions 41 through 43 are to be answered on the basis of the library card reproduced below.

```
                Working for yourself
658.1       Hewitt, Geof
  H             Working for yourself; how to be successfully
            self-employed. Photos by T. L. Gettinsts. Rodale
            [ c 1977 ] 304p illus

                Features the stories and advice of nearly one
            hundred self-employed people as well as guide-
            lines for selecting, promoting, financing, and
            managing a business or trade.

            1 Professions 2 Small business
        ISBN 0-87857-162-0

                              © THE BAKER & TAYLOR CO
```

41. The Dewey Decimal number you would use to locate this book on a library shelf is
    A. 1977
    B. 658.1H
    C. ISBN 0-87857-162-0
    D. 304

42. All of the following questions would be answered by reading this book EXCEPT:

    A. How have other people started their own businesses?
    B. How do I go about financing my business?
    C. What do I need to know to become a good manager?
    D. How should my boss treat me?

43. If you wanted additional books on the same topic, you would look in the card catalogue under the cross-reference

    A. Hewitt
    C. government service
    B. professions
    D. Rodale

Questions 44-45.

DIRECTIONS: Questions 44 and 45 are to be answered on the basis of the newspaper advertisement for a Broadway play shown below.

BOX OFFICE OPENS TOM'W at 10 AM

LIMITED ENGAGEMENT! 10 WEEKS ONLY!
PREVIEWS BEGIN WED. EVG., APRIL 29th
OPENS THURS. EVG., MAY 7th at 6:15
CHARGIT : (212) 944-9300
TICKETRON: (212) 977-9020 Group Sales: (212) 398-8383

MAIL ORDERS NOW!

Monday thru Saturday Evenings at 8 and Saturday Matinees at 2: Orchestra $30.00; Mezzanine $30.00, 27.50, 25.00. Wednesday Matinees at 2: Orchestra $28.50; Mezzanine $28.50, 25.00, 22.50. Please enclose a self-addressed, stamped envelope along with your check or money order made payable to: Martin Beck Theatre. List several alternate dates.

MARTIN BECK THEATRE 302 West 45th Street, New York, N.Y.

---

44. Missing from the ad is

    A. the times of the performance
    B. information on how to purchase tickets
    C. the name of the play
    D. the opening night of the play

45. For a Wednesday matinee performance, the LEAST expensive ticket is

    A. $30.00   B. $28.50   C. $22.50   D. $20.00

Questions 46-50.

DIRECTIONS: Questions 46 through 50 are to be answered on the basis of the following poem.

Summons

Keep me from going to sleep too soon
Or if I go to sleep too soon
Come wake me up. Come any hour
Of night. Come whistling up the road.
Stomp on the porch. Bang on the door.   5
Make me get out of bed and come
and let you in and light a light.
Tell me the northern lights are on -
And make me look. Or tell me clouds
Are doing something to the moon   10
they never did before, and show me
See that I see. Talk to me till
I'm half as wide awake as you
and start to dress wondering why
I ever went to bed at all.   15
Tell me the walking is superb.
Not only tell me but persuade me.
You know I'm not too hard persuaded.

Robert Francis

46. When the speaker says he is afraid he will "go to sleep too soon," he is really saying that he is afraid he will

   A. die suddenly
   B. lose his interest in life
   C. miss his friend's visit
   D. forget to get undressed

47. We can conclude that the speaker's friend is

   A. a woman
   B. more alive and curious about life than the speaker
   C. less alive and curious about life than the speaker
   D. disillusioned with life

48. The last line of the poem expresses

   A. difficulty   B. hope
   C. fear   D. disappointment

49. The title of the poem refers to a

   A. written notice to appear in court
   B. refusal to cooperate
   C. call for help to another person not present in the poem
   D. traffic violation ticket

50. Lines 3-5 in the poem are effective because they   50. _____
    A. rhyme
    B. are part of a pattern of requests for action
    C. start a new stanza
    D. make use of similes

KEY (CORRECT ANSWERS)

1.	C	16.	B	31.	said: "Every	46.	B
2.	A	17.	D	32.	contains	47.	B
3.	D	18.	A	33.	example, the	48.	B
4.	B	19.	C	34.	dying	49.	C
5.	A	20.	B	35.	you are/you're	50.	B
6.	B	21.	English	36.	C		
7.	D	22.	noticed	37.	B		
8.	A	23.	should have	38.	D		
9.	D	24.	going to	39.	C		
10.	B	25.	high school	40.	B		
11.	D	26.	ending. It	41.	B		
12.	B	27.	their	42.	D		
13.	A	28.	see	43.	B		
14.	D	29.	ending?	44.	C		
15.	B	30.	true, because	45.	C		

EXAMINATION SECTION
TEST 1

DIRECTIONS: Each question or incomplete statement is followed by several suggested answers or completions. Select the one that BEST answers the question or completes the statement. *PRINT THE LETTER OF THE CORRECT ANSWER IN THE SPACE AT THE RIGHT.*

Questions 1-5.

DIRECTIONS: Questions 1 through 5 are to be answered on the basis of the following passage.

The Grand Canyon carves through 279 miles of northern Arizona. No one expects what he finds here, and no one forgets what he sees and hears.

For more than ten years, Paul Winter has come to the Grand Canyon with his soprano saxophone. He has stood on the rim at Shoshone Point and played to cliffs that send back a triple echo. He has played with his fellow musicians in the side canyons, and together they have floated down the Colorado River. *I felt put back together on the river,* Winter says, *and I wanted to make music from that place. I wanted to make music of the canyon rather than just about it.*

Even when non-musicians come to these great spaces, they want to fill the stillness with sound. John Wesley Powell, first to describe the experience of a river trip through the canyon, wrote in 1895: *The wonders of the Grand Canyon cannot be adequately represented in symbols of speech, nor by speech itself.... It is the land of music.*

Winter and his group of musicians would certainly agree. On a fall evening, they play Japanese wood flutes, <u>improvisations</u> in answer to the local chorus of canyon tree frogs. Upstream the next morning the saxophone calls, sounding like a great bird, first raven, then great blue heron. The sounds of the wind mix with the rhythms of a frame drum. Much of this is recorded, and a small part will become part of a record the musicians are making.

The Grand Canyon is like a journey through time, life, Earth, underworld: It is any reality we care to invent. Paul Winter tries to recapture this in his music.

                         Adapted from PAUL WINTER'S CANYON CONSORT
                         by Stephen Trimble, SIERRA, March/April 1986

1. Paul Winter visits the Grand Canyon to

    A. trap ravens   B. take photographs
    C. record frogs and animals   D. play his saxophone

1.____

2. In 1895, John Wesley Powell suggested that

    A. only words could describe the Grand Canyon
    B. symbols are needed for nature
    C. music can best express the canyon's beauty
    D. stillness is required in nature

2.____

3. The word <u>improvisations</u> in this passage means

    A. producing high pitched sounds
    B. performing without preparation
    C. echoing the exact sound
    D. playing melodies

4. The musicians in this passage enjoy

    A. hiking in the wilderness
    B. playing old fashioned music
    C. responding in music to nature
    D. playing their music indoors

5. The author suggests that the Grand Canyon

    A. has many meanings
    B. stands for lack of freedom
    C. will be destroyed
    D. is a poor setting for art

Questions 6-10.

DIRECTIONS: Questions 6 through 10 are to be answered on the basis of the following passage.

Write about beauty and truth. Write about life, Miss Lowy had said.

Jeanie tore a page out of her notebook and opened her pen. Pulling over a chair she rested her book on the sooty window sill. She stared out at the dusk falling sadly, sadly, thickening into darkness over the coal yards.

A crash of the kitchen door caused a reverberation in the window sill. The notebook slipped out of her hands.

Where you get that soda? She heard her mother's voice, hard and more Southern-sounding than usual.

A lady give me a nickel. She come down the street and ask me–

You lyin'! I know where you got it. Gamblin? – that's what you was doin'!

I was pitchin' pennies, Ma. It's just a game.

Gamblin' an' stealin'! Takin' up with bad friends! I told you to stay away from them boys. Didn't I? Didn't I?

Her mother's voice rose. *I'm goin' to give you a beating you ain't goin' to forget for a good long time.*

Billy wailed on a long descending note.

Later, after the supper dishes were washed, Jeanie brought her books into the kitchen and spread them out under the glaring overhead light. Billy had been asleep, huddled in his clothes. Tears had left dusty streaks on his face.

Her mother sat in an armchair, ripping out the sides of a black dress. Her spectacles made her look strange. *Beauty is truth,* Jeanie read in her notebook. Hastily, carelessly, <u>defiantly</u> disregarding margins and doubtful spellings, letting her pen dig into the paper, she began to write: *Last night my brother Billy got a terrible beating....*

Adapted from BEAUTY IS TRUTH
by Anna Guest

6. The author suggests that Jeanie

    A. hated her mother
    B. was jealous of her brother
    C. had trouble writing at first
    D. enjoyed gambling

7. An overheard conversation serves to

    A. distract the writer
    B. inspire the writer
    C. involve the writer in a fight
    D. discourage the writer

8. The word <u>defiantly</u> as used in the passage means

    A. sadly   B. falsely
    C. fearlessly   D. carefully

9. Jeanie decides to write about

    A. life around her   B. her school experiences
    C. her secret dreams   D. an ideal family

10. The author suggests that a writer

    A. depends upon imagination
    B. finds inspiration in reality
    C. must ignore life experience
    D. needs a quiet place to work

Questions 11-15.

DIRECTIONS: Questions 11 through 15 are to be answered on the basis of the following passage.

LIFE

A crust of bread and a corner to sleep in,
A minute to smile and an hour to weep in,
A pint of joy to a peck of trouble,
And never a laugh but the moans come double:
    And that is life!

A crust and a corner that love makes precious,
With the smile to warm and the tears to refresh us;
And joy seems sweeter when cares come after,
And a moan is the finest of foils for laughter:
    And that is life!

by Paul Lawrence Dunbar

11. This poem is built on

    A. an abstract definition
    B. comparisons and contrasts
    C. a view of loneliness
    D. impressions of poverty

12. Lines 5 and 10 express

    A. the same meaning
    B. different meanings
    C. a unique message
    D. a poet's doubts

13. The rhyme schemes in stanzas 1 and 2 are

    A. totally different
    B. somewhat different
    C. the same
    D. difficult to identify

14. In line 4, sorrow is contrasted to

    A. suspicion   B. happiness   C. fear   D. insecurity

15. *And a moan is the finest of foils for laughter* means

    A. a moan is a prerequisite for happiness
    B. laughter follows tragedy
    C. sadness helps us appreciate joy
    D. unhappiness and happiness are equal

Questions 16-20.

DIRECTIONS: Read the following passage. In each question, select the word that BEST completes the passage.

    Immigration, which played an important part in America's rapid progress, increased greatly in the 1830's and 1840's. Europe suffered from a number of revolutions and crop failures during this period. Most of the revolutions failed, and many people with advanced ideas had to flee for their (16) . This was especially true in Germany, where absolute monarchy was still strong. The worst crop (17) occurred in Ireland. There, several million people faced starvation during the *potato famines* of 1845 and 1846.

Large numbers of Germans, Irish, and other Europeans were attracted to the United States by its cheap land, economic prosperity, and democratic government. But they met with an unexpected problem, a growing feeling among Americans of dislike for (18). Most of the Irish were very poor. Since they could not afford to buy farms, they (19) in the cities. There they performed the most difficult and unpleasant types of work for very low wages. Native American (20) resented the Irish for keeping wages down and for taking away jobs. The newcomers were also disliked because they were generally uneducated and had very low living standards.

16. A. wealth B. safety 16.____
    C. country D. importance

17. A. success B. likelihood 17.____
    C. failures D. knowledge

18. A. foreigners B. democracy 18.____
    C. farms D. dreams

19. A. farmed B. met C. bought D. settled 19.____

20. A. standards B. immigrants 20.____
    C. workers D. bosses

Questions 21-35.

DIRECTIONS: Each of the following sentences may have a mistake in it. The error may be in sentence structure, usage, capitalization, or punctuation. If there is an error, choose the CORRECT response, and write the letter of your answer in the space at the right. If the sentence is correct as it is written, choose the letter of the answer for *correct as is*.

SAMPLE: I have always <u>chose</u> to follow my <u>mother's</u> advice.
A. Correct as as
B. chosen; mother's
C. choosed; mothers
D. chose; mothers'

CORRECT ANSWER: B

21. We <u>should of stayed</u> home. 21.____

    A. correct as is B. should have stayed
    C. should of stay D. should have stay

22. John and <u>I</u> are going to my <u>uncle's</u> house. 22.____

    A. correct as is B. me; uncles
    C. me; uncle's D. I; uncles

23. <u>"How are you," she asked.</u> 23.____

    A. correct as is B. "How are you," she asked?
    C. "How are you? she asked." D. "How are you?" she asked.

24. If you had brought your homework, you wouldn't needed to do it over.   24.___

    A. correct as is
    B. have brought; wouldn't needed
    C. had brought; wouldn't need
    D. had brung; wouldn't need

25. She sung that song worse than anyone I ever heard before.   25.___

    A. correct as is   B. sung; worst
    C. sung; worser   D. sang; worse

26. More people than we expected.   26.___

    A. correct as is
    B. Many more people than we expected.
    C. More people than expected to the party.
    D. More people than we expected came to the party.

27. You can do that problem many ways, the teacher will explain them.   27.___

    A. correct as is
    B. You can do that problem many ways; The teacher will explain them.
    C. You can do that problem many ways. The teacher will explain them.
    D. You can do that problem many ways the teacher will explain them.

28. We was born in New York, but we are living in New Jersey for the last two years.   28.___

    A. correct as is
    B. we was born; we was living
    C. we were born; we are living
    D. we were born; we have been living

29. After the thief had robbed his wallet, he told the police of its contents.   29.___

    A. correct as is   B. robbed; it's
    C. stolen; it's   D. stolen; its

30. If you think he don't do nothing carefully, you're right.   30.___

    A. correct as is
    B. he don't do nothing careful
    C. he doesn't do nothing carefully
    D. he doesn't do anything carefully

31. I learned in English class that London was the home of the Globe theater.   31.___

    A. correct as is
    B. English class; London; Globe Theater
    C. english class; London; Globe Theater
    D. English Class; London; Globe Theater

32. He asked each of the men for their dollar contribution to the charity, like he had promised.   32.____

    A. correct as is
    B. their; as
    C. his; like
    D. his; as

33. John, as well as Mary, deserves credit for having past advanced math.   33.____

    A. correct as is
    B. deserves; having passed
    C. deserve; having passed
    D. deserve; having past

34. The dance was lovely all the students dressed in formals.   34.____

    A. correct as is
    B. The dance was lovely, all the
    C. "The dance was lovely," all the
    D. The dance was lovely. All

35. I do good on this kind of test.   35.____

    A. correct as is
    B. good; these kinds
    C. well; this kind
    D. well; these kinds

Questions 36-40.

DIRECTIONS: A dictionary page has been reprinted on the next page. Use the information on this dictionary page to answer Questions 36 through 40.

mer·ci·less \'mər-sē-ləs, 'mərs-l-əs\ *adj.* Without mercy; pitiless. — **mer·ci·less·ly,** *adv.*

mer·cu·ri·al \mər-'kyùr-ē-əl\ *adj.* 1 Having qualities associated with being born under the planet Mercury or attributed to the god Mercury; swift; clever; fickle; changeable. 2 Of, relating to, containing, or caused by the element mercury; as, *mercurial* medical preparations; a *mercurial* thermometer. — *n.* A drug containing mercury.

mer·cu·ric \mər-'kyùr-ik\ *adj.* Of, relating to, or containing mercury.

mer·cu·ry \'mərk-yər-ē, 'mərk-r(-)ē\ *n.; pl.* **mer·cu·ries.** 1 A messenger; a guide. 2 A heavy, silver-white metallic element, the only metal that is liquid at ordinary temperatures; quicksilver. 3 The column of mercury in a thermometer or barometer.

mer·cy \'mər-sē\ *n.; pl.* **mer·cies.** 1 Kind and gentle treatment of an offender, an opponent, or some unfortunate person. 2 A kind, sympathetic manner or disposition; a willingness to forgive, to spare, or to help. 3 The power to be merciful; as, to throw oneself on an enemy's *mercy*. 4 An act of kindness; a blessing.

— The words *clemency* and *leniency* are synonyms of *mercy*: *mercy* usually refers to a compassionate and forgiving attitude on the part of a person who has the power or right to impose severe punishment on another; *clemency* may indicate a habit or policy of moderation and mildness in one whose duty it is to impose punishment for offences; *leniency* often indicates a deliberate overlooking of mistakes or an overindulgent acceptance of another's faults.

mere \'mir\ *n. Archaic* or *Dial.* A sheet of standing water; a lake or pool.

mere \'mir\ *adj.; superlative* **mer·est** \'mir-əst\. Only this, and nothing else; nothing more than; simple; as, a *mere* whisper; a *mere* child.

mere·ly \'mir-lē\ *adv.* Not otherwise than; simply; only.

mer·e·tri·cious \,mer-ə-'trish-əs\ *adj.* Attracting by a display of showy but superficial and tawdry charms; falsely attractive. — **mer·e·tri·cious·ly,** *adv.*

mer·gan·ser \(,)mər-'gan(t)s-r\ *n.; pl.* **mer·gan·sers** or **mer·gan·ser.** A fish-eating wild duck with a slender, hooked beak and, usually, a crested head.

merge \'mərj\ *v.; merged; merg·ing.* 1 To be or cause to be swallowed up, combined, or absorbed in or within something else; to mingle; to blend; as, *merging* traffic. 2 To combine or unite, as two business firms into one.

merg·er \'mərj-r\ *n.* 1 The combining of business concerns or interests into one. 2 The resulting business unit.

me·rid·i·an \mə-'rid-ē-ən\ *adj.* 1 At or relating to midday. 2 Of or relating to a meridian. — *n.* 1 The highest apparent point reached by the sun or a star. 2 The highest point, as of success or importance; culmination. 3 An imaginary great circle on the earth's surface, passing through the North and South Poles and any given place between. 4 The half of such a circle included between the poles. 5 A representation of such a circle or half circle on a globe or map; any of a series of lines drawn at intervals due north and south or in the direction of the poles and numbered according to the degrees of longitude.

me·ringue \mə-'rang\ *n.* A mixture of beaten white of egg and sugar, put on pies or cakes and browned, or shaped into small cakes or shells and baked.

me·ri·no \mə-'rē-,nō\ *n.; pl.* **me·ri·nos.** 1 A fine-wooled white sheep of a breed marked by the heavy twisted horns of the male. 2 A fine soft fabric resembling cashmere and originally made of the wool from this sheep. 3 A fine wool yarn.

merino

mer·it \'mer-ət\ *n.* 1 Due reward or punishment; especially, deserved reward; a mark or token of excellence or approval. 2 The condition or fact of deserving well or ill; desert; as, each according to his *merit*. 3 Worth; excellence; as, a suggestion having considerable *merit*. 4 A quality or act worthy of praise; as, an answer that at least had the *merit* of honesty. — *v.* To earn by service or performance; to deserve; as, a man who *merited* respect.

mer·i·to·ri·ous \,mer-ə-'tōr-ē-əs, -'tor-\ *adj.* Deserving reward or honor; praiseworthy. — **mer·i·to·ri·ous·ly,** *adv.*

mer·maid \'mər-,mād\ *n.* [From medieval English *mermaide*, a compound formed from *mere* meaning "sea" and *maide* meaning "girl", "maid".] An imaginary sea creature usually represented with a woman's body and a fish's tail.

mer·man \'mər-,man, -mən\ *n.; mer·men* \-,men, -mən\. An imaginary sea creature usually represented with a man's body and a fish's tail.

mer·ri·ment \'mer-ē-mənt, -ə-mənt\ *n.* Gaiety; mirth; fun.

mer·ry \'mer-ē\ *adj.; mer·ri·er; mer·ri·est.* 1 Full of good humor and good spirits; laughingly gay. 2 Marked by gaiety or festivity; as, a *merry* Christmas. — **mer·ri·ly** \'mer-ə-lē\ *adv.*

mer·ry-an·drew \'mer-ē-'an-,drü\ *n.* A clown; a buffoon.

mer·ry-go-round \'mer-ē-gō-,raùnd\ *n.* 1 A circular revolving platform fitted with seats and figures of animals on which people sit for a ride. 2 Any rapid round of activities; a whirl; as, a *merry-go-round* of parties.

merry-go-round

mer·ry·mak·ing \'mer-ē-,māk-ing\ *adj.* Festive; jolly. — *n.* 1 The act of making merry; merriment. 2 A frolic; a festivity. — **mer·ry·mak·er** \-,māk-r\ *n.*

me·sa \'mā-sə\ *n.* A flat-topped hill or small plateau with steep sides.

mes·cal \mes-'kal\ *n.* 1 A small, spineless cactus

36. Which of the following groups contains ONLY adjectives?
    A. merciless, meritorious, merriment
    B. merciless, meridian, merry
    C. merit, meritorious, merry
    D. merciless, meritorious, merry

36.____

37. The word <u>clemency</u> is a synonym for

    A. mercurial   B. mercy   C. merit   D. merger

37.____

38. According to the pronunciation key for each word, the mark showing where the stress comes in the word occurs

    A. after the stressed syllable
    B. before the stressed syllable
    C. between stressed syllables
    D. at random

38.____

39. A word which means a sweet dessert is

    A. merge   B. meringue
    C. merit   D. merry-andrew

39.____

40. His invention was of such <u>merit</u> that the world honored him.
    Which is the CORRECT definition for the word <u>merit</u>, as used in the above sentence?
    Definition

    A. 1   B. 2   C. 3   D. 4

40.____

Questions 41-45.

DIRECTIONS: Select the BEST answer for each of the following media questions.

41. To find information on tonight's TV schedule, you should NOT look at

    A. this week's TV GUIDE
    B. this week's NEWSWEEK
    C. today's newspaper
    D. the weekend newspaper's TV section

41.____

42. An index

    A. gives an alphabetical list of topics and persons described in a book, with the pages listed
    B. gives the geographic location of all places in a book
    C. only lists the famous people mentioned in a book, with the appropriate page references
    D. gives the chapter headings found in the book

42.____

43. Magazines may concentrate on one particular subject such as

    A. sports   B. hobbies
    C. fashion   D. all of the above

43.____

44. People listen to the radio and watch television 44._____

    A. for information only
    B. for entertainment only
    C. lacking anything better to do
    D. for all of the above reasons

45. TV advertising frequently appeals to everything EXCEPT our desire 45._____

    A. to hear the whole truth about products
    B. to impress people
    C. to be up-to-date
    D. for the best in life

Questions 46-55.

DIRECTIONS: In each of Questions 46 through 55, only one of the words is misspelled. In each case, write the misspelled word CORRECTLY in the space at the right.

46. banana 46._____
    regional
    apolagize
    anticipate
    grievance

47. medicine 47._____
    interruption
    weird
    benifit
    fatigue

48. clothe 48._____
    religious
    aquarium
    brillianse
    vacuum

49. adjourn 49._____
    gorgeus
    precious
    category
    possess

50. diogram 50._____
    absence
    maturity
    pitiful
    intrusion

51. reccommend 51.____
    comparative
    assurance
    prisoner
    hilarious

52. attempt 52.____
    feminine
    independant
    orchestra
    hopeful

53. parallel 53.____
    transparent
    fantacy
    arguing
    hysterical

54. accidentally 54.____
    minimum
    cathedral
    responsable
    nuclear

55. approximatly 55.____
    committing
    fascinate
    minority
    privilege

KEY (CORRECT ANSWERS)

1. D	16. B	31. B	46. apologize
2. C	17. C	32. D	47. benefit
3. B	18. A	33. B	48. brilliance
4. C	19. D	34. D	49. gorgeous
5. A	20. C	35. C	50. diagram
6. C	21. B	36. D	51. recommend
7. B	22. A	37. B	52. independent
8. C	23. D	38. B	53. fantasy
9. A	24. C	39. B	54. responsible
10. B	25. D	40. C	55. approximately
11. B	26. D	41. B	
12. B	27. C	42. A	
13. C	28. D	43. D	
14. B	29. D	44. D	
15. C	30. D	45. A	

EXAMINATION SECTION
TEST 1

DIRECTIONS: Each question or incomplete statement is followed by several suggested answers or completions. Select the one that BEST answers the question or completes the statement. *PRINT THE LETTER OF THE CORRECT ANSWER IN THE SPACE AT THE RIGHT.*

1. The phrase "an incremental adjustment to meet a new stimulus level" (i.e., an increase in military strength) is an example of

    A. gobbledygook to make the idea seem more impressive
    B. propaganda for foreign consumption
    C. ambiguity to confuse foreign analysts
    D. distortion of the actual truth

2. Which word is spoken with the same stress both as a noun and as a verb?

    A. Permit   B. Desert
    C. Convert   D. Resort

3. Which term has become *least* specific in meaning because of excessive use?

    A. Happy   B. Nice
    C. Intelligent   D. Careless

4. Which level of language usage is illustrated in the sentences below?
   "Hula hoops used to be a hot item in toy stores."
   "The crook was driving a hot car."

    A. Specialized   B. Archaic
    C. Standard   D. Colloquial

5. Which prefix can be used to mean "artificial"?

    A. Quad   B. Tri
    C. Pseudo   D. Circum

6. Which word is *most* abstract?

    A. Sympathy   B. Ship
    C. Soil   D. Smudge

7. Which pair of prefixes has the same meaning?

    A. Sub and ultra   B. Ante and pre
    C. Intra and circum D. Hyper and tele

8. Which of the following is the *most* specific in meaning?

    A. Athlete   B. Girl
    C. Tracy Austin   D. Student

9. A writer's expressions of approval or disapproval of something are BEST regarded as

    A. inferences   B. reports
    C. allusions   D. judgments

QUESTIONS 10-24

In questions 10-24, the same idea is expressed in four different ways. Select the way that is BEST and print the corresponding letter in the space at the right.

10. A. Each time one of her cubs was threatened, the mother lion was ready to attack.
    B. Each time one of her cubs were threatened, the mother lion got ready to attack.
    C. Ready to attack, the cubs were protected from every threat by the mother lion.
    D. Protected from every threat, the mother lion was ready to defend her cubs every time one of them were threatened.

    10._____

11. A. Seatbelts, while unquestionably a good idea, it's sometimes a nuisance to use them.
    B. Seatbelts, while unquestionably a good idea, are sometimes a nuisance.
    C. Seatbelts are unquestionably a good idea and also they are sometimes a nuisance.
    D. Seatbelts, while it's unquestionably a good idea to have them, it's sometimes a nuisance to have them.

    11._____

12. A. While trimming the hedges, a bird's nest was discovered.
    B. He discovered a bird's nest trimming the hedges.
    C. Trimming the hedges, a bird's nest was discovered.
    D. As he was trimming the hedges, he discovered a bird's nest.

    12._____

13. A. Each person applying for a job must fill out a card listing his or her previous places of employment.
    B. Applying for a job, each person must fill out a card listing their previous places of employment.
    C. Listing his or her previous places of employment on a card, each person must do this when applying for a job.
    D. Each person, by filling out a card on which they list their previous places of employment, can apply for a job.

    13._____

14. A. A man, who's successful sets reasonable goals for himself.
    B. A man whose successful sets reasonable goals for himself.
    C. A man who's successful sets reasonable goals for himself.
    D. A man, whose successful sets reasonable goals for himself.

    14._____

15. A. I don't like hiking as much as I like cross-country skiing.
    B. I don't like to hike as much as I like cross-country skiing.
    C. I don't like hiking as much as I like to ski crosscountry.
    D. I don't like to hike as much as I like going crosscountry skiing.

    15._____

16. A. I wouldn't of gone if I had known about Emily.
    B. I wouldn't have gone if I had known about Emily.
    C. I wouldn't have went if I had known about Emily.
    D. I wouldn't of went if I had known about Emily.

    16._____

17. A. She planned a trip to the beach, a visit with her grandmother, and to take a long walk with her cousin.
    B. She planned to go to the beach, a visit with her grandmother, and a long walk with her cousin.
    C. She planned a trip to the beach, a visit with her grandmother, and a long walk with her cousin.
    D. She planned a trip to the beach, visiting with her grandmother, and to take a long walk with her cousin.

17.____

18. A. It is better to, I think, tell the truth than to lie.
    B. It is better to, I think, tell the truth than lying.
    C. Telling the truth, I think, is better than to lie.
    D. It is better, I think, to tell the truth than to lie.

18.____

19. A. He was not only a fine student but also a superior athlete.
    B. Not only was he a fine student but a superior athlete, also.
    C. He was not only a fine student but a superior athlete also.
    D. Also, he was not only a superior athlete, but a fine student.

19.____

20. A. Either Janice wanted to be student council president or valedictorian of her class.
    B. Janice either wanted to be student council president or class valedictorian.
    C. Janice wanted either to be president of student council or class valedictorian.
    D. Janice wanted to be either student council president or class valedictorian.

20.____

21. A. John having left school was without his father's permission.
    B. John left school without his fathers' permission.
    C. John left school without his father's permission.
    D. John having left school was without his father's permission.

21.____

22. A. Jane is the girl, who's purse was stolen.
    B. Jane is the girl whose purse was stolen.
    C. Jane is the girl who's purse was stolen.
    D. Jane is the girl, whose purse was stolen.

22.____

23. A. It's too bad that people are not more compassionate.
    B. Its to bad that people are not more compassionate.
    C. Its too bad that people are not more compassionate.
    D. It's to bad that people are not more compassionate.

23.____

24. A. The character who suffered the most was Laura.
    B. The character, which suffered the most, was Laura.
    C. The character which suffered the most was Laura.
    D. The character, who suffered the most, was Laura.

24.____

QUESTIONS 25-30
Questions 25-30 are based on the dictionary entry below.

of·fi'·cious *(o-fis h' us), adj.* (F. or L. ; F. *officieux;* fr. L. *officious.*) 1. *Obs.* Kind; obliging; dutiful. 2. Volunteering one's services where they are neither asked nor needed; meddlesome. 3. Of an informal or unauthorized nature; unofficial; as, an *officious* conversation. of·fi'cious·ly *adv.*

of·fi'cious·ness , *n.* Syn. Impertinent, imprudent, saucy, pert, cool

25. The expression "1., *Obs*. Kind; obliging; dutiful" means that

    A. at one time "officious" meant "kind"
    B. "officious" has a slang meaning
    C. a common meaning of "officious" is "kind"
    D. an important meaning of "officious" is "impertinent"

26. The vowel sound of the last syllable in "officious" is the same as the vowel sound in

    A. cute   B. loot   C. rub   D. ought

27. The expression "2. Volunteering one's services where they are neither asked nor needed; meddlesome" gives

    A. a meaning of "officious" as a verb
    B. a second meaning of "officious"
    C. an unusual meaning of "officious"
    D. an unauthorized meaning of "officious"

28. The expression "3. *Diplomacy.* Of an informal or unauthorized nature; unofficial ; as, an *officious* conversation" gives a meaning of "officious" which is

    A. authoritative   B. colloquial
    C. official   D. specialized

29. This entry suggests that today "officious"

    A. has a positive connotation
    B. can be used to mean "official"
    C. has almost no shades of meaning
    D. has a negative connotation

30. Which sentence BEST makes clear to a reader a current meaning of "officious"?

    A. How can you be so officious?
    B. He is a very officious person.
    C. Only an officious person would be so concerned with others' business.
    D. His kindness stamps him as one of the most officious people I know.

KEY (CORRECT ANSWERS)

1.	A		16.	B
2.	D		17.	C
3.	B		18.	D
4.	D		19.	A
5.	C		20.	D
6.	A		21.	C
7.	B		22.	B
8.	C		23.	A
9.	D		24.	A
10.	A		25.	A
11.	B		26.	C
12.	D		27.	B
13.	A		28.	D
14.	C		29.	D
15.	A		30.	C

EXAMINATION SECTION

TEST 1

DIRECTIONS: The questions that follow the paragraphs below are designed to test your appreciation of correctness and effectiveness of expression in English. The paragraphs are presented first in full so that you may read it through for sense. Disregard the errors you find as you will be asked to correct them in the questions that follow. The paragraphs are then presented sentence by sentence with portions underlined and numbered. At the end of this material, you will find numbers corresponding to those below the underlined portions, each followed by five alternatives lettered A, B, C, D, and E. In every case, the usage in the alternative lettered A is the same as that in the original paragraph and is followed by four possible usages. Choose the usage that you consider BEST in each case. *PRINT THE LETTER OF THE CORRECT ANSWER IN THE SPACE AT THE RIGHT.*

    The use of the machine produced up to the present time outstanding changes in our modern world. One of the most significant of these changes have been the marked decreases in the length of the working day and the working week. The fourteen-hour day not only has been reduced to one of ten hours but also, in some lines of work, to one of eight or even six. The trend toward a decrease is further evidenced in the longer weekend already given to employees in many business establishment. There seems also to be a trend toward shorter working weeks and longer summer vacations. An important feature of this development is that leisure is no longer the privilege of the wealthy few,—it has become the common right of most people. Using it wisely, leisure promotes health, efficiency and happiness, for there is time for each individual to live their own "more abundant life" and having opportunities for needed recreation.

    Recreation, like the name implies, is a process of revitalization. In giving expression to the play instincts of the human race, new vigor and effectiveness are afforded by recreation to the body and to the mind. Of course not all forms of amusement, by no means constitute recreation. Furthermore, an activity that provides recreation for one person may prove exhausting for another. Today, however, play among adults, as well as children, is regarded as a vital necessity of modern life. Play being recognized as an important factor in improving mental and physical health and thereby reducing human misery and poverty.

    Among the most important form of amusement available at the present time are the automobile, the moving picture, the radio, television, and organized sports. The automobile, especially, has been a boon to the American people, since it has been the chief means of them getting out into the open. The motion picture, the radio and television have tremendous opportunities to supply whole-some recreation and to promote cultural advancement. A criticism often leveled against organized sports as a means of recreation is because they make passive spectators of too many people. It has been said "that the American public is afflicted with "spectatoritis," but there is some recreational advantages to be gained even from being a spectator at organized games. Such sports afford a release from the monotony of daily toil, get people outdoors and also provide an exhilaration that is tonic in its effect.

2 (#1)

The chief concern, of course, should be to eliminate those forms of amusement that are socially undesirable. There are, however, far too many people who, we know, do not use their leisure to the best advantage. Sometime leisure leads to idleness, and idleness may lead to demoralization. The value of leisure both to the individual and to society will depend on the uses made of it.

The use of the machine <u>produced</u> up to the
                                     1

1.   A. produced   B. produces   C. has produced   1._____
       D. had produced   E. will have produced

present time many outstanding changes in our modern world. One of the most significant of these changes <u>have been</u> the marked
                                      2

2.   A. have been   B. was   C. were   2._____
       D. has been   E. will be

decreases in the length of the working day and the working week. <u>The fourteen-hour day not only has been reduced</u> to one of ten hours but also, in some lines of work, to one of eight or
         3
even six.

3.   A. The fourteen-hour day not only has been reduced   3._____
       B. Not only the fourteen-hour day has been reduced
       C. Not the fourteen-hour day only has been reduced
       D. The fourteen-hour day has not only been reduced

The trend toward a decrease is further evidenced in the longer week-end <u>already</u> given

4.   A. already   B. all ready   C. allready   4._____
       D. ready   E. all in all

to employees in many business establishments. There seems also to be a trend toward shorter working weeks and longer summer vacations. An important feature of this development is that leisure is no longer the privilege of the wealthy few<u>,—it</u> has become the common right of most people.

5.   A. ,—it   B. : it   C. ; it   5._____
       D. …it   E. omit punctuation

<u>Using it wisely</u>, leisure promotes health, efficiency, and happiness, for there is time for each
      6
individual to live <u>their</u> own "more abundant life" and <u>having</u> opportunities for needed recreation
                  7   8

6.   A. Using it wisely   B. If used wisely   6._____
       C. Having used it wisely   D. Because of its wise use
       E. Because of usefulness

3 (#1)

7. A. their   B. his   C. its   D. our   E. your   7.____

8. A. having   B. having had   C. to have   8.____
    D. to have had   E. had

Recreation, <u>like</u> the name implies, is a
           9

9. A. like   B. since   C. through   D. for   E. as   9.____

process of revitalization. In giving expression to the play instincts of the human race, <u>new vigor
and effectiveness are afforded by creation to the body and to the mind.</u>
                                10

10. A. new vigor and effectiveness are afforded by recreation to the body and to   10.____
       the mind
    B. recreation affords new vigor and effectiveness to the body and to the mind
    C. there are afforded new vigor and effectiveness to the body and to the mind
    D. by recreation the body and mind are afforded new vigor and effectiveness
    E. the body and the mind afford new vigor and effectiveness to themselves by
       recreation

Of course not all forms of amusement, <u>by no means,</u> constitute recreation. Furthermore, an
                                       11
activity that provides recreation for one person may prove exhausting for another. Today,
however, play among adults, as well as children is regarded as a vital necessity of modern life.

11. A. by no means   B. by those means   C. by some means   11.____
    D. by every means   E. by any means

<u>Play being recognized</u> as an important factor in improving mental and physical health and
        12
thereby reducing human misery and poverty.

12. A. . Play being recognized as   B. , by their recognizing play as   12.____
    C. . They recognizing play as   D. . Recognition of it being
    E. , for play is recognized as

Among the most important forms of amusement available at the present time are the
automobile, the moving picture, the radio, television, and organized sports. The automobile,
especially, has been a boon to the American people, since it has been the chief means of <u>them</u>
                                                                                          13
getting out into the open. The motion picture, the radio and television have tremendous
opportunities to supply wholesome recreation and to promote cultural advancement. A criticism
often leveled against organized

13. A. them   B. their   C. his   D. our   E. the people   13.____

sports as a means of recreation is <u>because</u> they make passive spectators of too many people.
                                                          14

14.   A. because   B. since   C. as   D. that   E. why   14.____

it has been said "<u>that</u> the American public is afflicted with "spectatoritis," but there <u>is</u> some
                      15   16
recreational advantages to be gained even from being a spectator at organized games.

15.   A. "that   B. "that"   C. that"   D. 'that   E. that   15.____

16.   A. is   B. was   C. are   D. were   E. will be   16.____

Such sports afford a release from the monotony of daily toil, get people outdoors and also provide an exhilaration that is tonic in its effect. The chief concern, of course, should be to eliminate those forms of amusement that are socially undesirable. There are, however, far too many people <u>who,</u> we know, do not use their leisure to the best advantage. Sometimes leisure
                                      17
leads to idleness, and idleness may lead to demoralization. The value of leisure both to the individual and to society will depend on the uses made of it.

17.   A. who   B. whom   C. which   D. such as   E. that which   17.____

KEY (CORRECT ANSWERS)

1.	C	11.	E
2.	D	12.	E
3.	E	13.	B
4.	A	14.	D
5.	C	15.	E
6.	B	16.	C
7.	B	17.	A
8.	C		
9.	E		
10.	B		

TEST 2

DIRECTIONS: The questions that follow the paragraphs below are designed to test your appreciation of correctness and effectiveness of expression in English. The paragraphs are presented first in full so that you may read it through for sense. Disregard the errors you find as you will be asked to correct them in the questions that follow. The paragraphs are then presented sentence by sentence with portions underlined and numbered. At the end of this material, you will find numbers corresponding to those below the underlined portions, each followed by five alternatives lettered A, B, C, D, and E. In every case, the usage in the alternative lettered A is the same as that in the original paragraph and is followed by four possible usages. Choose the usage that you consider BEST in each case. *PRINT THE LETTER OF THE CORRECT ANSWER IN THE SPACE AT THE RIGHT.*

    When this war is over, no nation will either be isolated in war or peace. Each will be within trading distance of all the others and will be able to strike them. Every nation will be most as dependent on the rest for the maintainance of peace as is any of our own American states on all the others. The world that we have known was a world made up of individual nations, each of which had the privilege of doing about as they pleased without being embarassed by outside interference. The world has dissolved before the impact of an invention, the airplane has done to our world what gunpowder did to the feudal world. Whether the coming century will be a period of further tragedy or one of peace and progress depend very largely on the wisdom and skill with which the present generation adjusts their thinking to the problems immediately at hand. Examining the principal movements sweeping through the world, it can be seen that they are being accelerated by the war. There is undoubtedly many of these whose courses will be affected for good or ill by the settlements that will follow the war. The United States will share the responsibility of these settlements with Russia, England and China. The influence of the United States, however, will be great. This country is likely to emerge from the war stronger than any other nation. Having benefitted by the absence of actual hostilities on our own soil, we shall probably be less exhausted that our allies and better able than them to help restore the devastated areas. However many mistakes have been made in our past, the tradition of America, not only the champion of freedom but also fair play, still lives among millions who can see light and hope scarcely nowhere else.

When this war is over, no nation will <u>either be isolated in war or peace.</u>
                                                 1

1. A. either be isolated in war or peace   1.____
   B. be either isolated in war or peace
   C. be isolated in neither war nor peace
   D. be isolated either in war or in peace
   E. be isolated neither in war or peace

   <u>Each</u> will be
     2

2. A. Each   B. It   C. Some   D. They   E. A nation   2.____

97

within trading distance of all others and will be able to strike them.
                    3

3. A. within trading distance of all the others and will be able to strike them   3.____
    B. near enough to trade with and strike all the others
    C. trading and striking the others
    D. within trading and striking distance of all the others
    E. able to strike and trade with all the others

Every nation will be most as dependent on

4. A. most   B. wholly   C. much   D. mostly   E. almost   4.____

the rest for the maintainance of peace as is
                  5

5. A. maintainance   B. maintainence   C. maintenence   5.____
    D. maintenance   E. maintanance

any of our own American states on all the others. The world that we have known as a world made up of individual nations, each
                                                                                   6

6. A. nations, each   B. nations. Each   C. nations: each   6.____
    D. nations; each   E. nations each

of which had the priviledge of doing about as
                        7

7. A. priviledge   B. priveledge   C. privelege   7.____
    D. privalege   E. privilege

they pleased without being
 8

8. A. they   B. it   C. they individually   8.____
    D. he   E. the nations

embarassed by outside interference. That
    9

9. A. embarassed   B. embarrassed   C. embaressed   9.____
    D. embarrased   E. embarrassed

world has dissolved before the impact of an invention, the airplane has done to our world what
                                                      10
gunpowder did to the feudal world. Whether the coming century will be a period of further tragedy or one of peace and

3 (#2)

10. A. invention, the B. invention but the C. invention: the   10.____
    D. invention. The E. invention and the

progress <u>depend</u> very largely on the wisdom and skill with which the present generation
        11

11. A. depend   B. will have depended C. depends   11.____
    D. depended   E. shall depend

<u>adjusts their</u> thinking to the problems immediately at hand.
   12

12. A. adjusts their   B. adjusts there   C. adjusts its   12.____
    D. adjust our   E. adjust it's

<u>Examining the principal movements sweeping through the world, it can be seen</u>
                      13

13. A. Examining the principal movements sweeping through the world, it can be   13.____
       seen
    B. Having examined the principal movements sweeping through the world, it
       can be seen
    C. Examining the principal movements sweeping through the world can be
       seen
    D. Examining the principal movements sweeping through the world, we can
       see
    E. It can be seen examining the principal movements sweeping through the
       world

that they are being <u>accelerated</u> by the war.
              14

14. A. accelerated   B. acelerated   C. accelerated   14.____
    D. acellerated   E. accelerated

There <u>is</u> undoubtedly many of these whose courses will be affected for good or ill by the
    15
settlements that will follow the war. The United States will share the responsibility of these
settlements with Russia, England and China. The influence of the United

15. A. is   B. were   C. was   D. are   E. might be

States, <u>however,</u> will be great. This country is likely to emerge from the war stronger than any
     16
other nation.

16. A. , however,   B. however,   C. , however   16.____
    D. however   E. ; however,

99

Having <u>benefitted</u> by the absence of actual hostilities on our own soil, we shall probably be
        17
less exhausted

17. A. benefitted   B. beniffited   C. benefited   17.____
    D. benifited   E. benafitted

than our allies and better able than <u>them</u> to help restore the devastated areas. However many
                                      18
mistakes have been made in our past, the tradition of America,

18. A. them   B. themselves   C. they   18.____
    D. the world   E. the nations

<u>not only the champion of freedom but also fair play,</u> still lives among millions who can
                    19

19. A. not only the champion of freedom but also fair play,   19.____
    B. the champion of not only freedom but also of fair play,
    C. the champion not only of freedom but also of fair play,
    D. not only the champion but also freedom and fair play,
    E. not the champion of freedom only, but also fair play,

see light and hope <u>scarcely nowhere else.</u>
                          20

20. A. scarcely nowhere else   B. elsewhere   20.____
    C. nowhere   D. scarcely anywhere else
    E. anywhere

KEY (CORRECT ANSWERS)

1.	D	11.	C
2.	A	12.	C
3.	D	13.	D
4.	E	14.	A
5.	D	15.	D
6.	A	16.	A
7.	E	17.	C
8.	B	18.	C
9.	B	19.	C
10.	D	20.	D

EXAMINATION SECTION
TEST 1

DIRECTIONS: On the basis of its use in the sentence, indicate the letter of the CORRECT or MOST NEARLY CORRECT grammatical description of the underlined expression in each of the following sentences. *PRINT THE LETTER OF THE CORRECT ANSWER IN THE SPACE AT THE RIGHT.*

1. Do you realize that the young man <u>now</u> addressing the audience is our principal?

    A. Adjective modifying *man*
    B. Adverb modifying a verb
    C. Adverb modifying a participle
    D. Preposition governing a gerund

2. <u>Their ammunition having been used up</u>, they were forced to retreat.

    A. Absolute phrase
    B. Phrase modifying *they*
    C. Adverbial phrase modifying *forced*
    D. Subordinate clause modifying *to retreat*

3. The wine tastes <u>sour</u>, if you are not accustomed to its flavor.

    A. Adverb
    B. Objective complement
    C. Predicate adjective
    D. Adjective modifying *flavor*

4. We asked <u>Dr. Jones</u> to be our sponsor.

    A. Object of *asked*
    B. Subject of *to be*
    C. In apposition with *sponsor*
    D. Indirect object

5. It was a night <u>when everything seemed enchanting</u>.

    A. Adverbial clause
    B. Adjective clause
    C. Participal phrase
    D. Noun clause in apposition with *night*

6. Although he has only a learner's permit, we let him <u>drive</u> to the camp.

    A. Infinitive
    B. Participle
    C. Gerund
    D. Predicate verb

7. His first contention, <u>that his group should be given preferential treatment</u>, was quickly disputed.

    A. Adjective clause modifying a noun
    B. Absolute construction
    C. Adverbial clause modifying an adjective
    D. Noun clause in apposition

8. *Notice Neptune, though,*
   Taming a sea-horse, thought a rarity,
   Which Claus of Innsbruck cast in bronze for me!

   A. Object of the verb
   B. Modifies the noun *sea-horse*
   C. Predicate verb
   D. Modifies the noun *Neptune*

9. *Let each new Temple, nobler than the last,*
   Shut thee from heaven with a dome more vast

   A. Participle   B. Infinitive
   C. Predicate verb   D. Adjective

10. *Beyond my window in the night*
    Is but a drab, inglorious street

    A. Pronoun   B. Preposition
    C. Conjunction   D. Adverb

11. *Are there no water-lilies, smooth as cream,*
    With long stems dripping crystal?

    A. Adjective modifying *stems*
    B. Object of the preposition *with*
    C. Adjective modifying *dripping*
    D. Object of *dripping*

12. *Pity me that the heart is slow to learn*
    What the swift mind beholds at every turn

    A. Adverbial clause containing a noun clause
    B. Noun clause containing an adjective clause
    C. Adjective clause containing an adjective clause
    D. Adjective clause containing a noun clause

13. *And I was filled with such delight*
    As prisoned birds must find in freedom

    A. Preposition   B. Conjunction
    C. Pronoun   D. Adverb

14. *And we are here as on a darkling plain*
    Swept with confused alarms of struggle and flight
    Where ignorant armies clash by night

    A. Adverbial clause modifying verb *are*
    B. Adjective clause modifying *flight*
    C. Adjective clause modifying *alarms*
    D. Adjective clause modifying *plain*

15. *Had I the heavens' embroidered cloths,*
    Enwrought with golden and silver light,
    The blue and the dim and the dark cloths
    Of night and light and the half-light,
    I would spread the cloths under your feet

    A. Absolute expression   B. Noun clause
    C. Adverbial clause   D. Independent clause

16. *Comrades, leave me here a <u>little</u>, while as yet 'tis early morn*

    A. Direct object   B. Adjective
    C. Adverb   D. Pronoun

17. *Yea, faileth now even <u>dream</u>*
    The dreamer, and the lute the lutanist

    A. Predicate verb   B. Subject of the verb
    C. Object of the verb D. Noun in direct address

18. There is a <u>but</u> attached to every statement he makes.

    A. Preposition   B. Relative pronoun
    C. Noun   D. Coordinating conjunction

19. The children were taught <u>that cleanliness is next to godliness</u>.

    A. Retained object   B. Predicate nominative
    C. Adjective clause D. Nominative absolute

20. His mother came home from the hospital the <u>day</u> before yesterday.

    A. Subject of the verb   B. Object of the verb
    C. Object of a preposition D. Adverbial objective

21. Let <u>us</u> go now that evening has come.

    A. Subject of infinitive   B. Subject of verb
    C. Object of preposition   D. Object of infinitive

22. Young people always talk of a time <u>when they will be rich</u>.

    A. Adjective clause B. Noun clause
    C. Adverbial clause D. Adverbial phrase

23. John Grove's attempt <u>to break</u> away from his family ended in failure.

    A. Modifies *John Grove* B. Subject of the verb
    C. Modifies *attempt*   D. Verb in dependent clause

24. Whatever <u>plans</u> we make now may have to be scrapped later.

    A. Nominative absolute B. Subject of a verb
    C. Object of a verb   D. Subject of an infinitive

25. Her face and hands were prematurely wrinkled from prolonged <u>tanning</u> at the beach.

    A. Participle   B. Infinitive
    C. Predicate verb D. Gerund

26. The teacher made the <u>very</u> mistake against which he had warned his pupils.

    A. Adverb
    B. Reflexive pronoun
    C. Adjective
    D. Noun in apposition

27. That red brick building at the end of the street is <u>where he works</u>.

    A. Adverbial phrase
    B. Adverbial clause
    C. Adjective clause
    D. Nominative clause

28. Our single and absorbing purpose now is <u>to complete</u> the spring planting.

    A. Modifier *of purpose*
    B. Objective complement
    C. Predicate nominative
    D. Subject of *is*

29. Tom's <u>seeing</u> his old enemy after a lapse of twenty years, during which he had no cause to retain his animosity, was no excuse for his uncontrolled behavior.

    A. Modifier of *enemy*
    B. Modifier of *he*
    C. Subject of main clause
    D. Nominative absolute

30. The teacher, having given each <u>pupil</u> an assignment, turned her attention to the visitor.

    A. Nominative absolute
    B. Indirect object
    C. Objective complement
    D. Direct object

31. The soup smelled so <u>good</u> that the children burned their tongues in their eagerness to taste it.

    A. Adverb of manner
    B. Noun used as an adjective
    C. Predicate adjective
    D. Retained object

32. On the table is where he left the purse.
    The subject of the above sentence is

    A. he
    B. on the table
    C. purse
    D. where he left the purse

33. He was glad <u>to go</u>.

    A. Adverb
    B. Adjective
    C. Appositive
    D. Predicate verb

34. When we finally found him, he was <u>but</u> half alive.

    A. Conjunction connecting subject and predicate
    B. Preposition introducing adverbial phrase *but half alive*
    C. Adverb modifying *half*
    D. Preposition governing pronoun *he*

35. He was awarded <u>the place I lost</u>.

    A. Object of *was awarded*
    B. Retained object
    C. Adverbial clause modifying *awarded*
    D. Indirect object

36. The parents named the child <u>Abraham</u> in the hope that he would develop the virtues and earn the affection of his grandfather.   36.____

   A. Direct object
   B. Predicate nominative
   C. Objective complement
   D. Object of an understood preposition

37. The decision, <u>unfortunately</u>, came too late.   37.____

   A. Adverb modifying the verb *came*
   B. Adverb modifying the adverb *too*
   C. Adverb modifying the adjective *late*
   D. Independent adverb

38. The building was old and dilapidated, a <u>condition</u> which made it necessary for us to close it.   38.____

   A. In apposition with the principal clause
   B. Subject of the subordinate clause
   C. Predicate nominative of the principal clause
   D. None of the above

39. There is not a school <u>but</u> is affected by this ruling.   39.____

   A. Adjective   B. Preposition
   C. Adverb   D. Pronoun

40. The speaker was unsatisfactory in many respects: <u>for instance</u>, he swallowed his words and wandered from the topic.   40.____

   A. Adverb modifying *swallowed*
   B. Conjunction
   C. Independent element
   D. Prepositional phrase

KEY (CORRECT ANSWERS)

1.	C	11.	D	21.	A	31.	C
2.	A	12.	A	22.	A	32.	B
3.	C	13.	C	23.	C	33.	A
4.	B	14.	D	24.	B	34.	C
5.	B	15.	C	25.	D	35.	B
6.	A	16.	C	26.	C	36.	C
7.	D	17.	B	27.	D	37.	D
8.	D	18.	C	28.	C	38.	A
9.	B	19.	A	29.	C	39.	D
10.	D	20.	D	30.	B	40.	B

TEST 2

DIRECTIONS: From the four answers listed below each of the following sentences, select the one which describes the syntax of the underlined part. *PRINT THE LETTER OF THE CORRECT ANSWER IN THE SPACE AT THE RIGHT.*

1. We planned to stay a <u>week</u> at Crawford Notch. 1.___

   A. Adverbial objective
   B. Object of *to stay*
   C. Object of *planned*
   D. None of the above

2. The proposition presented by Dan, <u>that no new member could run for office</u>, was voted down by the delegates. 2.___

   A. Adjective clause modifying *proposition*
   B. Noun clause, subject of *was voted*
   C. Noun clause in apposition with *proposition*
   D. Adverbial clause modifying *was voted*

3. The driver volunteered to take as many <u>as</u> wished to go. 3.___

   A. Adverb
   B. Conjunction
   C. Preposition
   D. Relative pronoun

4. Mr. Parker let us <u>see</u> his collection of antiques. 4.___

   A. Copulative verb
   B. Simple predicate
   C. Verb in (understood) subordinate clause
   D. Infinitive

5. The fickle mob wished to make Brutus <u>king</u>. 5.___

   A. Object of *wished*
   B. Object of *to make*
   C. Objective complement
   D. Retained object

6. <u>Being</u> new in town, he hesitated to speak out. 6.___

   A. Participle
   B. Nominative absolute
   C. Gerund
   D. Preposition

7. Though I wanted the victor to be <u>him</u>, I accepted her election without visible disappointment. 7.___

   A. Subject of *to be*
   B. Object of *wanted*
   C. Object of *to be*
   D. Predicate pronoun in agreement with *victor*

8. To err is human; <u>to forgive</u>, divine. 8.___

   A. Adverbial phrase
   B. Noun phrase
   C. Adjective phrase
   D. Elliptical clause

9. The teacher used <u>well</u> as five different parts of speech. 9.___

   A. Verb   B. Adverb   C. Noun   D. Adjective

10. The retiring president was given a watch by the club.   10.____
    A. Objective complement   B. Retained object
    C. Direct object   D. Predicate nominative

11. Were Ted and Bill voted the most popular officers the club ever had?   11.____
    A. Object of *were voted*
    B. Predicate nominative
    C. Subject in inverted sentence
    D. Object of *had*

12. Any man can be captain of his soul, be he king or commoner.   12.____
    A. Nominative absolute   B. Noun in apposition
    C. Predicate nominative   D. Subject

13. The secret agent telephoned me to come at once.   13.____
    A. Subject of infinitive   B. Retained object
    C. Direct object   D. Indirect object

14. However bad the weather may be, we shall have to fulfill our responsibilities.   14.____
    A. Independent element   B. Adverbial clause
    C. Noun clause in apposition D. Adjective modifier

15. The dean doesn't believe it any more than you.   15.____
    A. Object of *believe*
    B. Object of *than*
    C. Subject of elliptical clause
    D. In apposition with *it*

16. It was such a day as one rarely sees in this part of the country.   16.____
    A. Pronoun   B. Preposition
    C. Conjunction   D. Adverb

17. You had better not drive tonight on these icy roads.   17.____
    A. Main verb   B. Infinitive
    C. Imperative   D. Gerund

18. The door gunner of the helicopter aimed higher than on the first target sweep.   18.____
    A. Modifies *aimed*   B. Predicate adjective
    C. Part of connective phrase D. Adverbial objective

19. Take the money—there is no telling but you will need it.   19.____
    A. Clause in apposition   B. Independent clause
    C. Object of *telling*   D. Parenthetical element

20. On inspecting the accounts, the auditors found everything in good condition.   20.____
    A. Adjective modifier   B. Adverbial modifier
    C. Objective complement   D. Predicate nominative

21. Here there does seem to be, if not an absolute certainty, at least a real <u>possibility</u>. 21.____

    A. Subject
    B. Object of verb
    C. Predicate nominative
    D. Object of preposition

22. The unexpected visitors found the scientist <u>experimenting</u> with deadly bacilli. 22.____

    A. Gerund
    B. Participle
    C. Objective complement
    D. Main verb

23. The general made every effort to wrest from sure defeat victory and even the <u>spoils</u> of war. 23.____

    A. Object of the preposition
    B. Object of the infinitive
    C. In apposition with *victory*
    D. Objective complement

24. The puzzle remained impossible of solution, all our <u>efforts</u> notwithstanding. 24.____

    A. Predicate nominative
    B. Subject of subordinate clause
    C. Object of *notwithstanding*
    D. Parenthetical phrase

25. Completely <u>irreconcilable</u> were the viewpoints expressed by the board. 25.____

    A. Subject of the sentence
    B. Predicate noun
    C. Predicate adjective
    D. Modifies *completely*

26. <u>Why our military forces might not be equal to the test</u> none of us truly comprehends. 26.____

    A. Noun clause as subject
    B. Introductory adverbial clause
    C. In apposition with *none*
    D. Object of *comprehends*

27. Giving the manager a blank <u>look</u>, the salesman took his leave. 27.____

    A. Object of the gerund
    B. Object of the participle
    C. Object of the sentence
    D. Indirect object

28. The defendant chose an outstanding attorney as his <u>lawyer</u>. 28.____

    A. Subject of elliptical clause
    B. Objective complement
    C. Object of preposition
    D. Direct object

29. <u>For</u> the guests to leave early was a serious mistake. 29.____

    A. Subordinating conjunction
    B. Preposition governing *guests*
    C. Expletive
    D. Preposition governing *to leave*

30. I am very happy that you have reached the decision you have.   30._____

    A. Noun clause
    B. Adjective clause
    C. Adverbial clause
    D. Appositive

31. The speeding motorist was ordered to appear in court.   31._____

    A. Retained object
    B. Direct object of *was ordered*
    C. Complementary infinitive
    D. Modifies *was ordered*

32. The principal preoccupation was eavesdropping on the conversation of others.   32._____

    A. Gerund
    B. Participle
    C. Progressive form of verb
    D. Objective complement

33. His fumbling attempts to prove his point seemed pathetic.   33._____

    A. Prepositional phrase
    B. Noun phrase
    C. Adjective phrase
    D. Subject of *seemed*

34. The stone image of the God stood tall on the hill.   34._____

    A. Adjective
    B. Adverb
    C. Predicate nominative
    D. Object of the verb

35. After a stormy session, the men elected John their spokesman.   35._____

    A. Retained object
    B. Direct object
    C. Nominative absolute
    D. Objective complement

36. Although it almost cost him his life, the boy was true to his promise.   36._____
    Prepositional phrase used as a(n)

    A. adjective
    B. adverb
    C. noun in apposition
    D. predicate nominative

37. The children were shown pictures of the various birds of the region.   37._____

    A. Retained object
    B. Objective complement
    C. Direct object
    D. Predicate nominative

38. After dinner each evening, he wrote his son a letter.   38._____

    A. Indirect object
    B. Predicate noun
    C. Direct object
    D. Adverbial objective

39. We believed her to be the woman of whom you spoke.   39._____

    A. Object of verb *believed*
    B. Subject of infinitive *to be*
    C. Pronoun in apposition with *whom*
    D. Object of infinitive *to be*

40. I saw the car hit the dog.   40._____

    A. Infinitive
    B. Participle
    C. Predicate verb
    D. Gerund

KEY (CORRECT ANSWERS)

1.	A	11.	B	21.	A	31.	A
2.	C	12.	D	22.	B	32.	A
3.	D	13.	D	23.	B	33.	C
4.	D	14.	B	24.	C	34.	A
5.	C	15.	C	25.	C	35.	D
6.	A	16.	A	26.	D	36.	B
7.	D	17.	B	27.	B	37.	A
8.	B	18.	A	28.	B	38.	C
9.	C	19.	C	29.	D	39.	B
10.	B	20.	C	30.	C	40.	A

EXAMINATION SECTION
TEST 1

DIRECTIONS: From the choices listed below each of the following sentences, select the one which describes the syntax of the underlined part of the sentence. *PRINT THE LETTER OF THE CORRECT ANSWER IN THE SPACE AT THE RIGHT.*

1. After much urging for instructional materials, he gave us enough books <u>to distribute to our class</u>.   1._____

    A. Infinitive phrase used as a substantive
    B. Gerund phrase used as a substantive
    C. Prepositional phrase used as an adjective
    D. Infinitive phrase used as an adjective

2. Did they give the <u>boys</u> the scholarships?   2._____

    A. Indirect object
    B. Direct object
    C. Retained object
    D. Subject of sentence

3. Mrs. Dutton admits that England went through forty lean years <u>when food shortages were hard on British cuisine</u>.   3._____

    A. Adverbial clause
    B. Adverbial objective
    C. Adjective clause
    D. None of the above

4. It is a glorious form of excitement <u>to become a lion</u> without the tedium of being a lion cub.   4._____

    A. Infinitive in apposition with *being a lion cub*
    B. Infinitive phrase in apposition with *it*
    C. Infinitive modifying *excitement*
    D. Predicate nominative

5. <u>Released</u> on parole, Cook spent his remaining years lecturing.   5._____

    A. Participle modifying the subject
    B. Predicate verb
    C. Gerund
    D. Adjective

6. <u>Whatever you cannot understand</u>, you cannot possess.   6._____

    A. Noun clause, subject
    B. Noun clause, object
    C. Noun clause, predicate nominative
    D. None of the above

7. What Pythagorean discipline will ring from discord, <u>harmony</u>?   7._____

    A. Object of preposition *from*
    B. Appositive of *discord*
    C. Direct object of *ring*
    D. Nominative by direct address

111

8. The women looked so <u>attractive</u> in their Easter bonnets.   8.____

   A. Direct object
   B. Retained object
   C. Predicate noun
   D. Predicate adjective

9. He has no thought but to <u>succeed</u>.   9.____

   A. Verb of elliptical clause
   B. Object of preposition
   C. Apposition with *thought*
   D. Modifies *thought*

10. It is true <u>that he is not coming to school</u>.   10.____

    A. Adverbial clause modifying *true*
    B. Noun clause after *is*
    C. Noun clause used as objective complement
    D. Noun clause in apposition with *it*

11. The incumbent had been elected <u>president</u> because he was able to capture the votes of the industrial states.   11.____

    A. Predicate noun
    B. Direct object
    C. Objective complement
    D. Retained object

12. Here you should lie, ye <u>Kings</u> of old.   12.____

    A. Subject of *should lie*
    B. Direct object of *should lie*
    C. Nominative by direct address
    D. None of the above

13. His word portraits make the men <u>heroes</u>.   13.____

    A. Object of *to be* (understood)
    B. Direct object of *make*
    C. Retained object
    D. Objective complement

14. There was much tension in the air <u>that we could not relax</u>.   14.____
    Modifies

    A. *was*   B. *air*   C. *such*   D. *tension*

15. He went home, <u>for</u> his father had sent for him.   15.____

    A. Preposition
    B. Conjunction
    C. Expletive
    D. Appositive

16. The pitcher made the <u>batter</u> hit the ball.   16.____

    A. Subject of *hit*
    B. Direct object of *made*
    C. Retained object
    D. Indirect object of *made*

17. The paths of glory lead <u>but</u> to the grave.   17.____

    A. Relative pronoun
    B. Coordinate conjunction
    C. Adverb
    D. Preposition

18. His <u>decision</u> having been made, the President called for an itinerary for his trip.   18._____

    A. Subject of clause   B. Subject of sentence
    C. Objective noun   D. Nominative absolute

19. That <u>there</u> are threats to freedom in some types of planning cannot be gainsaid.   19._____

    A. Subject of *are*   B. Expletive
    C. Adverb   D. None of the above

20. He was urged <u>to leave</u>.   20._____

    A. Adjective phrase   B. Predicate complement
    C. Direct object   D. Retained object

21. She asks <u>us</u> to stop and consider.   21._____

    A. Subject of infinitive
    B. Direct object of verb
    C. Object of preposition understood
    D. None of the above

22. There was once a city <u>on the outskirts</u> of which lay a pestilential morass.   22._____
    Modifies

    A. *city*   B. *which*   C. *lay*   D. *morass*

23. <u>There</u> is no sugar left in the bowl.   23._____

    A. Expletive   B. Subject of *is*
    C. Adverb of place   D. Predicate adjective

24. If you decide to deliver a speech, please make it <u>brief</u>.   24._____

    A. Adverb modifying
    B. Objective complement
    C. Adjective modifying *speech*
    D. Predicate adjective

25. In the recent election, he was chosen <u>mayor</u> for a second time.   25._____

    A. Objective complement   B. Object of verb *was chosen*
    C. Predicate nominative   D. Noun in apposition with *he*

26. Here is such money <u>as</u> I have.   26._____

    A. Conjunction   B. Relative pronoun
    C. Preposition   D. Adverb

27. I am not able to walk another <u>mile</u> today.   27._____

    A. Object of infinitive *to walk*
    B. Adverbial objective
    C. Indirect object
    D. Objective complement

28. They judged him guilty, the evidence to the contrary <u>notwithstanding</u>.

    A. Present participle   B. Adverb
    C. Adjective   D. Preposition

29. <u>Provided</u> you follow this diet carefully, you can expect to lose weight gradually.

    A. Past participle   B. Preposition
    C. Conjunction   D. Verb

30. <u>All</u> told, there were twelve textbooks and five magazines for the entire class.

    A. Subject of clause
    B. Nominative absolute
    C. Adverb modifying *told*
    D. Adjective modifying *facts* (understood)

31. <u>To believe such a strange tale</u> was more than we were able to do.

    A. Noun clause   B. Noun phrase
    C. Prepositional phrase   D. Infinitive clause

32. None <u>but</u> the brave deserve the fair.

    A. Subordinating conjunction
    B. Adversative conjunction
    C. Preposition
    D. Relative pronoun

33. It was clear to all of us <u>that he was not telling the truth</u>.

    A. Adjective clause
    B. Participal phrase
    C. Adverbial clause
    D. Clause in apposition with *it*

34. My homework <u>will have been completed</u> before you return. Verb– _____ voice, _____ tense.

    A. active; future   B. active; future perfect
    C. passive; future   D. passive; future perfect

35. I was given a wrist <u>watch</u> on my sixteenth birthday.

    A. Direct object   B. Retained object
    C. Predicate nominative   D. Indirect object

36. I like TOM SAWYER better than <u>HUCKLEBERRY FINN</u>.

    A. Object of *than*
    B. Object in a dependent clause
    C. Subject of verb (understood)
    D. Noun grammatically coordinate with *TOM SAWYER*

37. <u>My mind being made up</u>, I sent in my resignation.

    A. Predicate nominative
    B. Nominative of direct address

C. Nominative absolute
D. Subject in a causal clause

38. He failed to reach financial success, <u>notwithstanding</u> his own efforts and his family's.   38.____

    A. Gerund   B. Preposition
    C. Conjunctive adverb   D. Participle

39. After all there is no one <u>but</u> has his faults.   39.____

    A. Coordinating conjunction   B. Adverb
    C. Pronoun   D. Subordinating conjunction

40. The time has come <u>when we must begin to think about Christmas shopping</u>.   40.____

    A. Adverbial clause
    B. Adjective clause
    C. Noun clause in apposition with *time*
    D. Noun clause used as an objective complement

KEY (CORRECT ANSWERS)

1.	D	11.	A	21.	A	31.	B
2.	A	12.	C	22.	C	32.	C
3.	C	13.	D	23.	A	33.	D
4.	B	14.	C	24.	B	34.	D
5.	A	15.	B	25.	C	35.	B
6.	B	16.	A	26.	B	36.	B
7.	C	17.	C	27.	B	37.	C
8.	D	18.	D	28.	D	38.	B
9.	B	19.	B	29.	C	39.	C
10.	D	20.	D	30.	B	40.	B

TEST 2

DIRECTIONS: From the choices listed below each of the following sentences, select the one which describes the syntax of the underlined part of the sentence. *PRINT THE LETTER OF THE CORRECT ANSWER IN THE SPACE AT THE RIGHT.*

1. The new assistant was made <u>director</u> of visual aids.   1.___

   A. Predicate noun
   B. Retained object
   C. Objective complement
   D. Indirect object

2. The <u>series</u> won, they settled down to a real winter vacation in the South.   2.___

   A. Subject of the verb *won*
   B. Noun in direct address
   C. Adverbial objective
   D. Nominative absolute

3. I was given a complete description and <u>explanation</u> of the situation by the principal.   3.___

   A. Predicate noun
   B. Object of a preposition
   C. Retained object
   D. Indirect object

4. The effects of the blast extended a hundred <u>miles</u> from its center.   4.___

   A. Adverbial objective
   B. Object of the verb *extended*
   C. Predicate noun
   D. Indirect object

5. Every move he made was <u>in defiance</u> of an order.   5.___

   A. Adverbial phrase modifying *made*
   B. Prepositional phrase used as predicate adjective
   C. Prepositional phrase, object of *made*
   D. Prepositional phrase modifying *order*

6. Whoever excelled in any art or science was sure to be regarded by him <u>as</u> a rival.   6.___

   A. Relative pronoun
   B. Subordinating conjunction
   C. Preposition
   D. Coordinating conjunction

7. I looked at my wrist watch or held it to my ear every few minutes, wondering <u>why it moved so slowly</u>.   7.___

   A. Noun clause
   B. Adverbial clause of cause
   C. Adjective clause modifying *reason*
   D. Coordinate clause

8. There was no one in the school <u>but</u> wished success to the brave child with such a handicap.   8.___

   A. Conjunction connecting coordinate clauses
   B. Conjunctive adverb
   C. Preposition
   D. Relative pronoun

9. Did the City Council grant the Transit Commission control over fare rises? 9.____

   A. Object of the verb *did grant*
   B. Objective complement
   C. Indirect object
   D. Adverbial objective

10. Teenage exuberance sometimes makes adults lose their patience. 10.____

    A. Object of the verb *makes*
    B. Subject of the infinitive *lose*
    C. Subject of the predicate verb *lose*
    D. Indirect object

11. Don't you think this fabric is several shades too dark? 11.____

    A. Noun in opposition with *fabric*
    B. Predicate noun
    C. Adverbial adjective
    D. Cognate object

12. He has a job to do and the spirit to do it well. 12.____

    A. Infinitive phrase with *spirit* as its subject
    B. Object of the verb *has*
    C. Objective complement
    D. Infinitive phrase modifying *spirit*

13. We know him to be undisputed master of the new technique. 13.____

    A. Object of *know*
    B. In apposition with *master*
    C. Subject of the infinitive
    D. Object of the infinitive

14. That music is for such as like mere novelty. 14.____

    A. Subordinating conjunction
    B. Relative pronoun
    C. Preposition introducing noun clause
    D. Conjunctive adverb

15. I shall give the paper to whomever you designate as your representative. 15.____

    A. Object of *designate*   B. Object of *give*
    C. Indirect object   D. Subject of *designate*

16. We never did know where we were going. 16.____

    A. Adverbial conjunction   B. Direct object
    C. Coordinating conjunction   D. D. Adverb

17. The corn grew tall and plentiful. 17.____

    A. Modified *grew*   B. Predicate adverb
    C. Predicate adjective   D. Part of prepositional phrase

18. <u>All</u> that a man owns will he give for his life.

    A. Subject of *owns*
    B. Object of *will give*
    C. In apposition with *that*
    D. Subject of *will give*

19. He is a year older, but I am an <u>inch</u> taller.

    A. Predicate adjective
    B. Predicate noun
    C. Modifies *taller*
    D. Adverbial objective

20. He was asked by the reporters <u>whether he would plead the Fifth Amendment</u>.

    A. Predicate adjective
    B. Predicate nominative
    C. Adverbial clause
    D. Retained object

21. He would take orders from no one but his <u>counselor</u> at camp.

    A. Subject of verb in an elliptical clause
    B. Object of *but*
    C. Object of *from*
    D. Object of verb in an elliptical clause

22. He likes Alfred better than <u>me</u>.

    A. Object of verb in elliptical clause
    B. Object of preposition
    C. Indirect object
    D. Objective complement

23. Did anyone so lavish a gift <u>as</u> Patrick?

    A. Relative pronoun, subject of verb understood
    B. Relative adverb
    C. Preposition governing *Patrick*
    D. Coordinating conjunction

24. These are the times <u>when all citizens must unite in the</u> common cause.

    A. Adverbial clause modifying *are*
    B. Noun clause in apposition with *times*
    C. Adverbial clause modifying the entire sentence
    D. Adjective clause modifying *times*

25. He became a concert <u>pianist</u> despite the handicap of an amputated right arm.

    A. Noun, object of verb
    B. Objective complement after verb *became*
    C. Predicate nominative
    D. Cognate object

26. Were you informed <u>that he was to be the new principal</u>?

    A. Object of verb *were informed*
    B. Retained object
    C. Adverbial clause
    D. Clause used as predicate nominative

27. Mr. Collins grew more and more <u>indignant</u> as he listened to the demagogue. 27._____

   A. Predicate adjective
   B. Adverb modifying the verb *grew*
   C. Appositive adjective
   D. Objective complement

28. <u>The</u> *better to see you with, my child,* said the wolf. 28._____

   A. Article
   B. Adjective modifying noun (understood)
   C. Adverb modifying *better*
   D. Adjective modifying *better*

29. Copernicus could not achieve great accuracy in his calculations, <u>instruments</u> still being at the time rather crudely constructed. 29._____

   A. Subject of participle
   B. Subject of subordinate clause
   C. Object of verb *constructed*
   D. Nominative absolute

30. *I declare <u>you</u>, my son, to be heir to my kingdom,* intoned the monarch. 30._____

   A. Object of *declare*
   B. Subject of *to be*
   C. In apposition to *my son*
   D. In apposition to *heir*

Questions 31-36.

DIRECTIONS: From the lettered choices given, select the one that identifies the nature of the error in grammar or in usage (if any) in the given sentence.

31. You might well have added that such indifference to the civic duty of voting is not confined only to the ignorant, but may be found even among the best educated of our citizenry. 31._____

   A. Wrong tense of verb
   B. Error in punctuation
   C. Misplaced modifier
   D. Use of superfluous word

32. Hamlet pretended madness, for he believed that by assuming an "antic disposition" the new king's guilt would more readily reveal itself. 32._____

   A. Incorrect sequence of tenses
   B. Dangling phrase
   C. Mistake in tense
   D. Misplaced modifier

33. To me, who have spent so many years in the cause of better education for our youth, the community's apparent indifference to our schools seems particularly reprehensible. 33._____

   A. Lack of agreement between subject and verb in the main clause
   B. Lack of agreement between subject and verb in the subordinate clause
   C. Faulty pronominal reference
   D. Correct

34. Everything had been taken care of: the rooms made ready, the materials provided, and the teachers properly trained for administering the tests.

    A. Lack of parallelism
    B. Incorrect punctuation
    C. Essential auxiliary verbs omitted
    D. Correct

35. He committed so many blunders during his campaign tour that his campaign manager curtailed the trip lest he be further embarrassed by his statements.

    A. Confused pronominal reference
    B. Incorrect mood
    C. Incorrect tense
    D. Correct

36. What angers me particularly, when I visit the classrooms in this school, are the frequent repetitions of the same errors.

    A. Subject of main verb misplaced
    B. Misplaced modifier
    C. Disagreement of subject and verb
    D. Correct

Questions 37-40.

DIRECTIONS: From each of the following groups of four items, indicate in the space at the right the letter of the CORRECT or MOST NEARLY CORRECT expression to complete each sentence.

37. In the phrase, *The more, the merrier*, the syntax of the word *the* is a(n)

    A. adverb
    B. expletive
    C. article
    D. preposition

38. In the sentence, *Despite the page's bantering manner, his story rang true*, the verb is

    A. transitive
    B. copulative
    C. passive
    D. unidiomatic

39. In the sentence, *Looking out of the plane window, we marvelled at the beauty of the flashing neon signs which gave me the impression of living jewels against a background of black velvet,*

    A. *beauty* is the object of the verb *marvelled at*
    B. *me* is an indirect object
    C. *impression* is an indirect object
    D. *velvet* is the object of the preposition *against*

40. In an English sentence, grammatical meaning

    A. cannot be expressed unless it contains a subject and predicate
    B. is essentially dependent on its noun and verb inflections
    C. depends largely on word order
    D. is essentially noun-centered

40. In an English sentence, grammatical meaning
    A. cannot be expressed unless it contains a subject and predicate
    B. is essentially dependent on its noun and verb inflections
    C. depends largely on word order
    D. is essentially noun-centered

KEY (CORRECT ANSWERS)

1. A	11. C	21. B	31. D
2. D	12. D	22. A	32. B
3. C	13. C	23. A	33. D
4. A	14. B	24. D	34. D
5. B	15. A	25. C	35. A
6. C, B	16. A	26. B	36. C
7. A	17. C	27. A	37. A
8. D	18. B	28. C	38. B
9. C	19. D	29. D	39. B
10. B	20. D	30. B	40. C

PREPARING WRITTEN MATERIAL

PARAGRAPH REARRANGEMENT
COMMENTARY

The sentences that follow are in scrambled order. You are to rearrange them in proper order and indicate the letter choice containing the correct answer at the space at the right.

Each group of sentences in this section is actually a paragraph presented in scrambled order. Each sentence in the group has a place in that paragraph; no sentence is to be left out. You are to read each group of sentences and decide upon the best order in which to put the sentences so as to form a well-organized paragraph.

The questions in this section measure the ability to solve a problem when all the facts relevant to its solution are not given.

More specifically, certain positions of responsibility and authority require the employee to discover connection between events sometimes, apparently, unrelated. In order to do this, the employee will find it necessary to correctly infer that unspecified events have probably occurred or are likely to occur. This ability becomes especially important when action must be taken on incomplete information.

Accordingly, these questions require competitors to choose among several suggested alternatives, each of which presents a different sequential arrangement of the events. Competitors must choose the MOST logical of the suggested sequences.

In order to do so, they may be required to draw on general knowledge to infer missing concepts or events that are essential to sequencing the given events. Competitors should be careful to infer only what is essential to the sequence. The plausibility of the wrong alternatives will always require the inclusion of unlikely events or of additional chains of events which are NOT essential to sequencing the given events.

It's very important to remember that you are looking for the best of the four possible choices, and that the best choice of all may not even be one of the answers you're given to choose from.

There is no one right way to solve these problems. Many people have found it helpful to first write out the order of the sentences, as they would have arranged them, on their scrap paper before looking at the possible answers. If their optimum answer is there, this can save them some time. If it isn't, this method can still give insight into solving the problem. Others find it most helpful to just go through each of the possible choices, contrasting each as they go along. You should use whatever method feels comfortable and works for you.

While most of these types of questions are not that difficult, we've added a higher percentage of the difficult type, just to give you more practice. Usually there are only one or two questions on this section that contain such subtle distinctions that you're unable to answer confidently. And you then may find yourself stuck deciding between two possible choices, neither of which you're sure about.

EXAMINATION SECTION
TEST 1

DIRECTIONS: Each group of sentences in this section is actually a paragraph presented in scrambled order. Each sentence in the group has a place in that paragraph; no sentence is to be left out. You are to read each group of sentences, so as to form a well-organized paragraph. Before trying to answer the questions which follow each group of sentences, jot down the correct order of the sentences. Then answer each of the questions by printing the letter of the correct answer in the space at the right. Remember that you will receive credit only for answers marked.

P. The infant only feels the positive stimulation of warmth and food and does not differentiate the warmth and food from their source, mother.
Q. The infant, at the moment of birth, would feel the fear of dying if gracious fate did not preserve it from any awareness of the anxiety involved in the separation from mother.
R. The infant's state, then, is what has been called narcissism.
S. Mother is warmth, mother is food, mother is the euphoric state of satisfaction and security.
T. Even after being born, the infant is not yet aware of itself, and of the world as being outside of itself.

1. Which sentence did you put before Sentence Q? 1._____

    A. P
    B. R
    C. S
    D. T
    E. None of the above. Sentence Q is first.

2. Which sentence did you put after Sentence S? 2._____

    A. P
    B. Q
    C. R
    D. T
    E. None of the above. Sentence S is last.

3. Which sentence did you put before Sentence P? 3._____

    A. Q
    B. R
    C. S
    D. T
    E. None of the above. Sentence P is first.

4. Which sentence did you put after Sentence P?

   A. Q
   B. R
   C. S
   D. T
   E. None of the above. Sentence P is last.

5. Which sentence did you put after Sentence R?

   A. P
   B. Q
   C. S
   D. T
   E. None of the above. Sentence R is last.

KEY (CORRECT ANSWERS)

1. E
2. C
3. D
4. C
5. E

TEST 2

DIRECTIONS: Each group of sentences in this section is actually a paragraph presented in scrambled order. Each sentence in the group has a place in that paragraph; no sentence is to be left out. You are to read each group of sentences, so as to form a well-organized paragraph. Before trying to answer the questions which follow each group of sentences, jot down the correct order of the sentences. Then answer each of the questions by printing the letter of the correct answer in the space at the right. Remember that you will receive credit only for answers marked.

P. Then it requires knowledge and effort.
Q. The former is my view.
R. Or is love a pleasant sensation, something one *falls into* if one is lucky?
S. The majority of people today, however, believe in the latter.
T. Is love an art?

1. Which sentence did you put second?

   A. P B. Q C. R D. S E. T

2. Which sentence did you put after Sentence S?

   A. P
   B. Q
   C. R
   D. T
   E. None of the above. Sentence S is last.

3. Which sentence did you put before Sentence Q?

   A. P
   B. R
   C. S
   D. T
   E. None of the above. Sentence Q is first.

4. Which sentence did you put before Sentence P?

   A. Q
   B. R
   C. S
   D. T
   E. None of the above. Sentence P is first.

5. Which sentence did you put after Sentence Q?

   A. P
   B. R
   C. S
   D. T
   E. None of the above. Sentence Q is last.

KEY (CORRECT ANSWERS)

1. A
2. E
3. B
4. D
5. C

TEST 3

DIRECTIONS: Each group of sentences in this section is actually a paragraph presented in scrambled order. Each sentence in the group has a place in that paragraph; no sentence is to be left out. You are to read each group of sentences, so as to form a well-organized paragraph. Before trying to answer the questions which follow each group of sentences, jot down the correct order of the sentences. Then answer each of the questions by printing the letter of the correct answer in the space at the right. Remember that you will receive credit only for answers marked.

P. Indeed, in his time, Freud's theories of sex had a challenging and revolutionary character.
Q. Sexual mores have changed so much that Freud's theories no longer are shocking to the middle classes.
R. Freud has been criticized for his overevaluation of sex.
S. But what was true sixty years ago is no longer true.
T. This criticism resulted from a wish to remove an element from Freud's system which might arouse criticism among conventionally-minded people.

1. Which sentence did you put last?
   A. P   B. Q   C. R   D. S   E. T

2. Which sentence did you put before Sentence Q?
   A. P
   B. R
   C. S
   D. T
   E. None of the above. Sentence Q is first.

3. Which sentence did you put after Sentence T?
   A. P
   B. Q
   C. R
   D. S
   E. None of the above. Sentence T is last.

4. Which sentence did you put before Sentence R?
   A. P
   B. Q
   C. S
   D. T
   E. None of the above. Sentence R is first.

5. Which sentence did you put after Sentence R?
   A. P
   B. Q
   C. S
   D. T
   E. None of the above. Sentence R is last.

KEY (CORRECT ANSWERS)

1. B
2. C
3. A
4. E
5. D

TEST 4

DIRECTIONS: Each group of sentences in this section is actually a paragraph presented in scrambled order. Each sentence in the group has a place in that paragraph; no sentence is to be left out. You are to read each group of sentences, so as to form a well-organized paragraph. Before trying to answer the questions which follow each group of sentences, jot down the correct order of the sentences. Then answer each of the questions by printing the letter of the correct answer in the space at the right. Remember that you will receive credit only for answers marked.

P. Early Scandanavian accounts, as well, are too mythological and legendary to serve as history.
Q. The first trustworthy written evidence of a kingdom of Denmark belongs to the beginning of the Viking period.
R. Ancient Roman knowledge of this remote country was fragmentary and unreliable.
S. Archaeology and the study of place names, however, provide a certain amount of information about the earliest settlements.
T. Everything before that is prehistory.

1. Which sentence did you put fourth?
   A. P   B. B. Q   C. C. R   D. D. S   E. E. T

2. Which sentence did you put after Sentence T?
   A. Q
   B. R
   C. S
   D. None of the above. Sentence T is last.

3. Which sentence did you put after Sentence Q?
   A. P
   B. R
   C. S
   D. T
   E. None of the above. Sentence Q is last.

4. Which sentence did you put before Sentence Q?
   A. P
   B. R
   C. S
   D. T
   E. None of the above. Sentence Q is first.

5. Which sentence did you put after Sentence P?
   A. Q
   B. R
   C. S
   D. T
   E. None of the above. Sentence P is last.

KEY (CORRECT ANSWERS)

1. A
2. C
3. D
4. E
5. C

TEST 5

DIRECTIONS: Each group of sentences in this section is actually a paragraph presented in scrambled order. Each sentence in the group has a place in that paragraph; no sentence is to be left out. You are to read each group of sentences, so as to form a well-organized paragraph. Before trying to answer the questions which follow each group of sentences, jot down the correct order of the sentences. Then answer each of the questions by printing the letter of the correct answer in the space at the right. Remember that you will receive credit only for answers marked.

P. In 1268, ambassadors were required to surrender all gifts they had received on their missions.
Q. In the 13th century, the Venetian republic began to lay down rules of conduct for its ambassadors.
R. In 1288, it was decreed that ambassadors were to report in writing on the results of their missions.
S. Such reports are a mine of historical material.
T. It is in Venice that the origins of modern diplomacy are to be sought.

1. Which sentence did you put second?

   A. P   B. Q   C. R   D. S   E. T

2. Which sentence did you put after Sentence R?

   A. P
   B. Q
   C. S
   D. T
   E. None of the above. Sentence R is last.

3. Which sentence did you put before Sentence P?

   A. Q
   B. R
   C. S
   D. T
   E. None of the above. Sentence P is first.

4. Which sentence did you put before Sentence T?

   A. P
   B. Q
   C. R
   D. S
   E. None of the above. Sentence T is first.

5. Which sentence did you put last?

   A. P   B. B. Q   C. C. R   D. D. S   E. E. T

KEY (CORRECT ANSWERS)

1. B
2. C
3. A
4. E
5. D

TESTS IN SENTENCE COMPLETION / 1 BLANK
EXAMINATION SECTION
TEST 1

DIRECTIONS: Each question in this section consists of a sentence in which one word is missing; a blank line indicates where the word has been removed from the sentence. Beneath each sentence are five words, *one* of which is the missing word. You are to select the letter of the missing word by deciding which one of the five words BEST fits in with the meaning of the sentence. *PRINT THE LETTER OF THE CORRECT ANSWER IN THE SPACE AT THE RIGHT.*

1. A man who cannot win honor in his own _____ will have a very small chance of winning it from posterity.   1.____

   A. right   B. field   C. country   D. way   E. age

2. The latent period for the contractile response to direct stimulation of the muscle has quite another and shorte value, encompassing only a utilization period. Hence it is that the term *latent period* must be _____ carefully each time that it is used.   2.____

   A. checked   B. timed   C. introduced
   D. defined   E. selected

3. Many television watchers enjoy stories which contain violence. Consequently those television producers who are dominated by rating systems aim to _____ the popular taste.   3.____

   A. raise   B. control   C. gratify   D. ignore   E. lower

4. No other man loses so much, so _____, so absolutely, as the beaten candidate for high public office.   4.____

   A. bewilderingly   B. predictably   C. disgracefully
   D. publicly   E. cheerfully

5. Mathematics is the product of thought operating by means of _____ for the purpose of expressing general laws.   5.____

   A. reasoning   B. symbols   C. words
   D. examples   E. science

6. Deductive reasoning is that form of reasoning in which the conclusion must necessarily follow if we accept the premise as true. In deduction, it is _____ the premise to be true and the conclusion false.   6.____

   A. impossible   B. inevitable   C. reasonable
   D. surprising   E. unlikely

7. Because in the administration it hath respect not to the group but to the _____, our form of government is called a democracy.   7.____

   A. courts   B. people   C. majority
   D. individual   E. law

8. Before criticizing the work of an artist one needs to _____ the artist's purpose.   8.____

    A. understand   B. reveal   C. defend
    D. correct   E. change

9. Their work was commemorative in character and consisted largely of _____ erected   9.____
   upon the occasion of victories.

    A. towers   B. tombs   C. monuments
    D. castles   E. fortresses

10. Every good story is carefully contrived: the elements of the story are _____ to fit with   10.____
    one another in order to
    make an effect on the reader.

    A. read   B. learned   C. emphasized
    D. reduced   E. planned

KEY (CORRECT ANSWERS)

1.	E	6.	A
2.	D	7.	D
3.	C	8.	A
4.	D	9.	C
5.	B	10.	E

TEST 2

DIRECTIONS: Each question in this section consists of a sentence in which one word is missing; a blank line indicates where the word has been removed from the sentence. Beneath each sentence are five words, *one* of which is the missing word. You are to select the letter of the missing word by deciding which one of the five words BEST fits in with the meaning of the sentence. *PRINT THE LETTER OF THE CORRECT ANSWER IN THE SPACE AT THE RIGHT.*

1. One of the most prevalent erroneous contentions is that Argentina is a country of _____ agricultural resources and needs only the arrival of ambitious settlers.   1.____

    A. modernized B. flourishing C. undeveloped
    D. waning E. limited

2. The last official statistics for the town indicated the presence of 24,212 Italians, 6,450 Magyars, and 2,315 Germans, which ensures to the _____ a numerical preponderance.   2.____

    A. Germans B. figures C. town D. Magyars E. Italians

3. Precision of wording is necessary in good writing; by choosing words that exactly convey the desired meaning, one can avoid _____.   3.____

    A. duplicity B. incongruity C. complexity
    D. ambiguity E. implications

4. Various civilians of the liberal school in the British Parliament remonstrated that there were no grounds for _____ of French aggression, since the Emperor showed less disposition to augment the navy than had Louis Philippe.   4.____

    A. suppression B. retaliation C. apprehension
    D. concealment E. commencement

5. _____ is as clear and definite as any of our urges; we wonder what is in a sealed letter or what is being said in a telephone booth.   5.____

    A. Envy B. Curiosity C. Knowledge
    D. Communication E. Ambition

6. It is a rarely philosophic soul who can make a _____ the other alternative forever into the limbo of forgotten things.   6.____

    A. mistake B. wish C. change D. choice E. plan

7. A creditor is worse than a master. A master owns only your person, but a creditor owns your _____ as well.   7.____

    A. aspirations B. potentialities C. ideas
    D. dignity E. wealth

8. People _____ small faults, in order to insinuate that they have no great ones.   8.____

    A. create B. display C. confess D. seek E. reject

9. Andrew Jackson believed that wars were inevitable, and to him the length and irregularity of our coast presented a _____ that called for a more than merely passive navy.

    A. defense   B. barrier   C. provocation
    D. vulnerability   E. dispute

10. The progressive yearly _____ of the land, caused by the depositing of mud from the river, makes it possible to estimate the age of excavated remains by noting the depth at which they are found below the present level of the valley.

    A. erosion   B. elevation   C. improvement
    D. irrigation   E. displacement

KEY (CORRECT ANSWERS)

1. C   6. D
2. E   7. D
3. D   8. C
4. C   9. D
5. B   10. B

TEST 3

DIRECTIONS: Each question in this section consists of a sentence in which one word is missing; a blank line indicates where the word has been removed from the sentence. Beneath each sentence are five words, *one* of which is the missing word. You are to select the letter of the missing word by deciding which one of the five words BEST fits in with the meaning of the sentence. *PRINT THE LETTER OF THE CORRECT ANSWER IN THE SPACE AT THE RIGHT.*

1. The judge exercised commendable _____ dismissing the charge against the prisoner. In spite of the clamor that surrounded the trial, and the heinousness of the offense, the judge could not be swayed to overlook the lack of facts in the case.   1.____

    A. avidity
    B. meticulousness
    C. clemency
    D. balance
    E. querulousness

2. The pianist played the concerto _____, displaying such facility and skill as has rarely been matched in this old auditorium.   2.____

    A. strenuous
    B. spiritedly
    C. passionately
    D. casually
    E. deftly

3. The Tanglewood Symphony Orchestra holds its outdoor concerts far from city turmoil in a _____, bucolic setting.   3.____

    A. spectacular
    B. atavistic
    C. serene
    D. chaotic
    E. catholic

4. Honest satire gives true joy to the thinking man. Thus, the satirist is most _____ when he points out the hypocrisy in human actions.   4.____

    A. elated
    B. humiliated
    C. ungainly
    D. repressed
    E. disdainful

5. She was a(n) _____ preferred the company of her books to the pleasures of cafe society.   5.____

    A. philanthropist
    B. stoic
    C. exhibitionist
    D. extrovert
    E. introvert

6. So many people are so convinced that people are driven by _____ motives that they cannot believe that anybody is unselfish!   6.____

    A. interior
    B. ulterior
    C. unworth
    D. selfish
    E. destructive

7. These _____ results were brought about by a chain of fortuitous events.   7.____

    A. unfortunate
    B. odd
    C. harmful
    D. haphazard
    E. propitious

8. The bank teller's _____ of the funds was discovered the following month when the auditors examined the books.   8.____

    A. embezzlement
    B. burglary
    C. borrowing
    D. assignment
    E. theft

139

9. The monks gathered in the _____ for their evening meal. 9.____

   A. lounge   B. auditorium   C. refectory
   D. rectory   E. solarium

10. Local officials usually have the responsibility in each area of determining when the need   10.____
    is sufficiently great to _____ withdrawals from the community water supply.

    A. encourage   B. justify   C. discontinue
    D. advocate   E. forbid

KEY (CORRECT ANSWERS)

1.	D		6.	B
2.	E		7.	D
3.	C		8.	A
4.	A		9.	C
5.	E		10.	B

TEST 4

DIRECTIONS: Each question in this section consists of a sentence in which one word is missing; a blank line indicates where the word has been removed from the sentence. Beneath each sentence are five words, *one* of which is the missing word. You are to select the letter of the missing word by deciding which one of the five words BEST fits in with the meaning of the sentence. *PRINT THE LETTER OF THE CORRECT ANSWER IN THE SPACE AT THE RIGHT*

1. The life of the mining camps as portrayed by Bret Harte—boisterous, material, brawling—was in direct _____ to the contemporary Eastern world of conventional morals and staid deportment depicted by other men of letters.

    A. model	B. parallel	C. antithesis
    D. relationship	E. response

2. The agreements were to remain in force for three years and were subject to automatic _____ unless terminated by the parties concerned on one month's notice.

    A. renewal	B. abrogation	C. amendment
    D. confiscation	E. option

3. In a democracy, people are recognized for what they do rather than for their _____.

    A. alacrity	B. ability	C. reputation
    D. skill	E. pedigree

4. Although he had often loudly proclaimed his _____ concerning world affairs, he actually read widely and was usually the best informed person in his circle.

    A. weariness	B. complacency	C. condolence
    D. indifference	E. worry

5. This student holds the _____ record of being the sole failure in his class.

    A. flagrant	B. unhappy	C. egregious
    D. dubious	E. unusual

6. She became enamored _____ acrobat when she witnessed his act.

    A. of	B. with	C. for	D. by	E. about

7. This will _____ all previous wills.

    A. abrogates	B. denies	C. supersedes
    D. prevents	E. continues

8. In the recent terrible Chicago _____, over ninety children were found dead as a result of the fire.

    A. hurricane	B. destruction	C. panic
    D. holocaust	E. accident

9. I can ascribe no better reason why he shunned society than that he was a _____.

    A. mentor	B. Centaur	C. aristocrat
    D. misanthrope	E. failure

10. One who attempts to learn all the known facts before he comes to a conclusion may most aptly be described as a _____.   10.____

    A. realist   B. philosopher   C. cynic
    D. pessimist   E. skeptic

KEY (CORRECT ANSWERS)

1. C   6. A
2. A   7. C
3. E   8. D
4. D   9. D
5. D   10. E

TEST 5

DIRECTIONS: Each question in this section consists of a sentence in which one word is missing; a blank line indicates where the word has been removed from the sentence. Beneath each sentence are five words, *one* of which is the missing word. You are to select the letter of the missing word by deciding which one of the five words BEST fits in with the meaning of the sentence. *PRINT THE LETTER OF THE CORRECT ANSWER IN THE SPACE AT THE RIGHT.*

1. The prime minister, fleeing from the rebels who had seized the government, sought _____ in the church.

    A. revenge B. mercy C. relief
    D. salvation E. sanctuary

2. It does not take us long to conclude that it is foolish to fight the _____, and that it is far wiser to accept it.

    A. inevitable B. inconsequential C. impossible
    D. choice E. invasion

3. _____ is usually defined as an excessively high rate of interest.

    A. Injustice B. Perjury C. Exorbitant
    D. Embezzlement E. Usury

4. "I ask you, gentlemen of the jury, to find this man guilty since I have _____ the charges brought about him."

    A. documented B. questioned C. revised
    D. selected E. confused

5. Although the critic was a close friend of the producer, he told him that he could not _____ his play.

    A. condemn B. prefer C. congratulate
    D. endorse E. revile

6. Knowledge of human nature and motivation is an important _____ in all areas of endeavor.

    A. object B. incentive C. opportunity
    D. asset E. goal

7. Numbered among the audience were kings, princes, dukes, and even a maharajah, all attempting to _____ another in the glitter of their habiliments and the number of their escorts.

    A. supersede B. outdo C. guide
    D. vanquish E. equal

8. There seems to be a widespread feeling that peoples who are located below us in respect to latitude are _____ also in respect to intellect and ability.

    A. superior B. melodramatic C. inferior
    D. ulterior E. contemptible

9. This should be considered a(n) _____ rather than the usual occurrence.   9.____

   A. coincidence   B. specialty   C. development
   D. outgrowth   E. mirage

10. Those who were considered states' rights adherents in the early part of our history,   10.____
    espoused the diminution of the powers of the national government because they had
    always been _____ of these powers.

    A. solicitous   B. advocates   C. apprehensive
    D. mindful   E. respectful

KEY (CORRECT ANSWERS)

1. E	6. D
2. A	7. B
3. E	8. C
4. A	9. A
5. D	10. C

TEST 6

DIRECTIONS: Each question in this section consists of a sentence in which one word is missing; a blank line indicates where the word has been removed from the sentence. Beneath each sentence are five words, *one* of which is the missing word. You are to select the letter of the missing word by deciding which one of the five words BEST fits in with the meaning of the sentence. *PRINT THE LETTER OF THE CORRECT ANSWER IN THE SPACE AT THE RIGHT.*

1. We can see in retrospect that the high hopes for lasting peace conceived at Versailles in 1919 were _____.

    A. ingenuous   B. transient   C. nostalgic
    D. ingenious   E. specious

    1.____

2. One of the constructive effects of Nazism was the passage by the U.N. of a resolution to combat _____.

    A. armaments   B. nationalism   C. colonialism
    D. genocide   E. geriatrics

    2.____

3. In our prisons, the role of _____ often gains for certain inmates a powerful position among their fellow prisoners.

    A. informer   B. clerk   C. warden   D. trusty   E. turnkey

    3.____

4. It is the _____ liar, experienced in the ways of the world, who finally trips upon some incongruous detail.

    A. consummate   B. incorrigible   C. congenital
    D. lagrant   E. contemptible

    4.____

5. Anyone who is called a misogynist can hardly be expected to look upon women with _____ contemptuous eyes.

    A. more than   B. nothing less than   C. decidedly
    D. other than   E. always

    5.____

6. Demagogues such as Hitler and Mussolini aroused the masses by appealing to their _____ rather than to their intellect.

    A. emotions   B. reason   C. nationalism
    D. conquests E. duty

    6.____

7. He was in great demand as an entertainer for his _____ abilities: he could sing, dance, tell a joke, or relate a story with equally great skill and facility.

    A. versatile   B. logical   C. culinary
    D. histrionic E. creative

    7.____

8. The wise politician is aware that, next to knowing when to seize an opportunity, it is also important to know when to _____ an advantage.

    A. develop   B. seek   C. revise
    D. proclaim   E. forego

    8.____

145

9. Books on psychology inform us that the best way to break a bad habit is to _____ a new habit in its place.

    A. expel
    B. substitute
    C. conceal
    D. curtail
    E. supplant

10. The author who uses one word where another uses a whole paragraph, should be considered a _____ writer.

    A. successful
    B. grandiloquent
    C. experienced
    D. prolix
    E. succinct

KEY (CORRECT ANSWERS)

1. A
2. D
3. A
4. A
5. D
6. A
7. A
8. E
9. B
10. E

BASIC FUNDAMENTALS OF ENGLISH EXPRESSION

TABLE OF CONTENTS

	Page
A. FUNCTIONAL INTRODUCTION TO GRAMMAR	1
<u>Classification</u>	1
1. Nominative Absolute ... 21. Verbals	1
<u>Syntax</u>	1
I. Uses of the Noun	1
II. Uses of the Pronoun	2
III. Uses of the Adjective	4
IV. Uses of the Adverb	4
V. Uses of Verbals	4
VI. Uses of Phrases	5
VII. Uses of Subordinate Clauses	6
VIII. Uses of the Verb	6
IX. Special Uses	7
B. BASIC SYNTAX	8
Rules 1-9	8
Rules 10-21	9
Rules 22-34	10
Rules 35-38	11
C. COMMON ERRORS IN USAGE	11

BASIC FUNDAMENTALS OF ENGLISH EXPRESSION

A. FUNCTIONAL INTRODUCTION TO GRAMMAR

For examination purposes, there are two clear-cut and yet related divisions in grammar: classification and syntax.

<u>Classification</u> refers to the required nomenclature for the proper identification and description of the <u>uses</u> of words or groups of words. <u>Syntax</u> refers to the relations of words and groups of words with one another in sentences.

The more usual terms of Classification are the following:

CLASSIFICATION

1. Nominative Absolute
2. Nominative of Direct Address
3. Nominative of Exclamation
4. Predicate Nominative
5. Predicate Adjective
6. Object of a Verb
7. Indirect Object
8. Object of a Preposition
9. Objective Complement
10. Adverbial Objective
11. Retained Object
12. Noun in Apposition
13. Auxiliary Verb
14. Copulative Verb
15. Progressive Forms of the Verb
16. Past Participle
17. Mood
18. Tense
19. Subject - complete subject, including modifiers
20. Predicate - verb and all modifiers and complements
21. Verbals

The more outstanding and the more frequently occurring types of syntactical relationships are defined in the illustrations appearing hereafter.

SYNTAX

I. <u>Uses of the Noun</u>
   A. Nominative Case:
      1. Subject of a verb: MARY bought a hat.
      2. Predicate Nominative: (Double Function)
         a. With a copulative verb: He became PRESIDENT. Is that the SORT of a person you take me for?
         b. With a verb in the passive voice: He was chosen PRESIDENT.
      3. Independent Constructions:
         a. Noun in Apposition with a noun in the nominative case: My sister, CLARA, is going with me.
         b. Nominative Absolute: The TRAIN having stopped, the passengers got out. James stood before me, his HANDS in his pocket
         c. Nominative of Direct Address: MARY, open the door.
         d. Nominative of Exclamation: What a MAN!

B. Possessive Case:
   1. To show ownership: MARY'S hat is brown.
   2. To indicate the relation of the doer to an act expressed in a particular noun: MARY'S having her homework saved the day. (See Predicate Complement of Copulative Verbal, below)
C. Objective Case: (Complements)
   1. Object of a
      a. Verb: The child ate the APPLE.
      b. Verbal:
         1. Infinitive: At times, it's a pleasure to eat an APPLE.
         2. Participle: Having lost the larger PART of his fortune, my friend found that economy was necessary.
         3. Participial Noun: Eating an APPLE is a pleasure.
      c. Preposition: She gave the book to CLARA.
      d. Cognate Object: He spoke his SPEECH well.
      e. Secondary Object of a Verb or Verbal: He told John the ANSWER. He asked John a QUESTION. He paid his workers good WAGES. (Differs from the indirect object because the secondary object can be dropped.)
   2. Indirect Object of a
      a. Verb: We gave JOHN our books.
      b. Verbal:
         1. Infinitive: He asked us to give CATHERINE the money.
         2. Participle: Giving my FRIEND the money I had borrowed, I heaved a sigh of relief.
         3. Participial Noun: Giving PEOPLE money makes most people happier.
   3. Subject of an Infinitive: I expect JOHN to be present. Let ME rest!
   4. Objective Complement: (See Predicate Nominative with Passive Verb) We elected him PRESIDENT. The Romans called Caesar FRIEND.
   5. Retained Object: (See 2a.) John was given our BOOKS.
   6. Adverbial Objective: I wanted to go HOME. The child is three YEARS old.
   7. Predicate Complement of Copulative Verbals:
      a. Referring back to the Subject of the Infinitive: I believed Allen to be the MAN.
      b. Referring back to the noun modified by a participle:
         Or lonely house,
         Long held the witches' HOME.
      c. Referring back to the Possessive with the Participial Noun: There is sense in your hoping to be SECRETARY. I was sure of John's being the AGGRESSOR.
   8. Noun in Apposition with a noun in the objective case: I gave the song, SOPHISTICATED LADY, to my friend to play.

II. Uses of the Pronoun
   A. Personal Pronouns: Similar to nouns in use, but, in addition, they must agree with the antecedent in <u>person, number,</u> and <u>gender</u>.
      1. Nominative Case:
         a. Subject of a verb: SHE bought a hat.
         b. Predicate Nominative with Copulative Verb: It is I
         c. Independent Construction:
            1. Nominative Absolute: SHE being ill, we decided to go.

2. Nominative of Direct Address: YOU, will you come!
   3. Nominative of Exclamation: I! You cannot accuse me!
  2. Possessive Case:
     a. To show ownership: HER hat is brown.
     b. To indicate relation of doer to an act or state expressed in a participial noun: HIS having a car saved the day.
  3. Objective Case:
     a. Object of a
        1. Verb: The child ate IT.
        2. Verbal:
           a. Infinitive: At times it is a pleasure to eat IT.
           b. Participle: Having lost IT, we hunted for another.
           c. Participial Noun: Taking IT in large doses is bad.
        3. Preposition: She referred me to HIM for an answer.
     b. Indirect Object of a
        1. Verb: We gave HIM our books.
        2. Verbal:
           a. Infinitive: He asked us to give HER the money.
           b. Participle: Giving HIM the money I had borrowed, I heaved a sigh of relief.
           c. Participial Noun: Giving HIM money made him unhappy.
     c. Subject of the Infinitive: I expected HIM to be present.
     d. Retained Object: He was given IT for his own use.
B. Uses of "it":
  1. Impersonal Pronoun, subject of a verb when no definite subject is expressed: IT rains.
  2. Expletive, serving to introduce the verb "is" when the real subject is in the Predicate: IT may be true that he did not commit the crime.
C. Compound Personal Pronouns:
  1. Intensively: I, MYSELF, will go.
  2. Reflexively: I have harmed MYSELF. The neighbors left us severely to OUR-SELVES.
D. Interrogative Pronouns: Similar to personal pronouns in use, but, in addition, they assist in asking a question. WHO is that? WHOSE is that? WHOM do you expect? WHICH is the better student? WHAT is your aim in life? He asked me WHAT I had meant by that statement.(Indirect) WHO do you consider is the best agent the company has?
E. Adjective (Demonstrative) Pronouns: Similar to personal pronouns in use. THIS is a new hat. THESE are very interesting books. The mountains of Colorado are higher than THOSE. I bought ONE, too.
F. Relative Pronouns: Similar to personal pronouns in use, but, in addition, they <u>connect</u> the adjective clauses they introduce with the nouns or pronouns modified.
   That is the girl WHO is going with me.
   The men WHOM you see there are marines.
   The men WHOSE lights are lit are seniors.
   Ask her for the book WHICH I recommended.
   Tell her WHAT you have told me. (That which)
   That's WHAT I did it for.
   The book THAT I gave her is lost.
   This is the pillow THAT I asked for.

Who do you consider is the best agent (THAT) the company has?
(Elliptical use)

Adjective clauses are also introduced by relative adverbs:
There was one time WHEN I almost caught you.
That is the house WHERE I was born.

G. Compound relative pronouns:
I will go with WHOEVER is going my way. (Implies own antecedent: HIM WHO)

III. Uses of the Adjective
A. Modifier of a noun (pronoun): That was an ORIENTAL rug. This dress is plainer than that PRETTY one. I must have the test-tube CLEAN. Of dark BROWN gardens and of PEEPING flowers.
B. Predicate Adjective:
1. With copulative verb: She was LAZY. This apple is RIPE.
2. Passive Voice: This man was pronounced GUILTY.
C. Objective Complement: I called the ship UNSEAWORTHY. I will make assurance doubly SURE. She wiped the plate DRY.

IV. Uses of the Adverb
A. Modifier of a verb: She walked RAPIDLY. This matter must be acted UPON.
B. Modifier of a verbal:
1. Infinitive: She attempted to walk RAPIDLY.
2. Participle: Having arrived SILENTLY, she overheard the conversation.
3. Participial Noun: Passing COMMENDABLY is our aim.
C. Modifier of an adjective: The ice was UNUSUALLY smooth this winter.
D. Modifier of another adverb: The wheels revolved VERY swiftly.
E. Modifier of a phrase or clause: He arrived JUST in time. That is EXACTLY what I expected of him.
F. As a relative or conjunctive adverb, introducing a clause and modifying the verb in this clause: I passed the house WHERE he was born. AS he rose from his chair, the audience burst into wild applause.
G. As an interrogative adverb, asking a direct or indirect question and modifying the verb: WHEN did you arrive? Tell us WHY he is always successful.

V. Uses of Verbals: Verbals take adverbial modifiers and complements.
A. The Infinitive.
1. As a noun
a. Nominative Case:
1. Subject of Verb: TO EXIST is a hard job these days.
2. Predicate Nominative: Copulative Verb: To work is TO EAT.
3. Independent Constructions: Apposition: Our ambition, TO ACT, was never realized.
4. Nominative Absolute: To ENJOY ourselves being impossible, we left the theatre.
5. Exclamation: TO SOAR! TO SOAR above the earth with wings!
b. Objective Case:
1. Object of a verb: The child asked TO SING. They expect TO TAKE one.
2. Object of a verbal:(Infinitive) It is never safe to ask TO GO. (Participle) Having asked TO LEAVE, he refused when the chance came. Bill Brown came asking
TO BE ADMITTED to the house. (Participial Noun) Learning TO FLY is amusing.

3. Object of a Preposition: There was nothing to do but TO GO.
4. Retained Object: He was told TO GO.
5. Apposition with noun in objective case: We never realized our ambition, TO ACT.
6. Special Use: With an object noun or pronoun as its subject: I wrote for him TO COME.(Such phrases introduced by "for" are used as nouns.) He felt the ground TREMBLE.
   2. As an adjective
      a. Modifying a noun: Houses TO RENT are scarce this year.
      c. Predicate Adjective: Our plan seemed TO WORK each day.
   3. As an adverb
      a. Modifying a verb: Folks would laugh TO SEE a cindermaid at a court ball.
      b. Modifying an adjective: The army was ready TO MARCH.
      c. Modifying a verbal: (Participle) Having gone out TO SHOP, he could not be found. (Participial Noun) Trying TO STUDY is impossible.
   4. As part of the complement of a verb or preposition with a noun as subject: Let me GO!
   5. As an Independent Expression: TO LIVE! To live in utter forgetfulness.
- B. The Participle: The participial form of a verb used as an adjective: The men HAVING WORKED steadily, the company decided to give them a raise. (Predicate Adjective) He appeared PANTING. (Objective Complement) I must have the test-tube CLEANED. Special Case: (1) With a noun in the nominative absolute construction: The day HAVING DAWNED, we started on our trip. (2) In rare cases, as an adverb: He ran CRYING down the street.
- C. The Participal Noun: The participial form of a verb used as a noun. (Subject) SEEING is believing. (Predicate Nominative)Seeing is BELIEVING. (Apposition) The sport, SKATING, is an exciting one. (Nominative Absolute) SKATING being over, the children went home. (With Possessive Pronoun) MARY'S swimming did not succeed very well. (Object of verb) I love SKATING. (Object of Verbal) He wanted to go SKATING. (Object of a Preposition) The pleasure lies in EATING. We went SKATING. (Retained Object) The children were given WEAVING to do. (Adverbial Objective) That is worth THINKING about. The water was BOILING hot.

VI. Uses of Phrases
- A. As nouns:
   1. The Infinitive Phrase: His aim is TO BE WELL.
   2. Participial Noun Phrase: His only pleasure is BEING WELL. MENDING BROKEN CHINA was his occupation.
- B. As adjectives:
1. Prepositional Phrase:(Modifier of a Noun) The trees OF THE FOREST are fading. (Predicate Adjective) The sun is IN ITS SPLENDOR.
2. Infinitive Phrase: (Modifier of a Noun) The house TO BE SOLD was burned. (Predicate Adjective) The house was TO BE SOLD.
3. Participial Phrase: (Modifier of Noun) RUNNING AWAY, he was shot.
- C. As adverbs:
   1. Prepositional Phrase: Frank came A-RUNNING. Tom ran crying DOWN THE STREET. The room was full OF PEOPLE.
   2. Infinitive Phrase: Folks would laugh TO SEE a cindermaid at a ball.
- D. As Independent Elements: It is true, TO BE SURE. It is better, IN MY OPINION, to face the situation directly.

VII. Uses of Subordinate Clauses
   A. Noun Clauses: Introduced by subordinating conjunctions such as THAT, WHETHER; interrogative pronouns in indirect questions, such as WHO, WHICH, WHAT; interrogative adverbs in indirect questions, such as WHERE, WHEN, WHY, HOW; all illustrated below.
      1. Subject of a Verb: THAT WE HAVE SURVIVED THE ORDEAL is evident.
      2. Predicate Nominative: The truth is THAT HE FAILED TO PASS.
      3. Noun in Apposition: The fact THAT THE EARTH IS ROUND is never disputed.
      4. Object of a Verb or Verbal: Tell me WHERE IS FANCY BRED. I wish HE WOULD HELP ME, I begged him to tell me WHAT HE WANTED. I asked him just WHAT HE REPORTED.
      5. Object of a Preposition: I am going there no matter WHAT YOU SAY. We came to the conclusion from WHAT WE KNOW.
      6. Retained Object: He was asked just WHAT HE REPORTED. I was asked WHETHER I ENJOY READING.
      7. Special Construction: In apposition with the expletive IT: It is commonly known THAT HE CANNOT BE TRUSTED.
   B. Adjective Clauses: Introduced by relative pronoun, WHO, WHICH, WHAT, THAT; relative adverb, WHERE, WHEN, AFTER.
      1. Modifier of a Noun: Thrice is he armed WHO HATH HIS QUARREL JUST. There is society WHERE NONE INTRUDES. I remember the house WHERE I WAS BORN. Who do you consider is the best agent THE COMPANY HAS?
   C. Adverbial Clauses: Introduced by relative (or conjunctive) adverbs; subordinating conjunctions such as BECAUSE, IF, SINCE, THOUGH.
      1. Modifier of a Verb, Verbal, Adjective, Adverb: Try AS WE MAY, we cannot swim to that rock. I intend to leave WHEN YOU GO. We are glad THAT YOU ARE WITH US. WHERE THE BEE SUCKS, there suck I.
   D. Independent Clause Element: Who DO YOU CONSIDER is the best agent the company has? He is, I THINK, able to do the work well.
VIII. Uses of the Verb
   A. Types of verbs
      1. Transitive verbs
         a. These require direct objects to complete the meaning: John ATE the apple, (direct object)
      2. Intransitive verbs
         a. These do not require an object to complete the meaning: The boy RAN down the mountain. (Common causes of error are the misuse of the intransitive verbs RISE, LIE, and SIT and/or the transitive verbs RAISE, LAY, and SET: She LAID on the bed, for She LAY on the bed.
      3. Copulative verbs
         a. These verbs, especially forms of the verb TO BE, are used to express simply the relationship between the subject and the predicate (or complement): She LOOKS good; The meat SMELLS bad; I FEEL better. (The most common copulative verbs are: BE, SEEM, PROVE, FEEL, SOUND, LOOK, APPEAR, BECOME, TASTE.)
      4. Auxiliary verbs
         a. These verbs assist in forming the voices, modes, and tenses of other verbs: She SHOULD go; They HAVE BEEN gone a month; We WERE given the information. (The most common auxiliary verbs are: BE,

HAVE, DO, SHALL, WILL, MAY, CAN, MUST, OUGHT, with all their inflectional forms.)
- B. Tenses of verbs (Verbs appear in different forms to indicate the time of the action):
  1. Present tense: The boy CARRIES the book; She EATS cookies.
  2. Past tense: The men COMPLETED the job; We VISITED him at home.
  3. Future tense: We WILL DO the job tomorrow; I SHALL GO alone.
     a. In speech and in informal writing, WILL and WOULD are now commonly used for all three persons except for the use of SHOULD to express obligation.
     b. In formal writing and careful usage, the following distinctions are observed between SHALL and WILL:
        1. To express simple futurity, use SHALL (or SHOULD) with the first person, and WILL (or WOULD) with the second or third persons: I SHALL be glad to go; They WOULD like to go.
        2. To express determination, intention, etc., use WILL (or WOULD) with the first person, and SHALL (or SHOULD) with the second and third persons: I WILL do it; You SHALL not go; They SHALL not pass.
        3. In questions, use SHALL with the first person: SHALL we see you tonight? SHALL I do it now? With the second person, use the form that is expected in the answer: WILL you lend us the car? (The answer that is expected here is: I WILL or I WILL not.) With the third person, use WILL to express simple futurity: WILL there be someone to meet him at the train?
        4. In indirect discourse, use the auxiliary that would be used if the discourse were direct: The company asked him whether he WOULD pay the bill. (Direct discourse: WILL you pay the bill?) He stated that he WOULD undertake the mission. (Direct discourse: I WILL undertake the mission.) His wife asked him whether he SHOULD be late for supper. (Direct discourse: SHALL you be late for supper?)
  4. Present perfect tense: I HAVE BEEN LIVING here for three years.
  5. Past perfect tense: He HAD BEEN CONVICTED of a crime many years ago.
  6. Future perfect tense: Before you arrive, I SHALL HAVE BAKED the pie.
- C. Mood (Mode) (The forms of a verb that indiqate the manner of the action):
  1. Indicative Mood (used to state a fact or to ask a question): The man FELL; ARE you well?
  2. Imperative Mood (used to express a command or an urgent request): DO it at once; ANSWER the telephone.
  3. Subjective Mood (used to express a wish, a supposition, a doubt, an exhortation, a concession, a condition contrary to fact): Wish: If only I WERE able to run faster!
     Supposition: They will be married provided their parents CONSENT. Condition contrary to fact: If you HAD more experience, you would know how to handle the problem.

IX. <u>Special Uses</u>
- A. Common Words Used as Different Parts of Speech:
  1. But: as relative pronoun: There is none BUT will answer.
     as adverb: You are BUT half awake, (only)
     as a preposition: Every man BUT him may leave, (except)
     I cannot BUT feel cherful.(except to feel)

as a coordinating conjunction: He leaves BUT I stay.
2. Like: (Never used as a conjunction)
   as a preposition: He talks LIKE his mother,
   as a verb: I LIKE his manner of speech.
3. As: as a relative pronoun: You own the same AS I.
   as an adverb: I am AS young as you are.
   as a subordinating conjunction: I am as young AS you are.
   as a preposition: He has frequently appeared AS Hamlet.
4. Than: as a preposition: He loves money more THAN learning.
   as a subordinating conjunction: He knows more THAN I.

B. BASIC SYNTAX

(NOTE: Rules are numbered for reference.)

A <u>noun</u> is the name of a person, place, object, or Idea.

A <u>pronoun</u> is a word used in place of a noun.

Nouns and pronouns are called <u>substantives.</u>

1. The subject of a verb is in the <u>nominative</u> case.
   The <u>boy</u> threw the ball.

Transitive verbs express action upon an object or product.

2. The direct object of a transitive verb is in the <u>objective (accusative)</u> case. <u>Whom</u> shall I fear?

Intransitive verbs are often followed by substantives which rename their subject. Such complements are called <u>predicate nominatives</u>, <u>predicate nouns,</u> or <u>attribute complements.</u>

3. A substantive used as attribute complement agrees in case with the subject to which it refers.
   It is <u>I</u>. <u>Whom</u> do you take me to be?

A substantive which helps to complete a verb but renames the object of the verb is called an <u>objective complement.</u>

4. An <u>objective complement</u> is in the <u>objective</u> case.
   The class elected him <u>president.</u>

5. The <u>object of a preposition</u> is in the <u>objective case</u>.
   Give it to me. The cat is under the <u>stove.</u>

The receiver of an action may sometimes be thought of as the principal word in an adverbial phrase from which the preposition <u>to</u> or <u>for</u> is omitted. Such a complement is called an <u>indirect object.</u>

6. An <u>indirect object</u> is in the objective case (dative object). Bring <u>me</u> a chair.

<u>Infinitives</u> and <u>participles</u> do not really assert action or being, but they imply it, and in this sense may have subjects.

Verbs of wishing, desiring, commanding, believing, declaring, perceiving, etc., are likely to be followed by objects which are at the same time <u>subjects of verbals.</u> It is this objective relation which justifies Rule 7.

7. The subject of a verbal is in the objective case. (Except in independent phrases.)
   She has <u>me</u> to protect her. We thought <u>him</u> to be honest.

8. Substantives used with verbals in independent phrases are in the nominative case. ("Absolute.")
   His <u>friends</u> advising it, he resigned.

An appositive is a noun or pronoun used as explanatory of or equivalent to another noun or pronoun.

9. An appositive takes the case of the substantive to which it is attached.
   The book was his, <u>Peter's.</u> (Possessive.)
   'Tis I, Hamlet, the Dane. (Nominative.)

Give it to me your brother.(Objective.)

10. A noun or pronoun <u>independent by address</u> is in the <u>nominative</u> case. ("Vocative".)
    <u>"Hens of Athens.</u> Him declare I unto you."
    <u>Mr. President,</u> I rise to a point of order.

11. A noun or pronoun used <u>independently with a following adjective, adverb, or phrase</u> may best be regarded as in the objective case, since it is virtually the object in a prepositional phrase from which the preposition is omitted.
    <u>Hat in hand,</u> he stood waiting
    <u>Beard unkempt, clothes threadbare,</u> he looked down and out.
    <u>Fences down, weeds everywhere,</u> the place was desolate.

12. Nouns or pronouns showing ownership are in the <u>possessive</u> case.
    <u>John's</u> farm; <u>your</u> shoes.

13. When an inanimate thing is personified, the <u>gender</u> of its noun or pronoun is determied by custom.
    <u>She's</u> a good old boat! (Feminine.)
    The <u>sun</u> is hiding <u>his</u> head. (Masculine.)

14. <u>Collective nouns are plural</u> when their units act separately as individuals; <u>singular</u> when the units act together as one. <u>Plural</u> titles are in this sense singular nouns.
    The class has had its picture taken. (All together.)
    The class have had their pictures taken. (Each person by himself.)
    "The Newcomes" is by Thackeray.

15. <u>Nouns used adverbially</u> to measure time or distance are in the <u>objective case.</u>
    <u>(Adverbial objective.)</u>
    We walked an <u>hour</u>, travelled four <u>miles</u>.

16. A <u>substantive</u> used as an exclamation is commonly held to be <u>nominative.</u> But if the exclamation repeats an idea already used, it will take the case of the term repeated.
    We shall be rich. We! think of that!
    "We'll make you do it!" <u>Me!</u> I guess not!

17. A <u>pronoun</u> must agree with its antecedent in <u>number, gender</u>. and <u>person</u>. Collective nouns take singular pronouns when the units act separately
    The Ship of State has refused to obey <u>her</u> rudder.
    <u>That</u> is <u>he whom</u> you seek. (All three are in 3rd Person, Masculine Gender, Singular Number.)
    The <u>case</u> of a pronoun does not depend upon its antecedent, but upon its use in the sentence.
    A verb is a word which asserts. (Tells something of its subject.)

18. A verb agrees with its subject in person and number. *I* am: You <u>are;</u> He <u>is;</u> She goes; They <u>go</u> .

19. A compound subject with <u>and</u> takes a singular verb if the idea of the combined subject is of <u>one</u> thing; if the compound subject is made of parts acting separately, the verb is <u>plural.</u>
    Roosevelt and Wilson <u>were</u> of opposing parties.
    The sum and substance of the matter <u>is</u> this.

20. A <u>distributive</u> subject with each, <u>every, everyone, either, neither</u>. etc., requires a verb in the <u>singular;</u> a disjunctive subject with <u>either-or. neither-nor,</u> takes a verb in the <u>singular</u> if the substantives are singular.
    <u>Either</u> the book or the teacher <u>is</u> wrong.
    <u>Each</u> of us must use his own judgment.

21. <u>Nouns plural in form</u> but singular in meaning commonly take a verb in the <u>singular.</u>
    Hydraulics <u>is</u> a practical study nowadays.

Mumps is contagious.
The news is discouraging.

22. When the subject acts upon an object, the verb is in the active voice; when the subject is a receiver or product of action, the verb is passive.
The hunter shot the door. (Active.)
The deer was shot by the hunter. (Passive.)

23. The indicative mood is used in questions and in simple assertions of factor matter thought of as possible fact.
Were you there?
You were there.
If you were there, I did not see you.(See subjunctive mood, Rule 24.)

24. The subjunctive mood expresses a wish, or a condition contrary to fact.
Would he were here!
If he were here, we would know about it.
(Implying denial. He has.not been here.)

25. The imperative mood states a command or request. Please_go at once.
The subject of an imperative verb is you understood; the you is seldom expressed, unless the mood is emphatic.

26. Infinitives may be used as subject, object of verb, attribute complement, object of preposition, appositive, adjective modifier, adverbial modifier, or in an independent phrase.
For examples, see discussion of Verbals in this section.

27. Gerunds (Verbal nouns in ing) have the uses of nouns together with the power of implying action, being or condition.
Examples have been given under uses of Verbals.

28. Participles may be used as adjectives, adverbs, subjective complements, objective complements, following a preposition, or in absolute phrases.
See examples under Verbals.

29. The comparative degree of adjectives and adverbs, not the superlative degree, is used in comparing two persons or things.
He is the taller of the two; in fact, the tallest of the three.

30. A coordinating conjunction connects words, phrases, or clauses of like rank, grammatically independent of each other.
I will come if I can and if the weather is good.

31. A subordinating conjunction joins a dependent clause to a principal one.
Make hay while the sun shines.

32. Interjections commonly have no grammatical relation in the sentence. In certain constructions, however, the interjection seems to have a phrasal modifier.
"Ah! for the pirate's dream of fight!"

33. Verbs become, feel, look, see, smell, taste, sound, grow may take an attribute complement to describe the subject, or an adverb to modify the assertion of the verb.
He grew tall. Poisonous mushrooms taste good.
"He looks well" may describe his own condition, and so the word well may be a predicate adjective relating to the subject; or the sentence may mean that he searches thoroughly. in which sense well is an adverb modifying looks.

34. Assertions of Simple Futurity take the form
I, we   shall
You   will
He, they   will

Assertions of Strong Purpose, Promise, Threat, Consent take the form I, we will You shall He, they shall

35. Adjectives should not take the place of adverbs, nor adverbs the place of adjectives.

36. The six tenses of English verbs in the Active Voice, Indicative Mood, are built up from the "principal parts" as follows:

<u>Present Tense, Past Tense,</u> as in Principal Parts, <u>Future Tense,</u> <u>shall</u> or will (Rule 34) with Present Infinitive (less "to").

<u>Present Perfect,</u> <u>have</u> or has. with Past Participle Past Perfect, <u>had,</u> with Past Participle.

<u>Future Perfect,</u> <u>shall</u> or <u>will</u> (Rule 34), with Present Perfect, the "have" form.

37. The six tenses of English verbs in the Passive Voice, Indicative Mood, invariably use the past participle of the given verb, preceded by an appropriate form of the verb "be."

38. <u>Gerunds,</u> being verbal nouns, are modified by adjectives and <u>possessive pronouns.</u>

Now do it without <u>my</u> watching you.

C. COMMON ERRORS IN USAGE

(Numbers refer to rules in the preceding section. Correct forms are given first.)

	RULE
This is the <u>better</u> of the two. *NOT* this is the <u>best</u> of the two	(29)
<u>You</u> and I, did it. *NOT* <u>you</u> and <u>me</u> did it, *NOR* <u>me</u> and <u>you.</u>	(1)
<u>We</u> boys will be there. *NOT* <u>us</u> boys will be there.	(1)
It was <u>I, she, he, they.</u> *NOT* <u>me, her, him, them.</u>	(3)
We believed it to be <u>her, him, them.</u> *NOT* <u>she, he, they.</u>	(3)
Between you and <u>me.</u> *NOT* between you and <u>I.</u>	(5)
She is taller than <u>I,</u> (am). *NOT* she is taller than <u>me.</u>	(1)
It was known to be <u>he.</u> *NOT* <u>him.</u> He agrees with "It."	(3)
We were sure of its being <u>him.</u> (Usage divided.)	(3,5)
Let everybody bring <u>his own</u> lunch. *NOT* <u>their own.</u>	(14,17,24)
We should all bring <u>our</u> lunches. (Action concerted.)	(17)
Every boy and girl should do his best. <u>Their</u> would be incorrect.	
<u>His</u> or <u>her</u> is correct, for formal,	(17)
Each of us <u>has his</u> problems. *NOT* <u>have their.</u>	(20)
The actor <u>whom</u> you saw was Otis Skinner. *NOT* <u>who.</u>	(2)
<u>Whom</u> did you call for? *NOT* <u>who.</u>	(5)
<u>Whom</u> did you select? *NOT* <u>who.</u>	(2)
<u>Who</u> do you suppose it is? <u>Who</u> agrees with <u>it.</u>	(3)
<u>Who</u> do you think I am? *NOT* <u>whom.</u> Agrees with <u>I.</u>	(3)
<u>Whom</u> did you take me to be? <u>Whom</u> agrees with <u>me.</u>	(3)
The tree looks <u>beautiful.</u> *NOT* beautifully.	(33)
The apple tastes <u>good.</u> *NOT* <u>well.</u>	(33)
The tune sounds <u>harsh.</u>	(33)
Roses smell <u>sweet.</u> *NOT* <u>sweetly.</u>	(33)
She looks <u>charming.</u> *NOT* <u>charmingly.</u>	(33)
We <u>shall</u> be drowned if we go there. *NOT* <u>we will be</u>	(34)
I <u>shall</u> be pleased to help you. *NOT* <u>will</u> be.	(34)
The senate has adjourned. *NOT* <u>have</u> adjourned.	(14)
There <u>are</u> all sorts of graft in town. *NOT* there <u>is</u> all sorts.	(18)
Here <u>are</u> wealth and beauty. *NOT* here <u>is.</u> (Unless taken separately.)	(18)
Neither of the men shows signs of giving *in. NOT* neither show.	(18)
In both cases, there <u>are</u> bad birth and misfortune. *NOT* there is. (Unless taken separately.)	(18)
Our class poet <u>believes</u> in symbolism. *NOT* <u>believe.</u>	(18)

He is one of the best actors that have ever been *here*. *NOT* has. (17,18)
Let him who will, come. *NOT* let he. (2)
The congregation were free to express their opinions, *OR* was free to
  express its opinions. (14)
I saw. *NOT* I seen. (36)
I did. *NOT* I done. (36)
We have gone. *NOT* have went. (36)
We were. *NOT* we was. (18)
You began it. *NOT* you begun it. (36)
The wind blew. *NOT* the wind blowed. (36)
The glass is broken. *NOT* broke. (37)
I caught, have caught. *NOT* catched, have catched. (36)
Have been chosen. *NOT* have been chose. (37)
We came along. *NOT* we come. (36)
We have come. *NOT* have came. (36)
The-baby crept. *NOT* creeped. (36)
You've done it. *NOT* you've did it. (36)
We drew. *NOT* we drawed. (36)
He has drunk a glassful. *NOT* has drank (36)
Have driven. *NOT* have drove. (36)
Have eaten. *NOT* have ate. (36)
I ate my dinner. *NOT* eat (36)
Eas fallen. *NOT* has fell. (36)
The boys fought. *NOT* fit. (36)
Has flown, *NOT* has flew. (36)
I've forgotten. *NOT* forgot. (36)
It grew. *NOT* it growed. (36)
You lie low. *NOT* lay low. (Lie, to recline; lay, to put down.) (36)
Have ridden. *NOT* have rode. (36)
We rang the bell. *NOT* we rung it. (36)
Had risen. *NOT* had rose. (36)
And then I ran away. *NOT* then I run away. (36)
Ve sang a song. NOT we sung it. (36)
Troubles sprang up. *NOT* troubles sprung up. (36)
Somebody has stolen my hat. *NOT* has stole. (36)
The place stunk. *NOT* stank. (36)
We swam a mile. *NOT* we swum. (36)
Who's taken my hat? *NOT* who's took? (36)
Have torn. .*NOT* have tore. (36)
Have written. *NOT* have wrote. (36)
Say it slowly. *NOT* slow. (35)
We can do that as easily as you please. *NOT* as easy. (35)
The horse threw my brother and me *out*.*NOT* my brother and I. (2)
We chose the foreman who we thought could handle the *men*. *NOW* whom. (1)
I never saw a taller man than he. *NOT* him. (1)
There isn't another girl in town so handsome as she. *NOT* her. (1)
MOSSES FROM AN OLD MANSE is a collection of essays and stories.
  NOT are a collection. (14)
Now skate without my helping you. *NOT* me helping. (38)
We ought to keep still about his being here. *NOT* him being. (38)

HANDBOOK OF ENGLISH EXPRESSION

CONTENTS

	Page
A ----- Amount	1
An ----- Awful	2
Badly ----- But	3
Calculate ----- Council	4
Counsel ----- Due	5
Each ----- Exceptionable	6
Exceptional ----- Gourmand	7
Habit ----- Its	8
It's ----- Line	9
Little ----- Myself	10
Near ----- Only	11
Onto ----- Petition	12
Place ----- Propose	13
Proposal ----- Purpose	14
Reason ----- Scarcely	15
Seem ----- Suspicion	16
Take ----- Unless	17
Up ----- Who	18
Whole ----- Without	19

HANDBOOK OF ENGLISH EXPRESSION

A

A - Do not use <u>a</u> before vowel sounds. Use it sparingly before <u>one</u> merely for the sake of emphasis. Do not use it after <u>sort of</u>, <u>kind of</u>, <u>type of</u>, <u>form of</u>, <u>manner of</u>, and similar expressions indicating class or distinction. Use it rarely after <u>such</u> when this word modifies an abstract noun followed by <u>as</u> or <u>that</u>: <u>Such a generosity</u> is wrong.

    The following are correct: The men joined a union... Not one of us arrived in time ... What manner of man art thou?... I never experienced such as that.

ABILITY - Power to accomplish (see CAPACITY). He has <u>ability</u> to do the work.

ABOUT - As an adverb <u>about</u> means around. As a preposition <u>about</u> means approximate or in the neighborhood of (see AROUND). Do not use after <u>discuss:</u> We discussed the subject thoroughly ... He strolled <u>about</u>, taking in the sights ... He told me <u>about</u> the letter he had received.

ACCEPT - To take something frankly and willing (see EXCEPT). I <u>accept</u> your invitation.

ADMISSION - The right of admittance. He was denied <u>admission</u> to membership in our club.

ADMITTANCE - The act of allowing to enter. He gained <u>admittance</u> to the theater after paying an exorbitant price for a ticket.

ADVERSE - Opposed or opposing or antagonistic or opposite. Accented on the first syllable. Customarily used of things and circumstances. Do not confuse with <u>averse</u>. He was discouraged by the <u>adverse</u> criticism of his work.

ADVICE - A noun meaning counsel or suggestion. We gave him some sound <u>advice</u> about letter writing.

ADVISE - A verb meaning to give counsel or guidance or suggestion. It is frequently wrongly used in the sense of conveying information. We <u>advise</u> you to look carefully after the placement of the letter parts. AFFECT - A verb meaning to move or influence. A verb meaning to feign or pretend (see EFFECT). The news in the morning papers will affect the stock market ... He will, of course, <u>affect</u> not to understand their derogatory remarks.

AGGRAVATE - To increase adversely, to make worse. Do not use for <u>exasperate.</u> Their enmity in business will <u>aggravate</u> their estrangement in sport.

ALL - This word refers, as a rule, to totality of number (see WHOLE). You have used <u>all</u> the pencils in the cabinet ... But <u>You have used all the paste in the pot</u> is also correct.

ALL RIGHT - Do not spell as one word with one "l". Almost all the apples are already stored away, and the barrels are <u>all right.</u>

ALLOW - Not to hinder (see PERMIT). Please <u>allow</u> me to pass. ALMOST - An adverb meaning not quite or less than or very nearly all (see MOST and MOSTLY). My work is <u>almost</u> done. (See second sentence above.)

ALONE - Solitary, without others (see ONLY). In scholarly achievement, this man stands <u>alone.</u>

ALONGSIDE - By the side of, close to, near to. Do not use <u>of</u> after this word. The ship came <u>alongside,</u> and the passengers disembarked.

ALTERNATIVE - This word refers to two only (see CHOICE). The <u>alternative</u> of surrender is death.

AMATEUR - One who engages in art or a sport, not professionally, but for the love of it, for the pleasure it affords, and for training in skill and experience (see NOVICE). His painting reveals him to be an <u>amateur</u> in the art.

AMONG - This word refers to three or more (see BETWEEN). <u>Among</u> the various works on exhibition, I like this best.

AMOUNT - This word refers to quantity. Not used, as a rule, to refer to number. He carried a large <u>amount</u> of money in his pocket ... A large number of people attended the party.

AN - Do not use <u>an</u> before consonant sounds. For other cautions regarding <u>an</u>, see A above. <u>An</u> honest man fears nothing... He presented a one-sided argument... What sort of apple is this?... Such emotion as he evinced was clearly understood.

ANGRY - An adjective meaning temporarily displeased or indignant. Do not confuse with <u>mad</u>. You are <u>angry</u> because he copied from your paper.

ANNOY - To trouble in a small way. Do not confuse with <u>aggravate</u> and <u>exasperate</u>. The dripping of the water <u>annoys</u> me.

ANOTHER - Used with <u>one</u> - <u>one another</u> - to denote succession or con-secutiveness of relationship. Custom may, however, justify its use interchangeably with <u>each other</u>. Do not use a plural verb or a plural reference with <u>one another</u>. The members of the diplomatic corps followed <u>one another</u> into dinner.

ANY - Do not phrase this word with superlatives. Do not say <u>best of any</u>. Used in comparative statements, this word requires <u>other</u> to follow it. Do not say <u>This paper is better than any I have used</u> ... Do not use with <u>place</u> for <u>anywhere</u>.

The following are correct: My last report is the best of those I have received ... This paper is better than <u>any</u> other I have ever used ... I cannot find my gloves anywhere (or in <u>any</u> place).

APPRECIATE - Do not use this word in the sense of <u>know</u> or <u>understand</u>. Do not use an adverb of degree with this word, such as <u>very</u> or <u>much</u>. The word itself means to value highly or to estimate correctly. I <u>appreciate</u> your kind remarks about me ... I sympathize with your feelings regarding your failure ... I <u>appreciate</u> your courtesies in my behalf.

APT - Tendency to, suitable or appropriate (see LIKELY and LIABLE). Also skillful or clever. He is <u>apt</u> at music and drawing ... His after-dinner talk was <u>apt</u> to the occasion.

ARBITER - This refers to an unprejudiced judge. ARBITRARY, however, means prejudiced, biased.

ARGUE - In arguing one depends upon cold facts (see PLEAD). He will <u>argue</u> from the figures of the last report.

AROUND - Encircled on all sides. Do not use for <u>about</u> in the sense of approximate (see ABOUT). He walked <u>around</u> the block in about ten minutes.

AS - (1) <u>As .. as</u> are correlatives in affirmative statements (see so ... <u>as</u>)
    (2) Do not use <u>as</u> for like when the latter is a preposition (see LIKE).
    (3) Do not use <u>as</u> for <u>that. I do not know as I am going</u> is wrong, (see THAT).
    (4) After such, <u>as</u> may properly be used as a relative pronoun (see SUCH). He has written <u>as</u> good a letter <u>as</u> it is possible to write ... He writes like me (or <u>as</u> I do) ... I do not know that I am going ... Such letters <u>as</u> you write should be written well.

ASCETIC - This word means self-denying. AESTHETIC means pertaining to the beautiful or beauty.

AT - Do not use before <u>about</u>. Do not use after <u>start, begin, commence</u>. He arrived <u>at</u> nine o'clock ... He began his work promptly.

AVERAGE - The mean of several, arrived at by numerical calculation (see ORDINARY). The <u>average</u> of his marks for the term was eighty. AVERSE - Reluctant, unfavorable toward in mind or feeling. Accented on last syllable. Customarily used of people and animals. Followed by preposition <u>to.</u> Do not confuse with <u>adverse</u>. John is <u>averse</u> to participation in social functions.

AVOCATION - Minor or subsidiary occupation (see VOCATION). After office hours he worked at radio as an <u>avocation.</u>

AWFUL - Custom is probably making permissible the use of this word in the sense of <u>very</u>, <u>execrable</u>, <u>supreme</u>. But such loose usage is not yet to be recommended. The word means awe-inspred. The heavy thunderstorm made an <u>awful</u> impression upon the company.

B

BADLY - Do not use this adverb for its adjective equivalent bad. Do not use in the sense of extremely or very much or a good deal. His record is bad ... He plays badly... I want to see you very much.

BALANCE - The difference between two sides of an account (see REMAINDER and REST). The accounts show a balance of fifty dollars in your favor. BAN - This means to prohibit. BANE, however, means woe. BECAUSE - Do not use to introduce a causal clause after reason followed by is or was or may be, or similar copulatives. The reason for his absence is because he is ill is wrong (see REASON).

The following are correct: He is absent because he is ill ... The reason for his absence is illness.

BEG - To ask alms, to entreat, to solicit, to request persistently and emotionally. Do not beg to inform in reply to a letter. We beg you not to eject this poor old man.

BESIDE - Near, close by, by the side of. Do not confuse with besides. He sat beside me at the circus.

BESIDES - Moreover, in addition to. Do not confuse with beside. He had four apples for lunch, and two pieces of cake besides.

BEST - Do not use this word loosely or too frequently. Do not use it in reference to things or individuals, instead of better. Say the better of two or the best of three or more (see ANY). Of all the fellows in my class I like Oliver best...The better of the two pictures in this room has been adjudged the best of all in the exhibition.

BETWEEN - Refers to two only (see AMONG). Requires the objective case after it. Between you and me there can be no quarrels, but among the members of that class there are always bitter bickerings. Between should not be used before any word or words by which singleness of meaning is denoted. Between each row is wrong.
But, Between one man and another and Between each couple are correct.

BID - An offer based upon an estimate (see ESTIMATE). After weighing very carefully the costs of labor and materials, the contractor placed a bid of ten thousand dollars on the job.

BIND - Refers to a decision forced or imposed through the agency of outside forces (see DETERMINE). His contract binds him to give eight American concerts.

BLAME - Used as a verb, this word should not be followed by on. Blame it on him is incorrect. Blame a person for an error, do not blame an error on some one. They blame John for the accident.

BORROW - A verb meaning to obtain temporary use of (see LEND and LOAN). May I borrow your umbrella?

BOTH - Refers to two persons or things considered jointly (see EACH). Both his parents will be present at commencement.

BRING - Refers to motion toward a speaker or writer or director (see FETCH and TAKE). Bring me a newspaper, please, when you return.

BUT - (1) As a preposition, but means except.

(2) As an adverb, but means only. Do not use but with this meaning after a negative. I haven't but two is wrong.

(3) As a conjunction, but gives contrasted or adversative meaning. But is frequently misused for and with that or what. We do not doubt but that (or what)you will be there is wrong. We don't know but what he will come is wrong. There is nobody but what (or who) he likes is wrong. Be careful, likewise, in the use of but after can. She can but come means that there is nothing else for her to do but to come. She cannot but come means that she cannot help coming.

The following are correct: Everybody went but me. . . I have but two . . . He was absent frequently, but he nevertheless passed ... We do not doubt that you will be there ... We don't know but that he will come... There is nobody that he likes (He likes nobody)... Observe, however, that but is used correctly before what and that in these two sentences: He delivered an address, but what the audience thought of it, I do not know ... He thought the book would disappoint me, but that is just the sort of book I like.

C

CALCULATE - To compute and estimate by more or less complicated devices (see RECKON). They calculate the cost of the building to be exactly $98,750.78.

CAN - Denotes power and capability (see MAY). I can operate a lathe.

CAN'T - Do not use with but in the same sense in which can but is used. Do not use with seem in the sense of being unable to do. I can't seem to get this is wrong.

The following are correct: I can't get this ... It appears that I can't get this... I seem unable to get this.

CAPACITY - Power to receive or hold (see ABILITY). He has the capacity to grow into a higher position.

CARRY - In relation to bring, fetch, and take (which see) carry refers to undetermined and indefinite action. He will carry your parcels.

CENSURE - This word means to find fault. CENSOR, however, means to purge or remove offensive passages.

CHARACTER - What a person really is by nature and temperament (see REPUTATION). His character qualifies him to hold the position.

CHOICE - Refers to two or more (see ALTERNATIVE). Of the dozen opportunities offered him, he cannot yet tell what his choice will be.

CLIENT - One whom a lawyer or a business agency serves (see CUSTOMER). The client questioned the legal advice given.

COMMODITY - Any product, or part thereof, that is movable and valuable, and thus made ready for the market. A new commodity has been placed on sale at the chain stores.

COMMON - Belonging to more than one (see MUTUAL). The employees use the library in common ...The two appetites common to all mankind are those for food and drink.

COMMONLY - Refers to the greater part of a class; generally (see UNIVERSALLY). The two men are commonly regarded as the best of friends.

COMPARE - To place together in order to discover likeness and unlike-ness (see CONTRAST). If you will compare this paper with that, you will find that one is almost a complete copy of the other.

COMPLACENT - This word means self-satisfied, smug. COMPLAISANT, however, means kindly, submissive.

COMPLEMENT - The act of completing (see COMPLIMENT). The complement of our Christmas stock has just come in.

COMPLIMENT - Praise or commendation or congratulation. Do not confuse with complement. He paid us a very high compliment by his visit.

CONSUL - An official representing a government in foreign parts (see COUNCIL and COUNSEL). The American consul at Algiers has resigned.

CONTEMPTIBLE - To deserve disdain or disregard. I think his behavior is contemptible.

CONTEMPTUOUS - To evince disdain or disregard. I think his attitude toward his teachers is contemptuous.

CONTRAST - To set in opposition in order to point out dissimilarity (see COMPARE). To contrast the two pictures effectively, you must place them in direct light.

COSMOPOLITAN - This word means sophisticated. METROPOLITAN, however, means pertaining to the city.

COUNCIL - A meeting or conference or consultation (see CONSUL and COUNSEL). The executive council is called at four o'clock.

COUNSEL - Advice; an adviser, usually in legal matters. (Do not confuse with consul and council). Lord Chesterfield gave his son the best of counsel ... Their counsel charged them a large fee.
CREDIBLE - Worthy of belief or acceptance. Your news is hardly credible.
CREDITABLE - Worthy of praise or commendation. His conduct is creditable from every point of view.
CREDULOUS - Too easily disposed to believe, making believable on slight and insufficient evidence. You are too credulous regarding market reports.
CUSTOM - Voluntary repetition of an act by a person or a group of persons, under the same circumstances, for the same reasons, and from the same underlying causes (see HABIT). The natives of a certain province in central Africa have the strange custom of using colored calico for money.
CUSTOMER - One whom a tradesman regularly serves. Used almost interchangeably with client in certain business relationships. Some banks refer to their depositors as clients; others refer to them as customers. He is a customer highly respected by the salesmen in the shop.

D

DATA - Plural for datum, a known or an assumed fact. The first ji is pronounced a, not a. Data for the debate are now ready in the library.
DEAL - Along with help, line, proposition (which see), this word is too loosely used. It does not refer to large transactions. It means to do business with a person, and is preferably a verb. I shall deal directly with you.
DEMURE - This word means pretending modesty. DEMUR, however, means to hesitate, raise objection.
DEPOT - A warehouse or storehouse. Usage has now justified its use in reference to a large railway station (see STATION). DEPRECATE - This word means to disapprove regretfully. DEPRECIATE however, means to undervaluate.
DETERMINE - To come to a decision by the exercise of one's own will (see BIND). After much deliberation, he has determined to pocket his pride and retain his position.
DIFFER - Do not use than after any form of this word. Differ and different and difference are not comparative forms. People differ with each other in opinion. They differ in judgment about a policy. They differ from their elders in a course of action taken. John and I differ from the principal regarding the game.
DIRECTLY - Do not use this word for as soon as. The word is properly used to refer to method, as well as to time (see IMMEDIATELY). It may also refer to proximity in space. He presented the case directly to the man... He will follow directly after us.
DISAGREE - Use with rather than from after this verb: We disagree with you in principle.
DISCREET - This word means judicious; prudent. DISCRETE, however, means separate.
DIVE - The past tense and the past participle of this verb is, preferably, dived. In occasional colloquial use only, dove is used. He dived, into the water is correct.
DISINTERESTED - This word means unprejudiced. UNINTERESTED, however, means not interested.
DIVERS - This word means several. DIVERSE, however, means varied.
DON'T - A contraction of do not. Do not use for doesn't. Some authorities claim that the somewhat common usage of he, she, or it don't is tending to make the expression acceptable. But it has not made it correct. They don't approve of his policy, and he doesn't approve of their practice.
DUE - Do not use this word unless it refers explicitly to a noun or a pronoun. It cannot refer to a verb, a phrase, or a clause. Due to his absence from the city he lost his vote is wrong.

The following are correct: His victory was <u>due</u> to his fine spirit ... He lost his vote as a result of his absence from the city.

E

EACH - This word refers to two or more individually (see BOTH). Followed by <u>other,</u> it should be used to indicate a certain equality of relationship among all referred to. <u>One another</u> means following or con-seductiveness or succession of relationship. Do not use a plural verb or a plural reference with <u>each. Each</u> boy has received his card ... The employees helped <u>each</u> other in every way.

EFFECT - (1) A noun meaning result.
(2) A verb, meaning to cause, to bring, to achieve (see AFFECT). His wide reading has shown its <u>effect</u> upon his writing ... His reading will <u>effect</u> a great improvement upon his writing.

EITHER - Refers to two persons or things, never more. Correlative of jor.. Do not use with nor. Used as an adjective pronoun, <u>either is</u> always singular (see NEITHER). <u>Either</u> John or James is to accompany you.... <u>Either</u> of the boys is to accompany you.

ELAPSE - Refers to the passing of time (see TRANSPIRE). Two hours have <u>elapsed</u> since you came in.

ELEVATED - High or lofty in situation or character. Usually a participle or an adjective, this word has properly come to be used as a substantive in reference to a railway that runs above ground level. Do not confuse with <u>elevator.</u> We went down town by the elevated or by the <u>elevated</u> train. ELEVATOR - One who or that which carries upward. A movable platform or "cage" in a building for carrying passengers or freight up and down. A grain warehouse. Do not confuse with <u>elevated.</u> <u>We went down town by the elevator</u> is wrong. Correct: We took the <u>elevator</u> to the tenth floor . The grain <u>elevator</u> is two hundred feet high.

ELICIT - This word means to extract. ILLICIT, however, means unlawful.

ELSE - In conjunction with <u>any one</u>, <u>everybody</u>, <u>somebody</u>, and similar words, should be given the sign of possession when the possessive case is used. <u>Anybody's else coat</u> is not the correct form. There is some good usage to contradict this, but the best authorities stand firmly for <u>Anybody else's coat.</u>

EMEND - This word means correct AMEND however, means change

EMPLOY - Do not use this verb for its noun equivalent <u>employment</u>. Try to <u>employ</u> your time profitably... We have eight men in our employment.

ENTHUSE - Do not use this word for <u>to be</u> or <u>to make</u> enthusiastic. The audience became <u>enthusiastic</u> at what he said.

EQUABLE - This word means even-tempered. EQUITABLE, however, means just.

ESTEEMED – Do not use this word to modify <u>favor</u> in reference to a letter. It means to value or regard. They <u>esteemed</u> your efforts highly.

ESTIMATE - To calculate in definite terms; to arrive at final judgment after the consideration of many factors (see BID). The contractor will <u>estimate</u> the cost of the new building to a fraction of a cent.

EVERY - Do not use with <u>place,</u> in the sense of <u>everywhere</u>. <u>In</u> is required before it when used to modify place. <u>Every</u> always implies singular number: He has looked in <u>every</u> place for his hat.

EXASPERATE - To vex or annoy extremely. Do not use for <u>aggravate</u> (which see). His gross carelessness and indifference <u>exasperate</u> me.

EXCELLENT - Do not use a modifier for <u>excellent,</u> such as <u>very</u>, quite, <u>most.</u> Do not use this word loosely to describe anything of which you think highly. He has made an <u>excellent</u> record ... He is a good friend of mine.

EXCEPT - (1) A verb meaning to exclude or omit.
(2) A preposition meaning at the exclusion or with the exception of
(see ACCEPT). I <u>except</u> your name from the list... The names are all listed except yours.

EXCEPTIONABLE - That may be objected to; subject or liable to objection. Do not confuse with <u>exceptional.</u> Correct: Certain people were offended at his <u>exceptionable</u> conduct.

EXCEPTIONAL - Unusual, of superior value, out of the ordinary. His <u>exceptional</u> conduct won promotion for him.
EXPECT - To look forward to as probable; to hold slight but justifiable belief that a certain thing will come to pass (see CALCULATE, RECKON, SUPPOSE, SUSPECT, etc.). In view of his telegram we <u>expect</u> him to arrive tonight.
EXULT - This word means to rejoice.
EXALT, however, means to raise, praise highly.

F

FARTHER - Refers to remoteness in space (see FURTHER). His shop is <u>farther</u> from the wholesale depot than I thought.
FAVOR - Do not habitually call a letter a favor or "your esteemed favor". Thank you for the <u>favor</u> you have just shown me.
FETCH - Motion from and toward a speaker or writer or director; to go from and return with (see BRING and TAKE). Please <u>fetch</u> my coat from the locker.
FEW - Refers to number (see LITTLE). There are <u>few</u> errors in your work.
FIND - To get something or to come upon somebody as a result of seeking (see LOCATE). I could <u>find</u> the place only after much difficulty.
FIX - To fasten or attach or secure firmly (see REPAIR). I shall <u>fix</u> the lamp above the mirror.
FLEE - To run away for safety. The parts of this verb are <u>flee, fled, fled</u>. He must <u>flee</u> to another country for safety.
FLOW - To move along quietly, as a stream of water. The parts are <u>flow, flowed, flowed.</u> Money <u>flows</u> in uninterruptedly.
FLY - To move through the air, or, figuratively, to move rapidly and more or less mysteriously. The parts are <u>fly, flew, flown.</u> The aviators will <u>fly</u> to Chicago overnight.
FORMER - Refers to one of two only; never to more than two (see LATTER). Both John and Bill received high marks, but the <u>former</u> was given greater commendation by his teachers.
FURTHER - Refers to remoteness in time, degree, or quantity. Refers also to something additional to what one has already said or written (see FARTHER). <u>Further</u> in the winter, we shall have snow... I shall give you <u>further</u> examination tomorrow ... He wants nothing <u>further</u> ... He says nothing <u>further</u> in his letter.

G

GAIN - Refers to transactions that are conducted on a large scale, income from which is attended with some irregularity and uncertainty (see PROFIT). His financial <u>gain</u> on his oil speculation has been unusual.
GOOD - This word is, as a rule, an adjective, and must therefore be used only in the modification of nouns and pronouns. Do not use in place of <u>well</u>. His work is <u>good</u> ... The plan works well.
GOODS - Any easily transferable articles that may or may not be offered for sale (see COMMODITY and MERCHANDISE). The <u>goods</u> were shipped to you promptly.
GOT - Use this word sparingly. Prefer it to the archaic past participle form <u>gotten.</u> Do not use <u>got</u> for <u>have</u>, except for emphasis or for conveying the meaning of <u>secured</u>. <u>We have got to bear it</u> is not good usage. Correct: We have to bear our troubles ... At last, after much struggling, we <u>got</u> the animal safely roped to a tree.
GOURMET - This word means lover of good food.
GOURMAND, however, means glutton.

H

HABIT - The tendency to repeat a certain act without volition on the part of the doer. CUSTOM usually refers to groups; HABIT to individuals. Acquire the <u>habit</u> of promptness if you would succeed in business.

HAD - Do not use of after had. <u>Had I of known</u> is incorrect. Do not use <u>ought</u> after <u>had</u>. <u>He had ought to go</u> is incorrect (see OF and OUGHT). Correct: <u>Had</u> I known you were coming, I could have met you ... He ought to go when he is told to go.

HANGED - Refers only to an individual who is executed by hanging (see HUNG). The murderer was <u>hanged</u> at dawn.

HARDLY - Do not use with a negative expression. We can <u>hardly</u> wait till he comes.

HAVE - Denotes possession. It is unnecessary, therefore, to combine with any other word to indicate possession (see GOT above). We <u>have</u> all the goods on hand that we can possibly sell.

HEALTHFUL - To be the cause of health (see HEALTHY and WHOLESOME). This is the most <u>healthful</u> climate in the world.

HEALTHY - To be in or to have good health (see HEALTHFUL and WHOLESOME). He is a strong and healthy man.

HELP - Do not use this word to mean <u>helpers</u> or <u>employees.</u> We need additional employees in our establishment to help us fill the large Christmas orders.

HERE - Do not use this word after <u>this</u> or <u>these</u> to reinforce your meaning. This sewing must be finished before these patterns are.

HUNG - Refers to anything that is fastened to a point above without supports from beneath (see HANGED). He <u>hung</u> his coat over the window.

I

IMMEDIATELY - With no delay in time. Both <u>directly</u> and <u>immediately</u> refer to immediacy in time and proximity in space, but the FORMER (see above) refers also to method of procedure as well. Usage has weakened both words (and the word <u>presently</u> also) to some extent, until they are frequently used now to mean <u>in a little while</u>. The Shakespearean <u>presently</u> meant <u>at once.</u> As used today, <u>presently</u> rarely means this. Correct: Please bring me the reports <u>immediately</u>... Please follow <u>immediately</u> after me ... I am too busy to see you now, but come to me presently.

IMPLY - To intimate a meaning not expressed; to convey, virtually (see INFER). Your behavior <u>implies</u> that you do not care for the good opinion of others.

IN - Indicates position, not motion (see INTO). We were sitting <u>in</u> the office when the bell rang.

INDIGENT - This word means poor. INDIGENOUS, however, means native.

INFER - To come to a conclusion or to make a deduction (see IMPLY). I <u>infer</u> from your behavior that you do not care for the opinion of others.

INFORMED - To have information. Do not say <u>well-posted</u> for <u>well-informed.</u> That man is wel <u>informed</u> in all matters pertaining to the parcel post.

INGENIOUS - Clever, skillful, with inventive genius. He is <u>Ingenious</u> at adjusting electrical devices.

INSIDE - Do not use this word to express time. Do not use <u>of</u> after it. The parcel will reach you <u>inside</u> of a week is wrong. Correct: He found the basket just inside the closet ... The parcel will reach you within a week.

INTERNMENT - This word means imprisonment. INTERMENT, however, means burial.

INTO - Indicates motion, not position or location (see IN). They went <u>into</u> the water in their street clothes.

ITS - The possessive singular of the pronoun <u>it</u>. Do not confuse with <u>it's</u>. The kitten has lost <u>its</u> ball of yarn.

IT'S - The contraction of it is. The apostrophe means that .i, has been omitted. It's a long lane that has no turning.

K

KIND - This is singular number. Do not precede it with a plural form such as these or those. Do not use a or an after kind of. This kind of cloth will wear well .... Those kinds are not so durable.
KINDLY - Be careful to place this word correctly when used in such expressions as this: Enclosed kindly find sample that you are asked to match. Kindly really modifies asked, and the sentence should read: Enclosed find sample that you are kindly asked to match.(See PLEASE.)

L

LAST - The final thing in a series. Last and first are frequently hyphenated with named to indicate reference to numbers in a series. The last game of the season will be played tomorrow ... Of the ten players you mention, the last-named has the best scoring record, and the first-named the best defensive record.
LATEST - The most recent. The latest game was played at Blaine Field; the next will be played in the gymnasium.
LATTER - Refers to one of two only, never to more than two (see FORMER). Both John and Bill received high marks, but the latter excelled the former.
LAY - To put or place. The parts are lay, laid, laid. I shall lay the map on the table.
LEAD -   (1) A noun, the name of a metal.
          (2) A verb meaning to guide by going on before. Unfortunately its past tense is led, pronounced exactly like the noun lead; hence, frequently confused with it (see LED). They melted the lead in a huge caldron ... They led the horse to water.
LEAVE - To go away (see LET), to part with, to submit, as a report. We shall leave by an early train ... We leave the report in your care.
LED - The past tense of lead (see above). Those who lead best have first been led.
LEND - A verb meaning to grant temporary use of (see LOAN and BORROW).
Please lend me your pen.
LET - To permit. Do not confuse with leave (see above). The master will not let them go to the game.
LIABLE - Dangerous, and unpleasant in results, disadvantageous (see APT and LIKELY). You are liable for damages if you run into my car.
LIE -   (1) A verb meaning to tell a falsehood. Its parts are lie, lied, lied.
          (2) A noun meaning falsehood.
          (3) A verb meaning to recline or rest. Its parts are lie, lay, lain. Do not confuse with lay (see above). Correct: If you say he cheated, you lie ... He has told a lie... I shall lie here for a little rest ... Yesterday I lay on the couch two hours.
LIKE -   (1) A preposition meaning similar to or in a similar manner to or resemblance to.
          (2) A verb expressing attitude.
          (3) An adjective indicating same.
          (4) A noun referring to kind or class, usually in the plural. Like should never be used for as in introducing a clause. He writes like I do is wrong. Correct: Clara is like Jane in appearance ... Clara will like Jane ... Like tastes beget like interests ...She has her likes and dislikes... He writes as I do, or like me.
LIKELY - Probably (see APT and LIABLE). It is likely to rain tomorrow.
LINE - This word is altogether too loosely used to indicate kind or brand or classification. Draw a line from this point to that one ... We shall travel by the Cunard Line ... What brand do you sell?

LITTLE - Refers to quantity, not number. Errors are frequently made in the use of the comparative less, and the superlative least (see FEW). I have little sugar and less molasses.

LOAN - A noun meaning the thing lent. Do not use as a verb, in place of lend (see above). The bank made him a loan of several thousand dollars.
LOCATE - To place in some particular position (see FIND). We shall locate our new factory on the block opposite.
LOOSE - To be free from anything that binds. Incoherence in thought or expression. Do not confuse with lose. Correct: His belt is loose ... Your sentences should not be loose and rambling.
LOSE - To fail, to be defeated, to part with anything unintentionally or unconsciously. If they lose, they will do so fighting hard.
LOT - A definite part, parcel, or quantity. A new lot of goods has just come in.
LOTS - Means definite parts, parcels, and quantities. Do not use loosely to mean much or many, or as a noun meaning abundance. We shall place all the lots on sale tomorrow.

M

MAD - Disordered in mind. Do not confuse with angry. Correct: He became mad at the death of his mother.
MAIZE - This word means corn. MAZE, however, means confusing network.
MAJORITY - More than half of any given number, as in election returns (see MOST and PLURALITY). He was elected over the Republican candidate by a large majority.

MANY - An adjective referring to number (see MUCH). There are many; errors in your letter.
MARTIAL - This word means warlike. MARITAL, however, means pertaining to marriage.
MAY - Denotes permission and possibility (see CAN). If I practice, I may some day be able to operate a lathe.
MENDACIOUS - This word means lying. MENDICANT, however, means begging.
MERCHANDISE - Goods prepared and offered for sale (see GOODS and COMMODITY). The new merchandise was placed on the market this morning. MERELY - Indicates the lack of something or the bare meeting of demand (see SIMPLY). Be sure to place merely as closely as possible to the word it modifies. "Quoth the raven: 'Nevermore!' Merely this, and nothing more." I merely want a book is wrong.
MOST - Superlative of the adjective much. Do not use as an adverb (see ALMOST, MOSTLY, and PLURALITY). Most letters are written without much thought as to form and content.
MOSTLY - An adverb meaning for the most part; principally (see MOST and ALMOST). The books in the corner closet are mostly old and torn.
MUCH - An adjective and an adverb referring to quantity and degree (see MANY, TOO, and VERY). There is much flour on the truck still to be unloaded ... We are much concerned about his condition.
MUTUAL - Pertaining reciprocally and interchangeably to both of two (see COMMON). John and I have mutual regard for each other.
MYSELF - Do not use this, or any other intensive form of pronoun, when the simpler form conveys the meaning desired. He spoke to you and myself about the work is wrong. Correct: He spoke to you and me about the work .... It was I myself who gave you the message.

N

NEAR - Do not use this word for <u>nearly</u>. <u>Near</u> may be used as an adjective, an adverb, a preposition, and a verb. <u>Near</u> relatives are not always agreeable ... There's his house, with the garage standing near ... He was sitting <u>near</u> me... We shall <u>near</u> the city by midday. NEARLY - An adverb only. <u>He is not near done</u> is wrong. <u>He is not nearly done</u> is correct.

NEITHER - Refers to two persons or things, never more. Correlative with <u>nor</u>. Do not use with <u>or</u>. Used as an adjective pronoun, neither is always singular (see EITHER). <u>Neither</u> of the boys is to go ... <u>Neither</u> John nor James is to accompany you.

NEW - A <u>new</u> thing is simply one more, one in addition (see NOVEL). He has just bought a <u>new</u> automobile.

NOTABLE - Worthily eminent or distinguished. He has made a <u>notable</u> record at college.

NOTED - Well and worthily known by report and reputation. He is <u>noted</u> for his fine work in athletics.

NOTORIOUS - More or less unfavorably known. Notoriety means unpleasant and disadvantageous publicity. As a result of his constant violation of rules, he has become <u>notorious</u> in athletics ... His bad behavior on the field has brought him much notoriety in athletic circles.

NOVEL - A <u>novel</u> thing is strange and unusual, in addition to being new. A <u>novel</u> device for beating carpets has just been invented.

NOVICE - One unskilled and inexperienced and still on probation (see AMATEUR). The works of a <u>novice</u> in the art of painting cannot possibly be entered at the exhibition.

NUMBER - Refers to units that are counted and countable (see QUANTITY). A <u>number</u> of trees could be seen in the distance.

O

OBSERVANCE - Keeping or celebrating, as certain feasts or holidays. We believe in the strict <u>observance</u> of legal holidays.

OBSERVATION - The act of seeing or looking at. On close <u>observation</u> you will see the four masts of a vessel on the horizon.

OF - Do not use this word for <u>have</u> after <u>may, might, must,</u> can, <u>could, will, would, shall, should.</u> Do not use it after <u>off, alongside, inside, beside, outside.</u> I must have met you outside the city limits ... Keep off the grass ... Keep away from the animals.

OFF - Do not confuse with <u>away from.</u> Say <u>The ship was wrecked a mile off shore,</u> not <u>away from shore.</u> Say <u>Keep away from me,</u> not <u>off me.</u>

OFFICIAL - Authoritative. Do not confuse with officious. Correct: This is the latest <u>official</u> report.

OFFICIOUS - Meddlesome. The newly appointed secretary is altogether too <u>officious</u> in his attitude.

ON - Do not use before <u>about.</u> Do not use after <u>blame.</u> Do not use in the sense (slang) of <u>from.</u> He will arrive about the fifteenth of May... He took it from me, not <u>on</u> me.

ONE - Inasmuch <u>a</u> and <u>an</u> mean <u>one,</u> it is unnecessary to precede one with either of these articles. I haven't <u>one</u> to my name, not I <u>haven't a one.</u>

ONES - Do not use <u>ones</u> for <u>these</u> or <u>those</u> (which see). Do not use <u>the</u> before <u>ones.</u> Use <u>those</u> instead of <u>the ones.</u> I mean those that you are wearing now.

ONLY - In no other time, place, or manner. Place <u>only</u> as closely as possible to the word it modifies. It is commonly misplaced in both conversation and writing. <u>I only asked for three is</u> incorrect(probably) for <u>I asked for only three.</u> Note that the placement of <u>only</u> may be varied in accordance with the varied meanings intended. <u>Only</u> John requested me to remove the chair ... John <u>only</u> requested me to remove the chair... John requested <u>only</u> me to remove the chair ...

John requested me only; to remove the chair. . . John requested me to remove only the chair... John requested me to remove the chair only.

ONTO - Do not use this word in the sense of place upon. The word on or upon is preferable. Onto, like ain't, is a vulgarism. Correct: He put his hat on the hook and jumped upon the table.

ORDINARY - Usual or common in occurrence (see AVERAGE). The ordinary events of the day held no interest for him.

OTHER - Preceded by each and every this word is singular (see EACH and ANOTHER). Every other boy in the class but John was prepared.

OUGHT - Do not use with or as an auxiliary verb. Had ought is a vulgarism. It is better never to use the ugly contraction oughtn't. Correct: She ought to have prepared dinner for two.

OUT - Do not use after start. They started on their six-day trip.

P

PART - A certain amount or number of anything (see PORTION). A part of his farm has been sold to a neighbor.

PARTIAL - Biased or prejudiced; also, incomplete. Since the word has these two distinctly different meanings, care should be taken to prevent ambiguity in its use. He made a partial report may mean either of two things. Do not confuse with partly. Correct: The report he made was partial to the negative side... He made only a partial report today, but he will complete it tomorrow.

PARTITION - A boundary or division wall or line, separating one room or apartment or larger space from another. Used as a verb it means to divide. Do not confuse with petition. Correct: They have built a partition between his half of the locker and mine...They will partition the locker.

PARTLY - Incomplete or in some degree. His work is partly done.

PARTY - Do not use to refer to an individual, except in legal phraseology. It should be used only to refer to a person or a group of persons who are actually concerned in some united action. There is an interesting old person sitting in the corner... The party of the first part agrees to pay to the party of the second part, fifty dollars.

PER - Do not use per for a in unabridged English expression. In abbreviated, technical, or commercial expression, it may be so used. We charge fifteen cents a copy for these brochures... Price, $15. per cwt.

PER CENT - Per hundred. Abbreviation of the Latin per centum. It may now be written as one word, and without the period after it. His money is invested at six percent interest. Do not confuse with PERCENTAGE.

PERCENTAGE - Rate percent, that is, rate by the hundred. The bonus amounted to a certain percentage of each man's salary.

PERMIT - To give express authorization, or, as a noun, the sign or token of such authorization (see ALLOW). The gateman will not permit you to enter the paddock ... My permit will admit two through the gate.

PERSECUTE - To pursue in order to injure or afflict; to hunt down (see PROSECUTE). The authorities have persecuted him until he is almost insane.

PERSONAL - This word means private. PERSONABLE, however, means attractive.

PERSPICACIOUS - This word means shrewd, acute. PERSPICUOUS, however, means clear, lucid.

PETITION - A formal request or appeal, usually addressed to some one in authority. Used as a verb, it means to request formally. Do not confuse with partition. Correct: They drew up a petition to present to the manager of the department... They are going to petition the manager for a holiday.

PLACE - Do not use after <u>any</u>, <u>every</u>, <u>some</u>, <u>no</u>, for <u>anywhere</u>, <u>everywhere</u>, <u>somewhere</u>, <u>nowhere</u>, without preceding with the preposition in. I have looked everywhere for my books, and cannot find them in any <u>place.</u>

PLEAD - Indicates the use of feeling and human-interest in an attempt to persuade. You argue a question but <u>plead</u> a cause (see ARGUE). He will <u>plead</u> the cause of the accused in terms that every mother will understand.

PLEASE - Be careful not to misplace this word in such expressions as this: Enclosed <u>please</u> find the sample that you are asked to match. (See KINDLY.) Correct: Enclosed find the sample that you will <u>please</u> match for me.

PLENTY - Do not use this word as an adverb, as in <u>This is plenty good enough for me.</u> Correct: This is quite good enough for me... We shall need <u>Plenty</u> of muslin.

PLURALITY - More than any other of three or more totals. If John received 600 votes and Bill 400 votes out of a total poll of 1000 votes, then John received a <u>majority</u>. If, out of 1000 votes, John received 600, Bill 250, and Jim 150, then John received a <u>plurality</u> of 350 votes, or so many more votes than his closest competitor. In other words, John received the most votes, whereas, in the case of his getting a majority of votes, he may be said to have received the greater number of votes. In the recent election, Thompkins had a <u>plurality</u> of twenty-two hundred.

PORTION - A share or an allotment (see PART). The father gave to his eldest daughter her <u>portion</u> of the estate.

POSTED - Do not use for <u>informed,</u> in the sense of <u>well-informed.</u> People are informed; ledgers and letters are <u>posted.</u> The timetables have been <u>posted</u> on the bulletin boards ... That man is well-informed in history.

PRACTICABLE - Capable of being put into practice; usable, feasible. It is used to refer to things only, never to persons. The device that he has invented for filling fountain pens appears to be most <u>practicable</u>. Do not confuse with PRACTICAL.

PRACTICAL - Useful and valuable as a result of having been tried out in actual practice. It is used of persons chiefly, but also of plans and things in opposition to the theoretical and visionary. <u>Practical</u> knowledge is knowledge that has grown out of useful and profitable practice; John is the most <u>practical</u> fellow I have ever met; his head is full of <u>practical</u> ideas.

PREFER - Do not use <u>than</u> or <u>rather</u> after <u>prefer</u>.It is not a comparative. It should always be followed by to, <u>above</u>, or <u>before.</u> I <u>prefer</u> red to blue, and round figures before square ones.

PRESCRIBE - To give, as a law or a direction. The noun form is <u>prescription</u> (see PROSCRIBE). He is going to prescribe rest, and I shall see that his prescription is carried out.

PRINCIPAL - (1) As a noun its meaning is chief, leader, employer, or prime mover in an undertaking of any kind.
    (2) As a noun it also means invested capital.
    (3) As an adjective its meaning is highest or best in rank or importance. Do not confuse with <u>principle</u>. Correct: The <u>principal</u> of the school is a thorough-going man... His <u>principal</u> is invested in gilt-edged bonds... The <u>principal</u> reason for my going is my mother's illness.

PRINCIPLE - A noun only, meaning truth, belief, policy, conviction, or general hypothesis. He is a man of high <u>principle</u>.

PRODIGAL - This word means wastefully lavish. PRODIGIOUS, however, means extraordinarily large.

PROFIT - Refers to income that accrues in a more or less regular manner, as a just reward for industry (see GAIN). His investments netted him a handsome semi-annual <u>profit.</u>

PROPOSE - To offer, to state a plan or a scheme for the consideration of others. Do not confuse this word with <u>purpose</u> (below). Correct: I <u>propose</u> that we build a new highway at this point for the relief of traffic.

PROPOSAL - Something placed before one, or more than one, for acceptance or rejection, usually concerning a course of action. My proposal for traffic relief is now ready to place before the committee for final vote. Do not confuse with PROPOSITION.

PROPOSITION - A formal statement or exposition presented for consideration rather than for immediate action. Do not use loosely in the sense of plan, task, question, problem. Correct: In outlining my proposition for your consideration, I want to call your attention particularly to pages twenty-two and twenty-three.

PROSCRIBE - To outlaw or ostracize. The noun form is proscription. Do not confuse with prescribe (see above). His criminal record makes it necessary for us to proscribe him, and to enter his works on the proscription list.

PROSECUTE - To follow up regularly and without injurious intent. To begin and carry out a legal procedure (see PERSECUTE). He will prosecute his studies with ardor... He will prosecute the offender to the full extent of the law.

PROVE - The past tense of this verb is proved. The past participle is likewise proved. The form proven is now not favored, though still much used. It has been proved that the best-looking letters receive the best attention.

PROVIDED - A conjunction meaning if, on condition that. We shall attend the performance provided it doesn't rain. Do not confuse with PROVIDING.

PROVIDING - Present participle of the verb provide.meaning to supply or furnish. The firm is providing the best stationery for its correspondence.

PURPOSE - (1) As a noun, it means aim, design, end or goal.
(2) As a verb, it means to decide or determine or intend in one's own mind. What we propose is open to others; what we purpose is not (see PROPOSE). I shall explain my purpose to the men when I meet them. ... I purpose to convert my old office into a den for. study and mediation.

Q

QUANTITY - Refers to things that are measured. Do not use for number. Amount, in contrast, refers to things in more or less indefinite bulk, while quantity connotes measurement, to a degree at least. We measured the quantity of grain he ordered, out of the large amount we had on hand.

R

RAISE - As a verb, always intransitive, this word means to move upward, to cause to rise; also, to breed, to revive, to excite, to alarm (see RISE). Its parts are raise, raised, raised. It is sometimes used colloquially as a noun to indicate increase. It is wrong to say He was so ill that he could not raise. Correct: He was so ill that he could not raise his head... He was so ill that he could not rise.

RARE - Uncommon or infrequent (see UNIQUE). The house is filled with rare tapestries.

RARELY - Do not say rarely ever, rarely or ever, or rarely or hardly ever. Ponder the meaning of the word, and use it consistently, either by itself or in combination. The idiom is rarely or never. Do not use with don't or doesn't. He doesn't rarely is wrong. Correct: We rarely, if ever,go there... We rarely or never go there ... We rarely go there.. We hardly ever go there.

REAL - Genuine, pure, authentic. Do not use for very. Correct: She wore a necklace of real emeralds.

REALLY - Be sure to place really always as closely as possible to the word it modifies. I really think that he is going at last is wrong. Correct: I think that he is really going at last.

REASON - This word, followed by is or other copulative verb, should not be explained by a causal clause. It requires, rather, a substantive attributable clause. In other words, do not use a phrase or a clause introduced by due or because in elaboration of reason. It is wrong to say The reason for his doing it was due to his ignorance (or because he was ignorant) of the law. Correct: The reason for his doing it was his ignorance of the law.

RECKON - To look upon or consider in a more general sense than by means of sheer computation or calculation. Do not use loosely for think, guess, believe, fancy. I reckon he'll come and I calculate it's going to rain are localisms. Correct: I reckon the loss to be very serious... I think he'll come... I think it's going to rain... I believe in what you say... I fancy he doesn't like me... I guess you have the ace in your hand.

RECOLLECT - To make a distinct mental effort to recall something (see REMEMBER). I am totally at a loss to recollect the date referred to.

REGARD - Refers to special esteem or kindliness toward equals, without consideration as to rank or position (see RESPECT). His colleagues hold him in high regard.

REMAINDER - A general term, meaning the part that is left, usually as a result of mathematical calculation (see BALANCE and REST). Do not say remainder of people. Correct: Please forward the remainder of my goods.

REMEMBER - To retain in the memory (see RECOLLECT). He remembered the meeting, and recollected the names of all those present.

REMIND - To recall, usually followed by of. Do not use reflexively, as I reminded myself. Correct: I must remind him of the meeting.

REMIT - To send in return for something (see SEND). On receipt of the bill I shall remit the amount due.

REPAIR - To mend (see FIX). He is going to repair the desk.

REPUTATION - What a person is said by others to be (see CHARACTER). His reputation disqualifies him to hold the position.

RESOLVE - To choose between action and inaction. Determine (see above) means, in contrast, to make a choice between one motive and another. I resolve to go to the meeting tonight, but I am determined not to speak.

RESPECT - Esteem felt toward one in a higher or a different station (see REGARD). The employees respect their president highly.

RESPECTFULLY - With deferential feeling and attitude. I respectfully request you to give me your decision as soon as you can.

RESPECTIVELY - Severally. Bill and Joe have respectively returned their reports to me.

REST - This is a still more general word than either balance or remainder. It refers in general to number or quantity that remains. The rest of the students will follow later.

RISE - (1) As a verb, always intransitive, it means to move upward or to advance; to appear above the horizon; to revolt or rebel; to be revived from the dead (as in Biblical use). The parts are rise, rose, risen. (2) As a noun, it means the act or degree of rising; advance, as in rank or prosperity. Tomorrow the sun will rise at seven-thirty... The rise of the waters this spring surpasses all past records.

S

SAME - This word should not be used as a pronoun, in place of it, they, that, and other pronouns. Exception may be made to this rule in legal phraseology. In reply to same is incorrect. Correct: In reply to your note I want, first, to thank you for your kindness... In pursuance to same, the legatee promises to leave such sum untouched until further notice.

SANCTION - This word means to authorize. SANCTITY, however, means holiness.

SCARCELY - Do not use with negative expression (see RARELY). I have scarcely any apples.

SEEM - Do not use with can't (which see). Use with caution in the sense of appear after couldn't, didn't, wouldn't. They seem to be coming toward us... He seems (or appears) unable to do the work.
SELDOM - Do not say seldom ever, seldom or ever, or seldom or rarely ever. These misuses of seldom in relation are incorrect substitutes for seldom or never, and seldom if ever. "Poor ear" is usually to blame for this error (see RARELY). Correct: We seldom or never attend church...We seldom, if ever, attend church... We seldom go to church.
SEND - To cause or direct to go or pass (see REMIT). Send me the following articles, and I shall promptly remit the amount due.
SET - To place in position; to cause to sit. Its parts are set, set, set (see SIT). Set the chair in the corner.
SIT - To seat; to rest, as in a chair; to take or occupy a seat. Its parts are sit, sat, sat (see SET). I shall sit here...I have sat here before.
SIZE - Do not use this noun as an adjective or a verb. Use, rather, sized or of size. How do the potatoes size up? is wrong. We carry every size shoe is wrong. Do not use the term size up in the sense of judge or estimate. I sized him up in a minute is wrong. Correct: We sell shoes of every size... We sell the larger-sized stockings... I judged him rightly at once.
SO - so...as are correlatives in negative statements (see AS...AS). He has not written so good a letter as this in a long time.
SOCIAL - This word means pertaining to human society. SOCIABLE, however, means companionable.
SOME - Do not use this word for somewhat. Do not use some place for somewhere. Do not use some as accentual slang in the sense of wonderful or remarkable. Correct: We shall take an outing somewhere tomorrow...There is in some place a fortune waiting for you... He made a remarkable speech.
SORT - This is singular number. Do not precede it with a plural form, such as these or those. Do not use a or an after sort of. Correct: This sort of calendar will not do, but those over there are just what I want.
STATION - A regular stopping place, used to designate the place for the starting and the stopping of trains (see DEPOT). The train came iato the station exactly on time.
SUCH - This word should be correlated with as in relative clauses, not with who, which, or that. In result clauses, such should be correlated with that alone. A and an should be used after such with some caution. Correct: Such students as see fit to do so, may accompany me... His reply was in such bad taste that I could not accept it... I never saw such curiosity as 'Jie evinces on the slightest provocation.
SUPERIOR - This word (with its superlative SUPREME) should be used with caution. Like best and very and excellent, it has been overused, especially in business expression, and its significance has consequently become weakened. Your report, placed side by side with others, shows you to have superior merit as a statistician... The constitution is the supreme law of the land.
SUPPOSE - Temporarily to assume that a thing is true. Do not use this word loosely for think, expect, reckon, calculate. Correct: Suppose A has had two hundred dollars.
SUSPECT - A verb meaning to mistrust, to imagine (usually unfavorably). Used more or less colloquially to mean the one suspected or mistrusted. I suspect him of intrigue in the matter that we have been discussing... They have been questioning the suspect.(The latter example is "jour-nalese.") Do not confuse with SUSPICION.
SUSPICION - A noun meaning mistrust, doubt, conjecture. It cannot be used as a verb. My suspicion of him has been justified by recent revelations.

17

T

TAKE - Do not use superfluously, as Take and shake, Take and apply, Take and heat... Motion from a speaker or writer or director (see BRING and FETCH). Heat the medicine before taking... Take this weight from my hand, and place it on the desk.

THAT - A relative pronoun referring to persons, animals, or things. That introduces restrictive clauses only. Do not use before there (see WHO and WHICH). Correct: The only man that can serve you is Jenkins... The only material that you can use is asbestos. ... The only dogs that care for are St. Bernards. ... That man, there on the bench, is the one I mean.

THERE - Do not use this word after that or those to enforce your meaning. Correct: Those men are about to be caught ...Those men, there by the wall, are the guilty ones.

THEREFOR - This word stands for a prepositional phrase, for that, for this, for it, for the matter referred to: I did the work, and am responsible therefor. Do not confuse with THEREFORE.

THEREFORE - A conjunction or reason, result, conclusion, addition, meaning (in the first two cases) for that reason or cause. I did the work, and am therefore responsible.

THESE - Do not use before ones or before here except for special designation. These are the books I want... These, here on the table, are the books I want.

THIS - Do not use before here. This is the book I want ...This book here is the one I want.

THOSE - Do not use before ones or before there except for special designation. Those are the books I want... Those, there by the window, are the books I want.

THROUGH - Do not use for a verb, in the sense of done, finished, angered, and the like. He waded through the tunnel, and declared that he would never take the coach again... I am done with you.

TILL - This word may be used interchangeably with until, meaning up to, to the time of, till such time as. They are adverbs, prepositions, and conjunctive adverbs, according to use. They never came till yesterday... He will be away until Thursday... We shall not go till they come.

TO - A preposition showing relationship. A sentence may properly end with to. He wrote a letter to me... I am the man he wrote to... Do not confuse with TOO.

TOO - An adverb meaning also, in addition to. Do not use too to modify a past participle. I was too disturbed to speak is incorrect (see MUCH and VERY). Correct: He wrote to her, too... I was too much disturbed to speak.

TOWARD - Used interchangeably with towards to mean in the direction of, in respect to, or regarding. Toward is sometimes used to mean apt, imminent, approaching fulfilment - usually negatively - as untoward. He walked toward the village ... His attitude toward his work is delightful ... Untoward events prevented his being present.

TRANSPIRE - To reveal, to bring to light, to make known something that was hidden. It now transpires that he was right in his opinions. Do not use in the sense of occur or happen.

TWO - An adjective meaning the number 2. He wrote two letters. Do not confuse with to and too.

U

UNIQUE - The only one of a kind. Do not confuse with rare meaning highly esteemed because of infrequency or incommonness. Rare can be compared; unique cannot be. I saw a duplicate of this vase in China; it is therefore not unique.

UNIVERSALLY - Refers to all of a class (see COMMONLY). His work has been universally praised.

UNLESS - A subordinate conjunction. It must be so used as to establish a relationship between two clauses. I shall not go to the theater unless you accompany me. Do not confuse with except and without.

UP - This word is used superfluously after build, divide, finish, open, settle, show, size, swell, write. Write up, however, seems to be settling into good usage. Show up and size up, for reveal and estimate respectively, are not good usage. Build your bridges... Divide your apple... Finish your work... Open the bottle... Settle your accounts... Show your hands... Write your story... Your gums will swell... Reveal your true character so that I can judge you fairly.

V

VACANT - Having nothing or no persons on it (see EMPTY). That is vacant that is without that which might fill or might be expected to fill (see the dictionary for extended exposition of the difference between empty and vacant). This loft has been vacant for two years... The children were playing on the vacant lot... The absent-minded man placed the empty bucket on the porch of the vacant house.
VENAL - This word means corrupt, mercenary. VENIAL, however, means pardonable.   VERY - Do not develop the habit of using this word to modify every adjective in your vocabulary. Like best and much and too it is greatly overused, and thus detracts from the intrinsic significance of the words it is thus brought to modify. In verbal modification, very, like too, should be followed by much. It is wrong to say I was very distressed or I was too distressed to see him. The insertion of much before distressed in each case makes the expression correct. Correct: I was very glad to receive your letter... I was very much disturbed at hearing of your illness.
VEX - To annoy or irritate. Do not use in the sense of aggravate (which see), or for so serious a meaning as exasperate. Correct: She was vexed at his conduct.
VOCATION - Major, systematic and remunerative employment. His vocation--salesmanship--makes such heavy demands upon his time that his avocation--music--is sadly neglected.

W

WAY - This word should be preceded by a preposition when used in the sense of manner. Do not behave that way is incorrect. Correct: Do not behave in that way.
WAYS - Do not use this word, preceded by a, to indicate distance. It is wrong to say He walked a little ways with me. Correct: He walked a short distance with me... He walked a little way with me... They delight to know my ways.
WHAT - Do not use for that after but (see BUT). Correct: They do not know but that he will come... He spoke to me, but what he said I do not know.
WELL - This word is an adverb, and must therefore be used only in the modification of verbs, adjectives, and other adverbs. Do not use in place of good. Correct: He looks well... He is a well-known author.. . It will be well worth your while to see him.
WHEN - Denotes definite time, past or present, and means at the very time of (see WHILE). When I entered, the click of typewriters suddenly ceased.
WHERE - Do not use this word for that as I see by the papers where the president has decided to veto the bill. Correct: I see by the papers that the president has decided to veto the bill. WHICH - A relative pronoun referring to both animals and things. It may introduce both restrictive and nonrestrictive clauses (see THAT and WHO). Do not use which to refer to persons. Correct: The dog which I bought of you has strangely disappeared... The machines which you sold me have given excellent service.
WHILE - Denotes passing of time; during the time of; progressive time (see WHEN). While I was going through the door, the click of typewriters suddenly ceased.
WHO - Refers to persons. It may introduce both restrictive and nonrestrictive clauses (see THAT and WHICH). Do not use who to refer to animals or things. Correct: The man who spoke to me is my secretary... He spoke to me, but who he is I do not know.

WHOLE - Indicates totality of quantity (see ALL). But this is by no means a hard and fast rule. We speak of a whole number, and of all the wheat in a granary: The whole field was covered with snow.

WHOLESOME - Generally used in reference to food or recreation or influence (see HEALTHFUL and HEALTHY). Eat plenty of wholesome food.

WHOSE - In general avoid whose as the possessive of which. It is the possessive of who only, unless the thing referred to by which is commonly personified (like ship, for instance), in which case whose may be used as the possessive of which. Where in which is awkward whose is, however, coming into general use. I opened the book the cover of which attracted my eye... The ship whose decks are cleared for action lies sleeping in the harbor.

WITHIN - This word should be used to indicate a period of time, rather than the incorrect expression inside of (see INSIDE). He will arrive within an hour.

WITHOUT - Do not use this word for unless. Without is usually a preposition, and, as such, it must have an object. It cannot serve as a subordinate conjunction. I am not going without your going is incorrect. Correct: I am not going without you ... I am not going unless you go.

www.ingramcontent.com/pod-product-compliance
Lightning Source LLC
Chambersburg PA
CBHW082036300426
44117CB00015B/2499